Development, Divinity and Dharma
The role of religion in development
and microfinance institutions

Development, Divinity and Dharma
The role of religion in development and microfinance institutions

Malcolm Harper, D.S.K. Rao
and Ashis Kumar Sahu

PRACTICAL ACTION
Publishing

Intermediate Technology Publications Ltd
trading as Practical Action Publishing
Schumacher Centre for Technology and Development
Bourton on Dunsmore, Rugby,
Warwickshire CV23 9QZ, UK
www.practicalactionpublishing.org

First published in 2008

ISBN 978 1 85339 655 7

A catalogue record for this book is available from the British Library.

The contributors have asserted their rights under the Copyright Designs and
Patents Act 1988 to be identified as authors of their respective contributions.

Since 1974, Practical Action Publishing has published and disseminated
books and information in support of international development work
throughout the world. Practical Action Publishing (formerly ITDG
Publishing) is a trading name of Intermediate Technology Publications Ltd
(Company Reg. No. 1159018), the wholly owned publishing company of
Intermediate Technology Development Group Ltd (working name Practical
Action). Practical Action Publishing trades only in support of its parent
charity objectives and any profits are covenanted back to Practical Action
(Charity Reg. No. 247257, Group VAT Registration No. 880 9924 76).

Cover design by Mercer Design
Typeset by S.J.I. Services
Printed by Replika Press

Table of Contents

Figures

Tables

Boxes

Acknowledgements

First, and so often forgotten, we should like to acknowledge the help we received from so many clients and members of the various organizations whose work we describe in this book. Some of their names are given in the text, but most are not. They are most unlikely ever to read the book, or indeed to have the time or inclination to do so, but we are very grateful for their time and their frank accounts of how their lives have been influenced by the programmes of the development institutions.

Dr Manjunath and Dr Veerendra Heggade of Shri Kshetra Dharmasthala Rural Development Programme first suggested that such a book should be written, and we must thank them for that, and them and their colleagues also for all the time they gave us when we were studying their work.

Fathers Marianus, Peter Jones, Michael Bogaert, Emanuel Baxla and Alex Ekka of the Society of Jesus provided valuable information about the Chotanagpur Catholic Co-operative Society, and we are particularly grateful to His Eminence Cardinal Telesphoro Toppo, Archbishop of Ranchi, for allowing us to study the institution. Saqib Aftab of Akhuwat Lahore, and Sister Rosily of the Holy Cross Social Service Centre in Hazaribag, gave us information and a great deal of their valuable time. We are grateful to Mr. A. Ranga Rao, Convenor, Andhra Pradesh Satya Sai Trust for sharing his intimate knowledge of Satya Sai Baba and the Seva Organization. We are very aware that it is more important to do good things than to write about them, and we hope that their work did not suffer as a result of the time they gave us.

Kim Wilson of Tufts University used her incomparable networking skills to lead us to numerous useful informants, and Kimberly Beth Priore of the Harvard department of theology assisted with data and analysis from American 'BINGOs'. S. Lalita Rao, microfinance consultant of Bangalore, dug deep into the history of Dakshin Kannada, Robb Davis of Freedom from Hunger and lately of the Mennonite Central Committee provided valuable insights on the reality of faith-based multinational NGOs, Y. M. Niranjan Babu helped with the material on SKDRDP and Rick James of INTRAC in Oxford showed the way to work of his own and others which helped us to avoid 'reinventing the wheel'.

The Livelihoods School generously allowed Ashis Kumar Sahu to give time to this work, and Shiela Rao, Kate Bulman and Uschi Kraus-Harper were usefully critical at various stages of the work. Many thanks to all of them.

About the authors

Malcolm Harper taught at Cranfield School of Management until 1995, and since then has worked mainly in India. He has published on enterprise development and microfinance. He was Chairman of Basix Finance from 1996 until 2006, and is Chairman of M-CRIL, the microfinance credit rating agency.

DSK Rao is the Regional Organizer for Asia-Pacific, Microcredit Summit Campaign. He has 22 years' experience in rural development banking with NABARD, the apex development financial institution in India. He has published extensively on farmer management of irrigation and self-help groups for the socio-economic empowerment of poor women.

Ashis Kumar Sahu has been a practitioner and researcher in microfinance and livelihoods for about 10 years, and is associated with The Livelihoods School, promoted by BASIX, Sa-Dhan, the Indian Association of Community Development Financial Institutions, RCDC in Orissa and Urmul Trust in Rajasthan.

Abbreviations

BINGOs	big international NGOs
BPL	below poverty line
CAPARV	Council for Anti Poverty Action and Rural Voluteers
COVA	Confederation of Voluntary Associations
CRS	Catholic Relief Services
DWCRA	Development of Women and Children in Rural Areas programme
ESAF	Evangelical Social Action Forum (of Kerala, southern India)
FBOs	faith-based organizations
GDP	gross domestic product
HCSSC	Holy Cross Social Service Centre
IRDP	integrated rural development programme
JVK	*Jnanavikasa Kendra* – women's groups run to raise awareness
LEAP	Local Enterprise Assistance Programme (of the Association of Evangelicals of Liberia)
MDGs	Millenium Development Goals
MMC	Mennonite Central Committee
MMW4P	make markets work for the poor
NABARD	National Bank for Agriculture and Rural Development
NGOs	non-governmental organizations
NMS	Norwegian Missionary Society
RUDSETI	Rural Development and Self Employment Training Institute
SGSY	Swarnjayanti Gram Swarozgar Yojana – a government self-employment programme
SHG	self-help groups
SKDRDP	Shri Kshetra Dharmasthala Rural Development Programme
UNHCR	United Nations High Commissioner for Refugees

Introduction

Abstract

This book is about the work of faith-based development NGOs. It examines the experience of a number of such institutions, in particular the Shri Kshetra Dharmasthala Rural Development Programme (SKDRDP), an offshoot of the temple of the same name in Karnataka in south India but also a number of other Christian and Hindu institutions, in south Asia and elsewhere. The potential conflicts between charity and the neoliberal search for 'sustainability', and the threat of radical extremism, in all religions, mean that this is an important contemporary topic.

Far in the south of rural Karnataka state in India, in a valley among the wooded hills and valleys that lead down to the Indian Ocean, stands a temple. It is a fairly modest building by the standards of such places, and is surrounded by a collection of hostels and shops that serve the thousands of pilgrims who visit the temple each and every day. The place is called the Shri Kshetra Dharmasthala, or, loosely, the 'place that is the abode of charity'.

There are many such places in coastal Karnataka. Shri Kshetra Dharmasthala is one of the more popular of them, and has many very special features. It is polytheist, and is revered by Hindus although it was established and has for six hundred years been managed by a Jain family. Their religion is one of the three Dharmaic faiths, together with Hinduism and Buddhism, but is strictly non-Brahminical and opposed to any notion of the hierarchy of caste.

This book, however, is not mainly about the history of this unusual institution, nor is it directly about the faith that is practised there or the pilgrims who visit it in such large numbers. It is about what is happening beyond the temple and its surrounding facilities, in the beautiful steeply sloping forests of the western *ghats*, the steep ranges of hills that stretch for many miles north and south of the temple.

The people who live around most temple towns in India, like similar places elsewhere in the world, may be spiritually blessed. In material terms, however, such places are usually notable for the contrast between the wealth and splendour of the holy places and the grinding poverty of the people who live around them. Millions of people, most of whom are poor, flock to them for spiritual sustenance, and some may perhaps also scrape a living by selling services to the pilgrims, or by begging. They do not expect, however, to acquire 'sustainable livelihoods'. They come for alms or grants, but not for loans which must be paid back.

Shri Kshetra Dharmasthala, however, is doing something very different. It is assisting almost half a million people who live in the surrounding area to escape from poverty, not with grants and handouts, but with one of India's lesser known but most successful and most comprehensive rural development programmes. This book is about this work, and the work of similar agencies which combine religion with development. Our purpose is to examine the role of religion in this work, and that of other faith-based development agencies, and to identify how their religious links strengthen, or perhaps weaken, their ability to help poor people to escape from poverty. We compare some aspects of 'multinational' faith-based development non-governmental organizations (NGOs) with the work of smaller local institutions, and our findings should help people who work in or support such agencies to take advantage of their undoubted strengths, to minimize their weaknesses, and thus to drive forward their mission of alleviating poverty.

We hope that the book will help faith-based development agencies, and perhaps SKDRDP itself, to see their future more clearly, in the context of the difficult environment which they face. It should also be useful to secular institutions, which can learn a great deal from their faith-based counterparts, to students of development, and to those who are responsible for making decisions about which agencies should be funded to undertake what types of work, with which kinds of client communities, over what periods.

This book does not in any sense claim to be a rigorous comparison between secular and faith-based institutions. There are too many contextual variables for such a study to have any meaning. What we do aim to do, however, is to examine certain issues, relating to the origins, governance, funding, staffing and above all the actual development activities and the clients of these institutions.

This examination is particularly important at this time, when development thinking runs so much against much of the basic philosophy of many faith-based institutions. The current trend in development is to aim for 'sustainability', which is in some sense the antithesis of long-term charity, and to work with businesses, or at least to hand over the development functions to for-profit businesses, as soon as possible. This is particularly difficult for faith-based institutions, whose origins lie in their founders' belief that it is morally good to give to the less fortunate, to be 'charitable'. The Sanskrit word *dharma* indeed includes the sense not only of religion, but also of charity, giving to those who are less fortunate than oneself.

It is true that charity, service to others, is usually portrayed as sacrifice, but can be of as much value to the server as to the served, and may even seriously damage those whom the servers profess to help. Professionals in the international 'aid trade' are often guilty of putting their own interests above those of them they purport to serve, and those who work for faith-based institutions are no more innocent than secular ones. Their good works sustain them, even as they profess to provide sustainable livelihoods and other benefits to the poor.

There are thousands of development agencies throughout the world whose overall aim is to alleviate poverty. Some are small and operate only in one village, others are large global institutions with multi-million or even billion dollar budgets, and operate worldwide. Some started in the country where they operate, while others were set up in wealthy countries, to help poor people in so-called 'developing countries'. Some are owned and run by governments, some by business corporations, and some by voluntary agencies, charities, or NGOs, the commonest if also the least informative label.

The difference which this book aims to examine, between faith-based and secular development agencies, is not clear-cut, but it is usually quite easy in practice to decide whether a given development institution is or is not 'faith-based'. In general, the institutions which most people would agree are faith-based, some of whose work is examined in this book, seem to share one or more of the following characteristics:

- They have been started by a temple, a church or other religious institution, or by an association of such institutions, or by an individual whose religious convictions have played an important part in his decision to start the institution.
- They work through or in close collaboration with locally based religious institutions, such as churches, mosques or temples.
- They raise most (but, quite importantly, not all) of their resources from members of the same faith, individually or through their home-based churches, temples or mosques.
- They often, but not always, incorporate the name of their religion, or some term associated with it, in their title.

It is equally important to note that there are certain things which many faith-based development agencies do not do, even though their religious origins might lead one to expect that they might.

These include:

- They do not restrict the benefits of their work to people who share the same faith. Some or even the majority of their clients may hold quite different beliefs, which in other contexts compete with the faith of the development agency.
- They do not depend wholly on funding from members of the same faith, or from funds raised by their institutions.
- Their staff, even at quite senior levels, do not necessarily share the same faith as that on which the agency is based.

Faith-based institutions do of course differ in many respects, and the strength of their religious base, and its impact on their work, can vary enormously. A group in the UK (Smith et al, 2002) suggested five categories of faith-based organization. These range from 'faith-saturated' groups, whose members believe that everyone should share their faith and should be persuaded to do so if necessary, through faith-centred, faith-background, faith-related and then to 'faith-secular partnerships', where some but not all of the staff are adherents of a particular religion and there is a general sense that this in some way affects their work. The institutions which are discussed in this book tend towards the more 'liberal' end of this spectrum.

The book examines the experience of Shri Kshetra Dharmasthala in south India and a number of other institutions of this type. They include Muslim, Hindu and Christian institutions, some of which operate internationally, and others only within one country, or more locally, in one part of a country.

We chose these three religions because they are by a large margin the world's most popular faiths. According to one estimate (www.adherents.com) there were in 2006 about 2.1 billion Christians, 1.3 billion Muslims and 900 million Hindus, making up 68 per cent of the world's total population. No other religion exceeds 500 million adherents.

We start with a brief financial analysis of a small sample of some of the largest 'multi-national' development agencies, both faith-based and secular, in order to find out if there are any broad indications of important differences in their fund-raising and remuneration policies.

We then examine the rural development work of Shri Kshetra Dharmasthala in particular detail, because it includes so many different activities and is apparently so successful. There is a great deal to learn from the work of SKDRDP, the development arm of the temple, but we also aim to throw some light on faith-based institutions in general. The Shri Kshetra Dharmasthala is actually a Hindu religious place managed by a Jain trustee in the Heggade's name. Jainism is in some respects similar to Hinduism, and many Jain communities share Hindu temples. This is something that different sects within other religions, such as Islam or Christianity, usually feel unable to do, and such openness is probably one of the features which enables SKDRDP to be so effective. Jainism only claims some four million adherents worldwide, and very few of these are themselves served by SKDRDP, which does not aim to reach only or even primarily its own adherents.

It is generally agreed that the best way for poor people to become less poor is to acquire 'sustainable livelihoods'. The institutions whose task is to assist the poor to become less poor should according to contemporary wisdom preferably themselves be businesses. They may need subsidy, or charity, but only for a limited time. The eventual goal, according to some adherents of the neoliberal paradigm, is to 'make markets work for the poor' (or, 'MMW4P' as this has become known in some circles) so that they can earn a living, and pay the full cost not only of their personal living expenses, but of water, schooling, health care, transport and other basic services which have traditionally been provided by governments. There is not a long-term role for charity in this scenario nor for traditional development agencies, particularly for faith-based institutions such as the Shri Kshetra Dharmasthala which is firmly based in a temple and totally and inseparably linked to the place where it stands.

Faith-based institutions are also challenged by the secularization of society which affects both those who finance and work for development agencies, and also their clients. This does not necessarily mean that people are less generous, or less willing to work long hours for very little in order to help those who are less fortunate than themselves. It does, however, mean that an appeal based on faith, for funds or for labour, has less resonance.

Similarly, today's clients of faith-based development agencies are more likely to question their motives than their parents. Religion is no longer 'the opium of the people', and it is sometimes easier to help people who are drugged than those who are fully alert. Faith-based institutions have to avoid being marginalized, being left with the more conservative and perhaps less progressive sections of society. This can happen to their sources of funding, to their staff and to their clients.

The growing radicalization of many religions also poses a major problem for faith-based development agencies. 'Fundamentalism' is affecting Christianity, Buddhism and Hinduism as well as Islam. In the short term, some people may be attracted to donate their money and their time to an institution which they believe will promote an extremist agenda, and clients may also be attracted by promises of radical societal changes in their favour. On the other hand, religious labels can often be misread, and any indication of an affiliation to a particular faith may be interpreted as being dangerously radical. When religious labels are suspect, it may be safer to work with secular institutions.

References

Adherents website, www.adherents.com [accessed 15.02.2007].

Smith, G. et al (2002), Working Group on Human Needs, University of East London, London.

CHAPTER ONE

Religion and development – can they go together?

Abstract

Religion is an important part of nearly every society, but there is no conclusive evidence that any one religion, or indeed any religion at all, is associated with economic and social 'development'. There may be reasons why faith-based institutions should or should not be successful in assisting in the process of development, whether for people of their own faith or others. Religions can be divisive, exclusive, hierarchical, badly managed and ultra-conservative, and they may use their development work as a means to convert poor people to their religion, rather than for secular development. Local religious bodies can be a very weak basis for the work of external development institutions which try to use them as a means of access to local communities. The converse can also be true; local churches, mosques and temples can provide a credible entry point for development initiatives, and can be a source of low-cost or volunteer staff and facilities.

The lessons of history

Before examining the effect of religion on institutions which attempt to assist other people to 'develop', we look briefly at the issue of how religion generally affects development. Is adherence to some religions more associated with economic and social development than others?

Theories abound as to the impact of different religions on development. Human beings are always anxious to find simple explanations for complex phenomena, and one of the great puzzles of mankind is why some people from some regions, countries and communities have 'developed', or become less poor, than others. It would be much easier to understand the world if we could say that people of a particular race, or those who live in particular climatic zones, or have benefited or suffered from particular historical backgrounds, are more likely than others to be 'developed'. But it is of course not that simple.

The term 'developed' is subject to many definitions. Religion itself plays a major part in defining what most people consider to be 'the good life', or even a tolerable existence. Apart from some extreme cases, however, most people would agree that the so-called 'basic needs' of adequate food, water, shelter and clothing, with primary healthcare and education and a fundamentally supportive social environment, are necessary for human dignity or even survival.

Why is it that some people, in some places, have achieved and indeed gone far beyond the satisfaction of these needs, while millions and indeed billions of others have not?

Religion has always been an attractive candidate for such speculation. Faiths cross racial and national boundaries, and religious beliefs have always played a major part in motivating behaviour. Members of a particular faith, or those who come from communities which are generally felt to belong to a certain faith, are also usually anxious to portray it in the best light, in order to encourage others to join them and to justify their own beliefs.

Max Weber argued in *The Protestant Ethic and the Spirit of Capitalism* (2005) that the critical rationalism of the Reformation destroyed the simple belief that salvation followed automatically from devotion and acceptance of the rituals and hierarchy of the Roman Catholic Church. Hard work, the acquisition and accumulation of wealth, and profitable investment in enterprises that produced further wealth, could be a vocation in itself. Charity, giving to poor people, could almost be seen as a sin, because it would discourage them from following the same path. This view is certainly borne out by the programmes and activities of many large development agencies with links to Protestant churches, particularly those based in the USA. We shall be examining their work later in this book.

There has of late been renewed interest in the whole issue of the relationship between faith and economic development. This is partly because of the apparent failure of many externally funded development initiatives, and because the new militancy of some adherents of Islam, mirrored by that of some Christians, poses difficult dilemmas for faith-based development institutions.

Some economists have viewed religion as a good which is subject to rational choice like any other, and they argue that when there is a free and competitive market in religion, with no state involvement, religions will be more effectively 'sold' because of the competition. This would seem to be confirmed by a comparison between active membership and participation in religions in the UK and the USA, and some parts of Africa. It is less clear in some Muslim countries such as Pakistan or Iran where Islam has a virtual monopoly position, sanctioned and reinforced by government, but where religious observance is widespread (Iyer, forthcoming).

The welfare and development work of many faith-based development NGOs, including some of those whose work we examine in this book, was initially inspired by their aim to bring converts into the fold. In a strictly economic framework, their development work can be perceived as a marketing tool. In most cases, however, the proselytizing motive is not apparent, and their work is extended to people of all faiths, irrespective of the religion of their founders.

An alternative but not necessarily inconsistent economic view sees religion as a form of social capital, or even as a separate form of capital on its own, which can be a valuable asset in any activity. This approach is highly relevant in our case, and it is clear that the interpersonal and interinstitutional links resulting from shared religious views are a very important resource for the institutions we describe.

Contemporary economic experience does not support Weber's argument, or any other which associates greater national wealth with religious beliefs of any kind. There is no consistent empirical evidence to suggest that Protestant Christian communities, or communities which adhere to any other religion, are more likely to be 'developed' than Catholic. Southern Germany is more Catholic than the north, but is equally economically successful if not more so. Northern Europe, including Scandinavia and the UK, is largely Protestant and is rich, but Italy, Spain and other southern European countries which are strongly Roman Catholic are also highly 'developed' by any standards.

So, is Christianity in general associated with development? The whole of Latin America, with few exceptions, is strongly Roman Catholic, and has been for several hundred years. This does not seem to have led to widespread 'development', and in spite of some recent successes all the nations of Central and South America are still very much 'developing countries'. The Philippines is and has been for some 200 years strongly Catholic, and is nevertheless quite rapidly falling behind its South-east Asian neighbours by many measures of development.

Much of sub-Saharan Africa is also Christian, both Protestant and Catholic, but the African development experience is almost universally bad, and much of the continent as a whole has become steadily poorer over the last two decades. Such wealth as has been achieved as generally been accumulated in the hands of a small minority; they share the same religions as their less fortunate fellow-countrymen, but have been individually much more successful.

The foregoing examples may suggest that colonialism holds the key. It can be and is still argued that countries which suffered from colonization are under-developed, and the countries which colonized them became and remain richer as a result. The English word 'development' can even be interpreted as an instrument of a continuing neocolonial process of under-development.

This argument obviously has some force in the context of recent history, but it begs the question of why some countries were the colonizers and others were colonized. Colonialism was, as neocolonialism still is, one of many instruments whereby the colonizing individuals and their nations became rich, and 'developed'. Their religions preceded their colonial adventures, by many centuries.

Christians were not, however, the only colonialists. Within a few years of the establishment of the first Muslim community in Medina, Muslim armies and traders had colonised most of Arabia. By the eigth century the whole Mediterranean region, from Spain in the west and as far east as Persia, was under the rule of the Muslim Umayyad dynasty. Their empire expanded much more rapidly than the empires of the European colonial nations did many centuries later.

Like many empires it suffered from internal problems over the ensuing years, but in the 16th century the Ottoman part of the Muslim empire still controlled much of the Mediterranean, as well as all the whole Balkan region, including as far north as the frontiers of Austria and reaching to what is now (or was) Iraq in the east. Muslim travellers and traders had also reached and converted people in far more distant places, such as Indonesia, Malaysia and much of India. They found that the people of Bali were already practising Hindus, and Chinese traders, adherents of Confucianism, has established outposts throughout the islands of eastern Asia. No religion has a monopoly of colonialism.

The biggest empire of the latter half of the 20th century, the Soviet Russian empire, controlled all of Eastern Europe and all of eastern, central and north western Asia. It had outposts in Arabia, Africa and even in the Americas. It was established and for some time maintained by an explicitly atheist regime. It has now more or less collapsed, as all empires do, but it further demonstrates that imperialism, which is one way of becoming 'developed', albeit at the expense of others, is not associated with religious beliefs. Particular cases may be impressive, but there is no convincing argument in favour of religion in general, or any particular religion, as being conducive to development.

The more dramatic recent national development successes also suggest that religion is irrelevant. Germany, Japan, China, Taiwan, Korea and Vietnam certainly do not share the same religious faith, and the Communist Party in China has attempted, albeit with limited success, to abolish religion. All these countries, however, share the experience of massive social and economic disruption and turmoil. This may have been the result of hideously destructive warfare, won or lost, or of self-inflicted harm. A national trauma of this kind is unlikely to be proposed as a stimulus to development, even if it was universally the case that prosperity was the inevitable result. Even this factor, however, is not always followed by development. There are all too many cases of countries which have been ravaged in this way, but have apparently been more or less permanently broken rather than revived by the experience.

Religion and development institutions

We can fairly safely conclude therefore that communities may or may not become developed irrespective of their religious affiliations. But what has religion to do with developers, with the people and institutions which attempt to assist others to develop? Why might an explicit religious affiliation help or perhaps hinder them in this endeavour?

There are many reasons why secular development organizations might be considered more effective than faith-based organizations, or 'FBOs' as they are now called in the 'development business'.

Religions are divisive. Past and recent history includes all too many occasions when people who have lived peacefully together for centuries have used religious differences as a pretext for conflict. Religion has also been the traditional basis of many long-standing injustices, such as in race and gender. Many if not most religious people believe that their own religion is the best, and that they are doing others a service if they try to convert them. Even if their charitable services come with no strings attached, and are available to all who need them, there is almost inevitably some implication that recipients should at least look favourably on the donor's religion. Not surprisingly, governments and donors may look askance at proselytizing of any kind.

Broadly, 'development' is primarily viewed as being about economic development, becoming less poor, and this is a materialist concept. Agencies which promote and assist development are not anti-spiritual, but they see themselves as promoting physical and social well-being. Any intrusion, however tangential, into the spiritual lives of those who are being 'developed' can be seen as unnecessary and inappropriate.

As a result of all these factors, many faith-based development agencies try to distance themselves from their religious roots, in order to establish their secular credentials with donors and governments. An official of the Aga Khan Foundation, for instance, which is led by His Highness the Aga Khan, the hereditary 49th Imam of the worldwide Ismaeli community, and whose core funding comes mainly from the wealthy Ismaeli diaspora, claimed that the institution was totally secular when he was asked to participate in this study. Their head office staff in Geneva are indeed not Ismaelis, and many of their projects are funded from secular government sources, but their single most important area of operation is with the predominantly Ismaeli communities of the northern Pakistan, and Tajikistan. Like many such institutions, they are at pains to stress their secular attributes in spite of their obviously religious roots, which play a vital role in their work.

Can religion help?

There has recently been some modification to this universally pro-secular view (James, 2005). This change falls into two rather separate strands. The government of the USA has encouraged USAID to provide more assistance through faith-based groups, in response to the increasing political influence of right wing or fundamentalist Christian groups. Other organizations, such as the World Bank, the Swedish govement development agency (SIDA) and British government development agency (DFID), have taken a broader view. The World Bank invited leaders of the world's nine leading religions to play some part in the preparation of the World Development Report for 2002 (James 2004) and DFID, SIDA and the Economic Commission for Africa have all called for more participation by faith-based groups and for more research into the role of religion and of faith-based institutions in development (Foster, 2005).

There are a number of reasons for this resurgence of interest in faith-based institutions by the major development agencies. Most obviously, the record of development assistance in general to date has been poor. This is not in itself a reason to believe that a faith-based approach would have been more successful, but clearly some major changes are needed. There seems to be more to 'development' than money and materialism.

Additionally, it is clear to any observer, however sceptical, that faith-based institutions have traditionally provided a major share of the services such as health care and education which are fundamental components of the Millennium Development Goals (MDGs). In the USA itself, the 1,400 agencies in the Catholic Charities network have a total annual expenditure of $7.5 billion, and are one of the largest non-governmental providers of social services, and their Lutheran equivalent employs 138,000 people in 280 agencies. Almost one-fifth of the 37,000 US NGO providers of social services are estimated to be faith-based. In 1999 these agencies were estimated to be spending about $17 billion annually on welfare services for the government (Wuthnow, 2004).

Until quite recently, the situation was not dissimilar in most of Europe. In the UK, it is estimated that there are several hundred registered NGOs providing Islamic education to Muslim children (Smith, 2003). In Malawi, three-quarters of all primary schooling and almost half of all health care is still provided by institutions with a religious basis. It has been estimated (Clarke, 2005) that half of all primary education and health care throughout sub-Saharan Africa is still provided by faith-based institutions. The finance for this comes from local congregations, and from foreign sources, including both Christian and Muslim institutions.

Even in India, which has a strong public commitment to secular government including presumably the approach to development, schools which have been established by religious bodies are considered to provide the highest quality secondary education, and many of the tertiary level institutions are also faith-based. 'Convent-educated' is a well-accepted statement of quality in marriage advertisements. Many hospitals are also faith-based, and health care and education appear to have been a natural complement to traditional missionary work, long before the modern notion of 'development' was first conceived.

As governments have withdrawn from many activities, in response to the neoliberal paradigm and simple economics, civil society has become much more important as a 'third way' between the weakening public sector and the increasing power of private corporations. Many, if not most, strong and well-established civil society institutions have religious origins. This in itself has increased their role in the development process. Development agencies are always searching for effective delivery channels through which to provide whatever services they have to offer. Even, and perhaps especially, in the poorest communities, churches, temples and mosques are a very potentially effective distribution channel for those agencies which are willing and able to make use of it.

The people who work with and are inspired by faith-based institutions are also more often willing to work without payment as volunteers, or for lower rewards, than those who support secular institutions. This applies, as we shall see later, to senior executives in multinational aid organizations as well as to workers in charity shops, to local fund-raisers, and to members of local congregations in poorer countries. Faith-based institutions can often 'turn on' armies of volunteers at short notice, in a way that their secular counterparts find very difficult.

Ordinary people tend to mistrust politicians and government officials, and they are all too aware that private corporations are in business to make money. There is no tradition of effective local government in many so-called 'developing countries', and the imam, the priest or the pastor may be the only person in authority whom they trust. Poor people are also in general more 'religious' than the rich, as is shown by the church attendance figures in Europe compared with most other Christian countries. If they believe in God and trust their religious leader, their faith can obviously play a major role in their acceptance of change and development interventions.

In many parts of Africa, poor communities are seeing large numbers of conversions to Islam and to Christianity (Deegan, 1995). This may in part be the result of poverty, of the failure of a materialistic secular development approach, but if development is ever to succeed, it can be argued that it should surely start where people are; in their church, their temple or their mosque. This view is echoed in the statement from the Office of the President of the United States by John Dilulio, the newly appointed leader of Charitable Choice, an agency whose purpose is to ensure that Government collaborates more effectively with NGOs, and particularly with local faith-based institutions:

> 'Our goal is to energize civil society and rebuild social capital, particularly by uplifting small non-profit organizations, congregations and other faith-based institutions that are lonely outposts of energy, service, and vision in poor and declining neighbourhoods and rural enclaves.'
> (Dilulio, 2001)

Social capital, which is often built around religion, is now recognized as being as important for development as more tangible forms of capital such as physical infrastructure, good health or education (Langsun Mate, 2006). The term 'social capital' has a materialistic ring, but development depends on loyalty, commitment, service, unity, justice and a sense of community as much as on entrepreneurship and technical skills. These are the essence of social capital, and are more likely to be found in faith-based groups than in companies or government offices. Faith can often provide a 'common bond', not only within but between communities. A well-paid development professional from 'the north' may have little in common with his local colleagues in 'the south', or with their clients, but their shared religious identity, of being part of some larger whole, can at least be the foundation on which effective mutual respect and good working relationships can be built. Development agencies can mobilize these resources if they work with faith-based institutions. The Director of the United Nations Millennium Development Goals Campaign advised:

> 'For the African state to become effective, it needs to understand what it is about religion that builds loyalty, creates infrastructure, collects tithes and taxes, and fosters a sense that it delivers material as well as spiritual benefits.'
> (Shetty, 2007)

Religion can be a powerful motivating force for development. It emphasizes compassion, service, unity, justice and reconciliation. The very word 'development' is often taken as being synonymous with 'economic development', income and its distribution, and gross national product. Religion brings in values and meaning. We are all familiar with people in poor communities who prefer to spend their little money on religious festivals and ceremonies rather than on better food or housing or education or health-care. Unless we believe they are simply wrong to do this, we must accept that there is more to development than gross domestic product (GDP).

Links to local institutions and communities

Faith-based development institutions are necessarily linked to religious communities in some way. This link may primarily be in their origins, their funding and their staffing, and they may also have links with local religious institutions to which the people they are trying to assist belong. This can give them significant comparative advantages in development work, through extensive community outreach and influence on people's behaviour. Some faith-based organizations are closely linked to local religious bodies, while others may have more tenuous local links or even none at all.

The closest link, which has great potential for sustained outreach and influence but is also fraught with potential challenges, is when the development institution works closely on a day-to-day basis with local places of worship, or is indeed an offshoot of such a place. This latter is the case with SKDRDP, which is a recent initiative of a 600 year old temple. It is more common for a large and often foreign-based development institution, such as Catholic Relief Services or World Vision, to work through smaller local religious institutions.

There are many very practical ways in which a development NGO can gain from working through local churches or other affiliated religious institutions. The management of Tuinuane, a savings and credit group programme run by the Free Pentecostal Fellowship in Kenya, have found that it is possible to achieve a satisfactory balance between total integration with the local churches and complete separation. The Foreign Pentecostal Mission in Norway was asked to assist with the development of a women's group revolving fund in association with existing literacy classes, but it was concluded that a traditional microcredit programme was unsuitable for both the donor and the Kenyan churches. They therefore set up a savings-only system, which is firmly based in one or other of the 500 Pentecostal churches in Kenya, although around 15 per cent of the group members are not themselves church members (Mersland, 2007).

The churches, like mosques and temples, are excellent meeting places; they are neutral and comfortable in a physical but also a social sense, since they are already familiar to the members as places where they can meet regularly and share their personal problems. The meetings can be combined with songs and other forms of worship, to enliven and vary the proceedings, and the groups can also be conveniently monitored and supported by specialist staff who are employed for the purpose but are closely allied to the churches.

Such relationships bring many opportunities and many challenges. The governance structures and organizational culture of the two institutions may be very different, and this can greatly complicate the interactions between the local religious leaders and the staff of the specialized development institution.

There is a range of types of linkages between local religious institutions, such as churches, mosques or temples, and larger faith-based development institutions which need to work with or through them in order to reach the people whom they wish to help.

At one extreme, the development work may be undertaken by the local religious institution itself, with guidance and assistance from the larger institution but with no formal legal or organizational separation between the existing pastoral role and the development work. This is common in many inner city churches in the UK and elsewhere, whose priests or other leaders, along with volunteer members of the congregation, spend a considerable part of their time on development work.

Alternatively, the development work may be partially within and partly outside the religious institution, perhaps with some independent and partly secular governance arrangements and possibly with a separate legal form. SKDRDP is an example of this; it is a separately registered body, managed by development professionals, but it was initiated and mainly funded by the Dharmasthala Temple. Dr Heggade, the hereditary leader of the temple, maintains close and regular contact with SKDRP, and is involved in all major decisions.

At the other extreme, the development operation is quite distinct and legally unrelated to the local entity. In many so-called 'developing countries', large and often wealthy international faith-based development institutions, such as World Vision, Islamic Relief or the Aga Khan Foundation, run their development programmes quite separately from the local churches, temples, mosques or other religious places. They must still relate closely to them, in order to benefit from their local credibility and contacts in the communities they serve, but their staff are quite different, often coming from abroad, and their organizational culture may be very different indeed from their local 'partner'.

There is no one correct type of relationship, and the chosen model will depend on factors such as the particular understanding of the development process by the local religious institution, the type of work being undertaken, and the age, size, and funding of each party. Funding and its sources, as well as the personalities involved, also play a very important part in determining the form of the relationship. Many of the cases described in this book suggest that it may be desirable to move towards quite separate institutional arrangements; shared religious beliefs do not necessarily translate into happy working relationships.

Although most faiths emphasize the importance of good relationships with fellow humans, there are many potential tensions and conflicts between local religious institutions and development organizations. These often relate to money, to power and to recognition.

Many development programmes are generously funded, particularly if they enjoy international support, and their staff, especially any expatriates, can be highly paid. Priests and others at the local level, on the other hand, tend to be very badly paid or may not be paid at all. The resources at their disposal are also very different. A quite junior staff member of the development institution may have access to a car, while the bishop, the leader of a large number of churches, may have to travel by train or bus.

Local churches may feel that they should be paid for access to their facilities, and to their networks and followers, while the development staff think that such facilities should be provided free of charge because the local people who 'own' their church are receiving the benefit of the development assistance. Should the local religious body pay the development institution for helping its followers, or should the development specialists pay the local body for its assistance?

Local religious bodies can also cause confusion and ill will through well-intentioned efforts to promote development for their people independently of their affiliated faith-based development institution. They may successfully appeal for relief or other supplies, which then have to be managed and distributed by the development organization, without any coordination with its existing programmes. In Malawi, one of Africa's poorest countries, a faith-based international development organization had to take on full responsibility for managing a $700,000 relief programme which had been independently solicited by local churches. Volunteers may also be successfully solicited by a local church, but then have to be managed and maintained by an international institution which has no real use for them.

Problems can also arise over recognition. Local religious bodies not unnaturally want to get credit and recognition for assisting their followers, but the funding and professional staff may have come from an international institution that needs to claim the full credit in order to maintain its fund-raising profile. If things go wrong, such as with poorly selected international staff or other issues, both sides not unnaturally want to avoid the blame.

Faith-based institutions, whether local or international, do of course share a common set of beliefs, which should and often does compensate for any potential tensions in the nature of their relationships. Faith has always been the inspiration for a great deal of development work, particularly among the poorest and most marginalized in any society. People's faiths can also influence the development methods they use. If they believe that people's religious beliefs are a vital source of inspiration for change and development, they will obviously take a different approach to development from that which secular development professionals will adopt.

Secular institutions also of course have their own values, which may or may not be written down in their formal mission statements but which can be as strong as some faiths. No development interventions are value-free, and members of the same religion may have very different values, but a shared religious belief can at least provide the beginnings of mutual understanding.

Some staff of faith-based institutions may believe that someone's faith is not only a means to development but is also an essential part of the end. This of course raises the awkward question of where spiritual development stops and conversion begins. Many religions want to proselytize, and to recruit more followers. If an overtly religious institution offers people an improvement in their economic position, particularly if their present religion has not helped them to become better off, they may be inclined to join the new religion. This can lead to very serious problems, to physical violence and the exclusion of potentially valuable development work. The authorities in the Hindu Kingdom of Nepal closed down clinics operated by Christian institutions because it was alleged that they encouraged conversion, and an Australian Christian missionary who worked with leprosy patients in Orissa was burned to death with his two sons in 1999. These valuable medical initiatives would presumably have survived had they been run on a purely secular basis.

Most religions encourage compassion and charity, but local bodies may have very different ideas from international institutions about how actually to operationalize compassionate behaviour in the optimum way. They may have very few resources to share, and their limited charitable activities may be effective with the few people whom they are able to assist. When a large international institution comes on the scene, however, particularly if it introduces some form of microfinance programme, there may be very real issues on how to deal with hard cases and defaults. Charitable donations may be virtuous, but are they 'empowering'?

Local churches, mosques or other religious institutions may also prefer to confine their assistance to their own supporters, members of their own faith, whereas most international faith-based development organizations aim to help everyone, regardless of his or her religion, and they may even be required to do this by the terms of the funding they receive from government sources. If an international programme is delivered through a local church or temple it may benefit from the existing outreach of the local entity but it may also at the same time inadvertently omit people of a different faith. If a programme is first announced in a church or mosque, those who attend will hear of it first and may benefit more than those who are informed later even if the programme is open to people of all religions. This has caused problems in many African countries and elsewhere. If the international institution bypasses its local co-religionists however, and works through its own or other secular networks, much ill will can result. There can be a trade-off between professionalism and religious affiliation.

Leadership and management

There are also problems, as well as opportunities, related to leadership. Religious leaders have spiritual as well as temporal authority, and the leaders of some faiths, such as the Roman Catholic Church or some branches of Islam, are seen as being above the authority of the state and even as infallible. Many believers feel that if they question the guidance of their spiritual leader, they are questioning God. This gives religious leaders the power to promote change, or the maintenance of the status quo, for good or for ill. Many religious institutions are also strongly hierarchical, and their leaders are expected to act autonomously and even autocratically. This may or may not lead to good management, but it is certainly inconsistent with the liberal management style which is adopted by most development institutions.

Many people are willing to work harder and for less money for faith-based institutions than or secular ones, because their religion gives them a deep commitment to their work. This can also lead to problems in selection and recruitment, particularly if the development institution is generously funded and jobs with it are eagerly sought after. If the institution hires only people of the same religion, it may be considered discriminatory, but if it hires irrespective of faith it may lose the sense of collegiality and shared commitment which is a major strength.

Even if they admit staff of different faiths, most faith-based development institutions restrict senior leadership positions to practicing members of the same faith. This helps to preserve the identity of the institution, in the eyes of local people and local religious institutions and perhaps even more important in the eyes of any 'mother' institution in another country, and financial supporters. This too can lead to problems, and there are all too many examples of people with very limited competence being hired because they are loyal members of the church, temple or mosque.

Religious institutions tend to pay low salaries, and priests and other leaders may even work for nothing, or for their bare expenses. Many secular development organizations pay quite generously, but the directors of faith-based institutions may wish to restrict salaries in order to maintain some parity with their own remuneration and that of other servants of the faith, as they see it. This can make it hard to recruit competent staff, and if salaries are at a relatively high level can erode the sense of vocation and commitment which is seen to be an essential strength of faith-based institutions.

Problems can also arise in staff behaviour outside of work. Irrespective of their personal beliefs, they are perceived as being part of a religious institution and expected to behave accordingly. Their private lives are not considered to be private by their employer, and all manner of difficult issues can result from this conflict.

There can also be inconsistencies between the management systems of local religious institutions and their affiliated development organizations. Good systems are expensive to install and maintain, and they need trained people; religious bodies are often unable to afford this. Autocratic leaders may also regard such systems as unnecessary and undesirable restrictions on their own authority and behaviour. They see themselves as being trustworthy, and accountable to God, not to donors or accountants. Even if they are convinced that their God is concerned with the welfare of everyone, and not just their co-religionists, it is highly unlikely that they and their staff will accept that their spiritual progress can be captured in measurable performance indicators as stipulated by the donors. Many donor-imposed systems are also very cumbersome and bureaucratic, and this exacerbates an already difficult situation.

There are thus a number of critical differences between secular and religious development institutions, and between the religious institutions and their local temples, mosques or churches. These can result in creative tensions, which eventually benefit both staff and those who are intended to benefit from their work. They can also be very destructive.

References

Clarke, G. (2005) 'Faith Matters: Development and the complex world of faith-based organisations', paper presented at the conference of the Development Studies Association, the Open University, Milton Keynes.

Deegan, H. (1995) Contemporary Islamic influences in sub-Saharan Africa, An alternative development agenda in the Middle Eastern environment, St Malo Press, Cambridge.

Dilulio, J. (2001), in http://www.whitehouse.gov/news/reports/faithbased.html [accessed 12.02.07]

Foster, G. (2005) 'Study of the response of Faith Based Organizations to orphans and vulnerable children, preliminary report to World Conference of Religions for Peace', Tokyo.

Iyer, S. (forthcoming) 'Religion and Economic Development', in S. Durlauf and L. Blumer (eds.) *The New Palgrave Dictionary of Economics*, Palgrave McMillan, London.

James, R. (2004) *Reflections on current thinking on spirituality in organizations*, Swedish Mission Council, Stockholm.

James, R. (2005) *What is Different about Faith-Based Organization Development? Reflections on experience in Malawi*, INTRAC, Oxford.

Langsun Mate, T. (2006) 'Microfinance, A Strategy for sustainable development', *The ICFAI Journal of Business Strategy*, ICFAI, Hyderabad.

Mersland, R. (2007) 'Innovations in savings and credit groups – evidence from Kenya', *Small Enterprise Development*, vol. 18.

Shetty, S. (2007) 'How Anglicans can help achieve the MDGs?', Proceedings of TEAM Conference, Johannesburg.

Smith, G. (2003) *Faith in the Voluntary Sector: A common or distinctive experience of religious organizations?* Centre for Institutional Studies, University of East London.

Weber, M. (2003) *The Protestant Ethic and the Spirit of Capitalism*, trans. T. Parsons, Dover Publications, Mineola.

Wuthnow, R. (2004) *Saving America: Faith-based services and the future of civil society*, Princeton University Press, Princeton.

CHAPTER 2
How does religion affect the 'BINGOs'?

Abstract

The published figures of a sample of faith-based and secular development NGOs, based in the UK and the USA, show that the faith-based institutions generally rely less on government funds than the secular ones, and more on voluntary contributions which are often accessed through their local churches or mosques. They pay lower salaries, and employ fewer highly paid staff in relation to their total revenues. Their fund-raising costs are similar. Donor governments have been reluctant to channel a large proportion of their foreign aid through faith-based institutions, in order to avoid claims of religious bias. There has recently, however, been a move towards increased use of these religious NGOs, because of the high cost and ineffectiveness of many 'projects' which are undertaken by secular NGOs.

Financial indicators

We shall now examine the quantitative financial impact of religious links on the faith-based international development NGOs; on their funding, their staffing, their activities, their clients and their governance.

The big international development NGOs, or 'BINGOs' as they have been called, stand at the apex of the non-government development pyramid. They have their head offices in the donor countries, notably the USA but also in the UK and continental Europe, and some have developed global brands which are familiar high street names.

Many are multinationals, such as CARE, Save the Children or World Vision. Many of them are actually federations, made up of more or less independent national entities which share a common brand but raise their own funds and manage their own overseas programmes. They raise large sums through voluntary donations and trading activities, from legacies and a whole range of fund-raising initiatives, but they also receive substantial project grants from government bilateral donor agencies which may in some cases exceed their 'voluntary' funding.

The majority of these BINGOs are secular, but some of the largest, with international incomes of over a billion dollars, are faith-based. These include Catholic Relief Services (CRS), which is the major but by no means the only US-based Roman Catholic development NGO, and World Vision which is its Protestant equivalent.

The power and fund-raising capacity of these overtly faith-based BINGOs may seem inconsistent with the decrease in religious practice in most wealthy countries. The proportion of the population who regularly attend a place of worship has dropped heavily over the last 50 years in 19 of the world's 20 most 'developed' countries, as measured by the UNDP Human Development Index. In the UK, for instance, only about 8 per cent of the population say that they regularly attend a church, a mosque, a temple or other religious centre, and all religions, not only Christianity, are experiencing this decline. Some three-quarters of the population, however, claim that they have a religious faith; they seem able to 'believe without belonging'.

The USA is the big exception to this trend, and 44 per cent of its population claim to attend a place of worship at least once a week. The biggest and best known of the faith-based development NGOs originated from the USA, but so too did many of the secular NGOs. Great wealth may be more important than religious observance. There has also been a great increase everywhere in what might be called 'spirituality', as measured by people's statements about themselves and their beliefs, and the adoption of 'quasi-religious' practices such as yoga, meditation and reiki. Generosity and concern for others are in no way the exclusive preserve of the religious, and they need not be expressed through donating to a faith-based charity.

There are nevertheless some important differences between the faith-based and the secular BINGOs. Many of these differences are of practical importance, and some appear to confer a competitive advantage over their secular counterparts. Faith-based institutions can use their churches or other places of worship as a base for fund-raising, and they can call upon the loyalty of adherents to the same faith for donations and for voluntary or semi-voluntary labour. They may, on the other hand, make the task of the institutions more difficult. Governments in most 'developed' countries, perhaps currently with the exception of the USA, have tended until recently to avoid using faith-based institutions as channels for their funding, since they wish to avoid appearing to favour any particular religion.

Some continental European countries, where the state still channels tax payers' donations to churches and other religious institutions, avoid this by having carefully balanced state-recognized development institutions for Catholic and for Protestant Christians, but this becomes more difficult as traditional religious affiliations weaken and are diversified.

We attempted to make a very approximate quantitative assessment of these factors by comparing data from the 2004/5 or 2005/6 financial reports of a total of 11 secular and 11 faith-based development agencies, based in the UK and in the USA. Some of these, such as Save the Children and World Vision, have the same name but are actually separate and independent institutions, being part of international confederations using the same brand names and subscribing to similar principles.

British charity regulations require that registered charities over a certain size should declare the identity of their major donors, including 'official' government sources, and that they should also declare the amount they spend on fund-raising. Additionally, British charities must state how much they spend on salaries, how many people they employ, and, critically, the numbers of people

Table 2.1 Some UK-based faith-based and secular NGOs – some comparisons

NGO	Income	From governments	Fund-raising cost	Average staff salary	Highest paid staff
Faith-based NGOs					
Christian Aid 2004	£80 million	£13.5 million/17%	£13 million/16%	£21,860	1 at £50,000–60,000
Islamic Relief Worldwide 2005	£35 million	£1.3 million/4%	£3.7 million/11%	£17,900	1 at £50,000–60,000
Tearfund 2004	£53 million	£5.5 million/9.5%	£4.2 million/8%	£30,000	1 at £50,000–60,000 and 1 at £60,000–70,000
World Vision UK 2005	£43 million	£5.1 million/12%	£8.4 million/19.5%	£25,600	1 at £50,000–60,000, 4 at £60,000–70,000 and 1 at £80,000–90,000
CAFOD 2005	£47 million	£4.4 million/9%	£4 million/8%	£34,000	1 at £50,000–60,000
Muslim Aid 2005	£4.8 million	Nil	£0.38 million/8%	Not given	None
Muslim Hands '04	£4.5 million	£45,000/1%	£457,000/10%	£20,000	None
Secular NGOs					
Action Aid 2005	£126 million	£34 million/27%	£19 million/15%	£12,460	8 at £50,000–60,000
SCF(UK) 2005	£134 million	£50 million/37%	£18 million/13%	£7,650	8 at £50,000–60,000, 4 at £60,000–70,000, 1 at £70,000–80,000, 1 at £80,000–90,000 and 1 at £90,000–£100,000
CARE (UK) 2005	£40 million	£35 million/87.5%	£3 million/7.5%	£29,850	1 at £50,000–60,000 and 1 at £70,000–80,000
Concern	£58 million	£6 million/10%	£8 million/14%	£28,000	1 at £60,000–70,000, 1 at £70,000–80,000 and 1 at £80,000–90,000
Oxfam 2005	£181 million	£62 million/34%	£18.5 million/10%	£26,300	19 at £50,000–60,000, 12 at £60,000–70,000, 2 at £70,000–80, 000, 1 at £80,000–£90,000 and 1 at £90,000–100,000
Plan (UK) 2005	£31 million	£2.3 million/7.5%	£5 million/16%	£26,500	1 at £60,000–70,000 and 1 at £70,000–80,000

whose annual salaries are above £50,000 (about $100,000) which is about double the average national earnings figure. The data for the US institutions was not available in the same format, but similar figures are published in a number of indices from various sources.

The NGOs, and the salient figures, are shown in Table 2.1. The data was obtained from the websites of the respective institutions, and the sterling figures can be approximately doubled to give their dollar equivalents.

The figures in Table 2.2 for 10 US institutions are not directly comparable since the disclosure requirements are not the same, particularly in relation to staff numbers and salaries. The conclusions are broadly similar, but they do differ significantly in certain respects.

Some of the figures for staff salaries may be deceptive because they include volunteers, semi-volunteers and part time workers, such as those who work in charity shops, but this applies to both secular and faith-based institutions.

One conclusion from this brief analysis is that government funding in faith-based NGOs makes up a smaller proportion of total funding than it does in secular ones. The average figure for the six British-based secular institutions is about one-quarter, whereas for their faith-based equivalents the figure is under 10 per cent. The comparison was less extreme in the USA, where the secular organizations drew an average of 56 per cent of their support from government sources, while the faith-based average was only 36 per cent.

The findings for the USA seem odd given the current political landscape in that country surrounding faith-based international NGOs. A recent *Boston Globe* series on federal funding to religious charities observed that the Bush administration has nearly doubled the percentage of US foreign-aid dollars to faith-based NGOs:

> 'A *Globe* survey of more than 52,000 awards of contracts, grants, and cooperative agreements from the US Agency for International Development – which distributes tax payer-funded assistance overseas – provides the first comprehensive assessment of the impact of Bush's policies on foreign aid. The survey of prime contractors and grantees, based on records obtained through the Freedom of Information Act, shows a sharp increase in money going to faith-based groups between fiscal 2001, the last budget of the Clinton administration, and fiscal 2005, the last year for which complete figures were available. Faith-based groups accounted for 10.5 per cent of USAID dollars to nongovernmental aid organizations in fiscal 2001, and 19.9 per cent in 2005.'
>
> (*Boston Globe*, October 8, 2006)

The apparent inconsistency may arise from the fact that the reported figures relate to contracts rather than actual flows of funds, which show up much later.

The longer term position in the USA seems more similar to that in Britain, where faith-based NGOs are less able than their secular counterparts to secure government funding, from the likes of DFID, USAID, the European Union or the United Nations, because the official agencies are reluctant to appear to be

Table 2.2 Some US-based faith-based and secular NGOs – some comparisons

NGO	Income	From government	Fund-raising cost	Average staff salary	Highest paid staff
Faith-based NGOs					
Adventist Development Relief Association 2004	$101 million	$49 million/49%	$800,000/0.8%	$37,000	$106,000
World Vision 2004	$807 million	$285 million/35%	$63 million/8%	$59,000	$385,000
Christian Children's Fund 2004	$191 million	$8 million/4%	$20.6 million/11.2%	$24,000	$223,000
Catholic Relief Services 2004	$568 million	$406 million/71%	$18 million/3%	$26,000	$225,000
Food for the Hungry 2004	$94 million	$17 million/18%	$4 million/4%	$35,000	$170,000
Secular NGOs					
Pathfinder International 2005	$78 million	$38 million	$1 million/1.3%	N/A	$284,000
Mercy Corps 2005	$168 million	$98 million/58%	$7.25 million/4.4%	N/A	$220,000
International Rescue Committee 2005	$204 million	$97 million/47%	$6.2 million/3.4%	N/A	$325,000
Africare 2005	$49 million	$29 million/71%	$980,000/2%	N/A	$160,000
Save the Children 2004	$271 million	$142 million/52%	$16 million/7%	N/A	$322,000

supporting particular religions. This can also be because faith-based agencies do not want to rely on official sources of funds. They value their political and ideological independence, and official money often comes with 'strings' attached, even if they are not overt.

Whatever the reasons, however, many people at both the giving and the receiving end of development assistance appreciate support which is in no sense 'tainted' by public sector money. Governments are quite naturally anxious that foreign aid, direct or through multilateral agencies, should achieve positive goals for their own national economies as well as for the recipients. This may be achieved by 'tying' aid to national sources of supply, or national institutions, or the aid itself may be directed to activities that serve donor interests rather than those of the poor in the recipient countries.

The average costs of fund-raising are more or less the same for both groups of British institutions, amounting to about 12 per cent of their total income; the figures for the USA were less than half this. The secular US institutions spent an average of 3.2 per cent of their income on fund-raising, while the faith-based organizations spent an average of 6.3 per cent. The apparently greater efficiency in the USA may arise in some cases from their far larger scale of operations, and the differences between secular and faith-based institutions, as in all this data, may be influenced more by other factors than the faith or secular base of the institution.

Child sponsorship is a particularly expensive (but nevertheless very effective) way of raising funds, and World Vision's use of this technique means that it costs their British operation about £20 to raise £100. The figure for World Vision in the USA is much lower, but it, and Christian Children's Fund, both use child sponsorship, thus making the fund-raising costs well over the other US institutions of all kinds. CARE (UK) and Africare are also unusual in that well over half of their funding comes from official sources, such as USAID, the British Government and European Union aid. Fund-raising of this sort is much less expensive than raising voluntary donations from the public.

Average staff salaries in the UK are also fairly similar, at about £22,000 per year per employee. Equivalent information was not available for the secular institutions in the USA, but the US faith-based NGOS pay their staff an average of $36,000, which is somewhat lower than the British figure at present rates of exchange, and well above it in purchasing power. All NGOs, both secular and faith-based, benefit from the services of large numbers of volunteers. Comparative figures for the scale of voluntary work are not available, so it is not possible to hazard a guess as to whether faith-based NGOs receive more assistance of this type.

The British salaries are not high by the standards of the private nor even the public sector, but £50,000 is almost twice average full-time earnings in the UK. Two secular NGOs, Oxfam and Save the Children (UK), are paying their highest paid employees between £90,000 and £100,000 a year. This is almost four times the average wage for all earners, and approaching five times the average salary in the sample. The average salary of the highest paid employee of the British faith-based NGOs in our small sample is between £50,000 and £60,000, and the figure for secular NGOs is between £70,000 and £80,000. This difference cannot be wholly explained by the larger scale of the secular institutions, and presumably owes something to the higher level of voluntarism and commitment of leaders of faith-based institutions.

The US figures are much higher, even though the total funding of the institutions is not very different from that of the British institutions. Three of the five faith-based institutions, and two of the secular ones, pay their chief executives over $200,000 which is over what any of the British executives earn, and the chief executives of World Vision, the International Rescue Committee and Save the Children are paid almost four times what similar British managers are paid. Unlike the British case, there does not seem to be any great difference between the top salaries paid by faith-based and by secular NGOs.

Although charities are obliged to report the numbers and salary bands of their higher-paid staff, they are not required to declare the actual salaries of their chief executives. Comparisons may be misleading, but Christian Aid and Concern have very similar incomes of around £80 million. Christian Aid pays one person between £50,000 and £60,000, while Concern has one each in the three brackets from £60,000–£70,000, from £70,000–£80,000 and from £80,000–£90,000.

Similarly, Islamic Relief and Plan (UK) both have incomes of around £30 million. Islamic Relief pays one person between £50,000 and £60,000 a year, while Plan (UK) pays one person between £60,000 and £70,000 and another between £70,000 and £80,000 a year.

Any comparison of these figures must obviously make an allowance for the size of the charity. This is most conveniently measured by its annual income. According to this measure, the secular NGOs in our list had an average of just over one person receiving over £50,000 a year for every £1 million of income, while the equivalent figure for the faith-based NGOs was just under one-third of a person. In other words, in the faith-based NGOs one highly paid manager could deal with £3 million worth of activity, while their secular equivalents could only deal with £1 million worth.

The chief executive of the Salvation Army is paid approximately £10,000 a year. The Salvation Army is larger in financial terms than all but one of the institutions in our analysis, and is far larger than all of them in terms of numbers employed, but is not included in our analysis because the data for its home-based welfare and religious activities are combined with its social and development work. This is an extreme case, but it does demonstrate the potential impact of religious commitment on salaries and costs.

These figures suggest that faith-based institutions are able to recruit senior management at substantially lower cost than their secular equivalents. These lower-paid managers may be less competent than those who work for secular institutions, but there is no evidence that the management of faith-based NGOs is weaker than others. For want of other evidence, we can conclude that senior managers in faith-based international development institutions are willing to work for less than their secular counterparts.

The data from published reports and accounts shows only a very partial picture. We have thus far considered only a small number of very large multinational institutions, both secular and faith-based, which fall into cells A and C of Figure 2.1. We have examined them only in the context of their published financial data. This data says little about the actual work the institutions perform, or which they support, and our emphasis shifts now to local and generally smaller faith-based institutions which fall into cell B of Figure 2.1.

Figure 2.1 Local vs. multinational and faith-based vs. secular

	Multinational	Local
Faith-based	A	**B**
Secular	C	D

We start by examining in some detail the work of Shri Kshetra Dharmasthala in India, and we then compare this with the principles and programmes of development as practiced by other institutions which are guided by variants of Hinduism, and by the world's two major multinational religions, Islam and Christianity.

References

www.adra.org/ (accessed 20 November 2006)
www.africare.org/ (accessed 20 November 2006)
www.care.org.uk (accessed 21 September 2005)
www.christainchildrensfund.org/ (accessed 21 September 2005)
www.christianaid.org.uk (accessed 21 September 2005)
www.concern.net (accessed 21 September 2005)
www.crs.org/ (accessed 20 November 2006)
www.freedomfromhunger.org/ (accessed 20 November 2006)
www.islamic-relief.com (accessed 20 November 2006)
www.mercycorps.org (accessed 20 November 2006)
www.muslimaid.org (accessed 21 September 2005)
www.muslimhands.org (accessed 21 September 2005)
www.oxfam.org.uk (accessed 21 September 2005)
www.pathfind.org/ (accessed 20 November 2006)
www.savethechildren.org (accessed 20 November 2006)
www.savethechildren.org.uk (accessed 21 September 2005)
www.tearfund.org (accessed 21 September 2005)
www.theirc.org/ (accessed 21 September 2005)
www.wvi.org/ (accessed 20 November 2006)

CHAPTER 3
Dakshin Kannada and Dharmasthala Temple

Abstract

The Dharmasthala Temple is in the southern part of the state of Karnataka in India, in the hills close to the port city of Mangalore. The area has always been open to foreign influences and to trade, and there has always been a strong banking tradition. Many of the bankers belong to the Jain religion, which is one of the three Dharmaic religions, along with Hindusim and Buddhism. Jains have a strong respect for all living things, and are total vegetarians. They have a long tradition of charitable activity. The temple was established in the 15th century by the Heggade family, and has been managed by the family ever since. It welcomes thousands of pilgrims every day, and the incumbent Heggade also acts as a judge in local disputes; his verdicts are respected by the civil courts and are never questioned. The Heggades have always dispensed charity to the neighbouring village people, who have only recently secured ownership of their small plots on the steep hillsides, and generally lack the resources to develop their land.

South Canara district

The Shri Kshetra Dharmasthala Temple is located in Dakshin Kannada district in the state of Karnataka on the west coast of India.

Dakshin Kannada, or South Canara, consists of three rather different areas. The most thickly populated part is the belt of low-lying land along the coast, which is intersected by numerous ranges of hills which stretch westwards from the hilly area, known as the western *ghats*. This area is very fertile, with broad alluvial plains between the hills, and its economy is centred on the port town of Mangalore, the largest town in the district and second only to Bangalore in the whole state.

The middle belt is more hilly but is also fairly fertile, and has many small farms with tree crops such as rubber, coconut and betel nut, an important constituent of 'paan', the betel leaf 'chewing gum' which is so important in India. There are also many small rice paddy fields between the hills, but the area is substantially less fertile and poorer than the coastal belt. Finally, the higher hills of the summits of the western *ghats* run along the eastern side of the district. They are rocky and steeply sloping, and quite sparsely populated, but they have a number of small but highly productive spice gardens, growing pepper and many other spices.

In the district as a whole less than a third of the total land area is available for agriculture. The average landholding in the district is less than one hectare, 70 per cent of the farmers have under one acre, and a further 18 per cent have between one and two acres. The total population of the district is nearly two million, and only 10 per cent of these belong to the 'scheduled tribes' and 'scheduled castes'.

Unlike much of India, where the number of women is much less than men, because of life-long habits of discrimination, there are 1,022 women to every 978 men. The literacy rate is also high by Indian standards: only 10 per cent of men and 13 per cent of women are illiterate. There are three major local languages, Tulu, Kannada and Konkani, in addition to Hindi, the nominal national language, and English.

The coastal belt of south Karnataka was the first point of contact in India for many of the early voyagers from Europe and the Middle East. They came primarily for trade, but they also brought their religions and their language along with them. There were many different waves of migration and settlement in this area, from the tenth century onward, and this has resulted in wide diversity of cultures, religions and languages.

Hinduism is the faith of the majority of the people in the region. The indigenous local kings were generally very religious, and they also relied on religious institutions to strengthen and legitimize their positions as heads of their various kingdoms. As a result, many important temples were established in the area, and several of them are still very popular with the local people and with visitors from elsewhere in Karnataka state and throughout India.

In addition to the four major castes, there are also a number of important local sub-castes, such as Dalits, who are usually field labourers, Tulus and Maplahs, who are landowners and cultivators, and Bants, who are typically the smallest scale independent farmers.

In addition to Hinduism, and often closely related to it, many other religions have a strong presence in the area. The Jains are particularly influential, in spite of their quite small numbers, and they are concentrated in a few areas of the middle hilly belt of south Karnataka, and in the city of Mangalore. There are also over 200,000 Muslim people throughout the district, and nearly every small town and many villages have an active mosque. Their culture has become an integral part of local society. Seven per cent of the population, or around 150,000 people, are Christians. Most are Roman Catholics, and are concentrated around Mangalore, where the Portuguese established an outpost in the 16th century, but there are also smaller groups of Protestants, who are mainly members of the Church of South India.

The banking tradition

South Karnataka has been a centre of international commerce for at least 1,000 years. Until the beginning of the 20th century, many of the import and export merchants relied on local moneylenders for credit. Interest rates were around

50 per cent annually, but the moneylending community, many of whom were Jains, had a tradition of donating a certain percentage of their interest income to local temples in their area. This was confined to unsecured loans, without mortgages, since these were generally made at a higher rate of interest than secured loans, and were also felt to be more risky. If a part of the interest was given to a temple, the risk might therefore be reduced by divine intervention, and the borrower might also feel less aggrieved at the high cost he was paying for the loan.

There was also a well-developed system of cooperative financial institutions known as *nidhis*, and the poorer people had and indeed still have rotating savings clubs, known as *chits*, where one member would collect the pooled savings of all the others on a rotating basis, or on the basis of an informal auction.

These informal financial services were gradually replaced by formal banks, several of which were established in the late 19th and early 20th centuries in southern Karnataka. Modern banking was introduced to the region in 1868 when the Presidency Bank of Madras, which had been founded in 1843, opened a branch in Mangalore to cater to the needs of British firms involved in exporting plantation produce. In 1921, this bank became part of the Imperial Bank of India, the precursor to the State Bank of India.

Because the region was primarily agricultural, with few possibilities for industry, and was also somewhat cut off from the rest of the country by the sea on the west and the mountains to the east, the main outlet for entrepreneurial activity was trade and its financing. Many of the early entrepreneurs, therefore, started selling financial services, and even today the coastal areas maintain a strong banking culture.

The west coast of India, extending from Goa, south of Mumbai (Bombay) to Kanyakumari at the southern tip of the country, is also home to a community known as the Gowd Saraswat Brahmins who are known for their administrative abilities and integrity. Before independence, many of them were employed by the British as revenue collectors for villages. In 1800, Sir Thomas Munro, the first district collector of Canara, wrote that their accounts were so perfect that they furnished a complete record of land revenues for a period of 400 years. This group were born to accountancy and record keeping, and this provided a further impetus to the successful establishment and management of formal banks in the area. Between 1880 and 1935, 22 banks were established in coastal Karnataka, nine of them in the coastal port city of Mangalore and the others in smaller towns in the neighbouring plains and hilly areas (Chatterjee, 1998).

After India's independence in 1947, the national banking industry gained momentum. Several of the smaller banks were merged with larger ones, and in spite of its location on the south western edge of the country the institutions which had started in south Canara rapidly became national leaders. This trend was maintained even after the major banks were nationalized in 1969. Canara Bank, India's fifth largest and by some measures its most successful public sector bank, was started in Mangalore although it has now shifted its head office to

Bangalore, and Syndicate Bank, Corporation Bank, Karnataka Bank and Vijaya Bank were all also originally started in Mangalore. Karnataka Bank was promoted by a group of agriculturists, lawyers and businessmen as the common man's bank, with a strong social and political mandate, and was an offshoot of the *Swadeshi* movement of 1905, which aimed to set up indigenous institutions to rival the imperial establishments of the British rulers.

Syndicate Bank is a particularly important example in the context of rural development. It was established in 1925 in Udupi, quite near to the town of Belthangady where the Dharmasthala Temple is located. It now has almost 2000 branches throughout India, and is one of the fastest growing and most successful of India's public sector banks. Its deposits, its loans and its profits grew by around 20 per cent during the three years to 2005. It was originally established by wealthy trading families in the Dakshin Kannada area, but the bank had a strong social mandate from the very beginning. One of the main initial objectives of its founders was to mobilize small savings and provide affordable credit to local artisans and farmers, including the local weavers who were crippled by a crisis in the handloom industry.

In 1928 the bank started a daily doorstep collection service to help the very poorest people to save, accepting deposits of as little as two annas, or one-eighth of a rupee. This was called the Pigmy Deposit Scheme, and is still offered today by many of the bank's branches, working through some 3,700 agents.

In 2005, Syndicate Bank was every day collecting about Rs.20 million (Indian rupees) (over $500,000) from over one million daily deposit customers (note: in this and subsequent chapters Indian rupees have been approximately converted to US dollars at the rate of Rs.50=$1.00). The minimum daily deposit had by then been increased to Rs.1, and the outstanding balances of daily savers amounted to about $250 million. These deposits mature after seven years, and small penalties are chargeable for earlier withdrawals. Balances can however be converted to fixed deposit accounts without penalty, and with higher interest rates. Small depositors such as those who save under the Pygmy daily collection scheme, and whose balances amount to under Rs.1500 (just over $30) make up over 90 per cent of Syndicate Bank's depositors (Brunton 2004; *Business India*, 4–17 July 2005, Syndicate Bank website). In some of the more remote hill villages loans are still given in kind. The borrower takes 42 seers of rice, and six months or so later, when he has harvested his own crop, he repays 56 seers.

India's rural cooperative banks are not generally very successful; they have been used and often misused by local and state government interests, and many of the 93,000 rural primary societies in the country are moribund or only operate on a very small scale. The South Canara district cooperative bank is a notable exception. The bank and most of its 171 associated primary savings and credit societies are profitable, and it stands second in all of India's cooperative financial institutions for its microfinance business, through the almost 15,000 women's self-help groups to which it has extended credit, with some 200,000 members. The bank has made a major commitment to microfinance, and has appointed a team of 50 full-time group animators to promote and support the groups.

This generous gesture has no doubt enhanced the reputation of the bank, and it may have contributed to the high level of group savings. The Mangalore area is well known for its people's propensity to save, and members' savings in their primary societies in the area are much higher than in other parts of India and have materially improved their profitability. This is good business, it is good for the group members who have few other secure and accessible savings facilities or sources of affordable loans, and it is also good politics. The president of the bank has political ambitions and the extensive outreach to village women has undoubtedly help to build his popularity. Unlike so many cooperative banks elsewhere in India, however, there does not seem to be any fundamental contradiction between politics, business or social welfare; all can coexist.

Fig. 3.1 Map of India, showing the location of institutions described.

There is thus a long tradition of financial intermediation and banking, often with a strong social mandate, and in most parts of South Canara there are a number of institutions competing for business with small farmers and landless labourers. This competition has undoubtedly improved the services which are available to the local people. Institutions can only compete if they offer accessible financial products, at reasonable cost. This has had an important influence on the evolution of the rural development activities of the Dharmasthala Temple in Belthangady.

The Shri Kshetra Dharmasthala Temple

The Shri Kshetra Dharmasthala Temple is located in a valley near the small town of Belthangady in the central hilly belt of Dakshin Kannada, about 300 km west of Bangalore, the state capital of Karnataka which is sometimes known as the Silicon Valley of India, and about 75 km from the sea.

The Belthangady area is heavily forested and only a very low proportion of its land can be farmed. Because the little available cultivable land is generally very hilly, it is only suitable for a limited number of crops. These are mainly tree plantation crops such as rubber, and betel nut, locally known as 'areca nut', the main ingredient of *paan* which is the small leaf wrapped packets of chewing material which are so popular in India. These crops can be very profitable, and one family can make a decent living from a hectare or even less of good land planted to these crops if it is well cared for. The main problem is that like most plantation crops they require a long gestation period of between five and seven years after they have been planted before they yield any income. The process of clearing the land and preparing it for these crops, and planting the seedlings, as well as caring for them before they bear any fruit, also requires some cash inputs and a great deal of labour.

This is financially impossible for most small farmers, so they have to plant much less profitable annual crops, for which the land is not wholly suitable, but which can be harvested after six months or one year. The area has quite high rainfall but only for a very limited period of the year, and it is often unreliable.

Most of the families around Belthangady live in isolated huts or houses on their own plots of land, so that each village occupies a rather large geographical area. They either farm their own small patches of land, or if they do not own their own land, they are employed as daily wage workers on other people's land. The women take care of their families, and help on the land. They also roll *beedis* [local hand-made cigarettes]; this is a major occupation for women in the area because there are some large *beedi* producers in the district.

Up until 1974, the situation was very different. Before then, most of the land was owned by quite substantial landowners. Some of these managed their own land, and employed large numbers of agricultural labourers. Others leased their land to sharecroppers. In the early 1970s there was a major move towards land reform throughout southern India, and in 1974 the Karnataka Land Reform Act set strict limits on the amount of land that could be owned by any single owner.

This Act provided the erstwhile labourers and tenants with land of their own. This was not however sufficient to enable them to cultivate their new land profitably, because of the high investment and long gestation period that tree crops demanded. This problem was compounded by the fact that many of the farmers were drunkards. Excessive drinking was in some ways legitimized by the common practice of drinking during the rituals for some of the local gods which were worshipped in the smaller village temples.

The Dharmasthala temple was originally established at some time in the 15th century. A local farmer, one Barmana Heggade, lived there, in a village which was originally called Kuduma, and was well known in the area for his piety and generosity.

It is said that two travelling strangers, who were actually angels in the form of human beings, came to Heggade's house and asked for hospitality. They were generously received and entertained, and after they had gone the angels reappeared to Heggade in a dream. They thanked him for his kindness, and said that they wished to return in their spiritual form and to live in the place. They asked Heggade in his dream to build a small temple for them next to his house, and to offer hospitality to everyone who came in the same way as he had received them.

Heggade was overwhelmed by this honour and did exactly as the angels had told him. He built a small temple and offered food to anybody who came to see what he was doing, and the place soon became a place of pilgrimage for the local people. Some time later the angels sent another special messenger who brought a sacred *lingam* [stone idol] from Mangalore and installed it in Heggade's temple. This made the temple a place for the worship of Lord Shiva as well as the spirits of the original angels, and enormously widened its popular appeal. The temple became famous in the area, and the name of the place was changed from Kuduma to Dharmasthala, or the place where piety and service to mankind are the way of life.

Since that time, the Heggade family have maintained their position as owners and trustees of the temple and its surrounding area, and as the spiritual rulers of the region. There are a number of not dissimilar places of worship in that part of south Karnataka, but Dharmasthala is unique in having being governed by the same family for such a long period.

The Heggade family, like many of the better-off families in southern Karnataka, are Jains. Jainism is a Dharmaic religion which originated in India in the sixth century BC. There are only about four million Jains in the world today, most of whom live in India, but they have had an influence which is out of all proportion to their numbers. There are growing numbers of Jains in the Indian diaspora in the Europe and North America, and in Africa and South-east Asia.

Jains have significantly influenced the religious, spiritual, economic and political life of India for more than 2,000 years, and the apparently anomalous position of the Heggade family controlling a Hindu temple is not inconsistent with their history.

Like Hindus and Buddhists, the other two main Dharmaic religions, Jains aim towards achieving total release from self and desire, or nirvana. They believe, however, in equality and non-violence, and in respect for all living things, irrespective of caste or even of species. One major reason for their breaking away from mainstream Hinduism was their rejection of the notion of caste. They are total vegetarians, and prefer when possible not even to eat plants, such as root crops, which must be killed in order to be harvested.

Jains believe that all souls are equal because they all possess the potential of being liberated and attaining self-realization. Every human being is believed to responsible for his or her actions, rather than being pre-ordained to behave in a particular way. They do not believe in an omnipotent supreme being or creator, but rather in an eternal universe which is governed by natural laws.

Compassion for all life, human and non-human, is central to Jainism. Human life is valued as an opportunity to reach enlightenment. To kill any person, no matter what crime he may have committed, is considered unimaginably abhorrent. Jainism is the only religion that requires all its adherents to be vegetarian. Some parts of India, including south Karnataka, have been strongly influenced by Jains, and this is one reason why so many Hindus in southern India are vegetarians.

Jains accept and respect other faiths, and are often prominent in interfaith activities. A number of non-Jain temples in India are managed by Jains, including Dharmasthala, and Mahatma Gandhi was strongly influenced by the non-violent tradition of Jainism. Most of the staff at Dharmasthala, including the temple servants and priests, are not Jains, but are Hindu Brahmins, and Lord Shiva is of course a Hindu God. This exemplifies the pantheist approach of Dharmasthala, and of much of Hinduism generally.

Many, if not most, of the pilgrims are local people, and Dharmasthala has in its 600 years of history never acquired the same international reputation as some other similar places, such as the celebrated Sai Baba has acquired for his ashram at Puttarpathi in one generation. The pilgrims make such donations as they can afford, and some are quite generous, but Dharmasthala has not accumulated enormous wealth in the same way as the Sai Baba ashram, Tirupathi or some of the better-known temples elsewhere in India. Nevertheless, over its long history, the family and the temple have become very wealthy. This has enabled the family to maintain the temple, and, in recent years, to finance and run their remarkable rural development programme.

The management of many of the larger Indian temples has been taken over by the Indian Government, because of claims of inefficiency, misuse or malpractice, but Dharmasthala has so far remained independent, and is in legal terms under the sole control of the Heggade family. The state authorities have made some moves to take over control as they have in other places, but they have been unable to find any cause for intervention. The very fact that Heggades are Jains, a separate minority religion although it is part of the Dharmaic tradition, has helped to maintain the independent status of Dharmasthala.

Around 10,000 or even 20,000 pilgrims come to Dharmasthala every day, or almost three million people every year. There is a range of accommodation for those who wish to stay overnight, from simple dormitory rooms to well furnished lodges of 'five star' standard. Those who cannot afford the cost are fed and accommodated without charge, as the angels are said to have commanded 600 years ago. Nearly every devotee leaves some donation, however small. Many also follow the tradition of having their heads shaved before paying their respects to the God in the Temple; Dharmasthala runs a large barbers establishment for this purpose, and the mass of hair which is cut from the pilgrims' heads is sold for industrial purposes. Even this raises a substantial sum every year.

The Heggades are said to have discharged their sacred responsibilities without fail ever since the 15th century, and this has enabled them to acquire an aura of divinity which extends into non-spiritual affairs. The 'reigning' Heggade is also known by the honorary title of 'Manjunatha who speaks', since the family has the honour of functioning as the earthly representatives of Lord Manjunath.

The Heggades are said always to have followed the example of the founder of the dynasty by providing the four traditional charitable gifts of food, health care, education and economic security. As a result, the leader of the family has also acquired temporal powers. The local people, and even some people from quite distant places, regard Veerendra Heggade, the current leader of the dynasty, as a totally impartial judge. This custom is said to have been followed for over 600 years, and the Heggades' decisions are accepted and honoured by the civil courts. It is a local tradition that when two people cannot resolve a dispute, if one of them invokes the name of Manjunatha they must both stop their arguments forthwith and go to present the issue to him at Dharmasthala during his daily audience. These disputes often relate to caste, as well as to civil and criminal matters. When one party lodges a complaint with the Heggade, the other party to the dispute is informed and is requested to come to the temple to state if there is any truth in the complaint which has been lodged. Both parties appear before the Heggade and present their cases, and he gives his verdict. This is accepted as final, not only by the affected parties, but by the Indian civil courts.

So far as is known, nobody has ever dissented from his judgment, or appealed back to a civil court. The Heggade's decisions are always accepted without further argument, since any further questions would be perceived as sacrilegious disregard for the holy Manjunatha. Many Christians and Muslims, as well as Hindus, use Dharmasthala as a source of legal judgments in this way. Hundreds of other postulants come to Dr Heggade's daily audiences, to ask for his blessing, or to request his assistance in personal problems. He or his staff may intercede with local authorities, often with success, or he may give people small sums of money to deal with their immediate needs.

The Heggade family have been in charge of the Dharmasthala Temple for 20 generations. Their position is unique, and there is nothing like it anywhere else in India. It is a hereditary position, generally passed on from the father to the eldest son, and they have also always occupied an important place in civil affairs in the local area. In addition to individual donations to needy people, the family has also contributed to improvements in health, education and general infrastructure activities in the area. Hindus believe that serving food to travellers, to beggars or to the poor and the needy, is a virtuous act in itself. Many temples include the serving of food as an integral part of their ritual, and the food is always offered first to the idol of the God, before it is distributed to the devotees. Many Hindu temples in South Canara distribute free food twice a day to the visiting pilgrims, who regard the food as God's *Prasad,* which is sanctified by being offered first to the Lord, rather as with the food and wine of the Christian Holy Communion. It is fundamental also that no charge is levied for the food. In Dharmasthala everyone who visits the temple may eat for free.

The *Dharmadhikaris,* as the guardians of the temple have always been known, have always been known for their charity. This is financed from the donations of the thousand of pilgrims who visit the temple every day. Most of these pilgrims are not rich people themselves, but the total of their small donations amounts to a very large income every year. After meeting the establishment and maintenance expenditures of the temple, the balance of the money is given away as charity.

Jains have traditionally been regarded as local chieftains, in a temporal sense, and they were often employed as managers of temples because of their well-known respect for people of all religions. As a result of the high status they acquired from this, many Jains later became traders and financiers, and occupied prominent positions in local society. The Heggade dynasty is unusual in many respects, but it follows the tradition of the mingling of spiritual and economic power which Jains have traditionally occupied in South Canara.

The thousands of pilgrims who come to Dharmasthala regard it as a place of total religious tolerance; they are welcomed regardless of their caste, their sect or their religion. The *Theerthankara,* the earliest follower of Jainism, is worshipped on the same consecrated ground as Lord Manjunatha, the reincarnation of Lord Shiva. The priests are Brahmins and the guardian of the temple is a Heggade, a Jain by faith. The place has a highly charged religious atmosphere, but it is a place of all religions, not merely one.

References

Brunton, P.D. (2004), *Financing small-scale rural manufacturing enterprises,* FAO, Rome.

Chatterjee R. (1998) *Lifescapes of India: Religions, customs and laws of India,* Frandsen Humanities Press, Reno.

Syndicate Bank website, www.syndicatebank.com [accessed 14.02.2007].

CHAPTER 4
SKDRDP, the rural development programme

Abstract

When Veerendra Heggade, the present hereditary leader of the Dharmasthala Temple took over, he reaffirmed his father's commitment to the spiritual roots of the temple He was also concerned to improve the livelihoods of the people in the surrounding areas rather than merely to help them with charitable donations. The farmers had recently gained ownership of the land on which they had for generations been labourers, but they lacked the capital, and the skills, to use the land and were worse off than before. Heggade started a small programme to help them, but the benefits were not sustained, and most of the farmers spent the benefits on liquor. In the late 1990s it was totally restructured and professionalized, under the title of the Shri Kshetra Dharmastahala Rural Development Programme, or SKDRDP. The range of initiatives was broadened, to include microfinance, shared labour and women's groups, alcohol de-addiction, insurance, education and religious meetings. The sevaniratha field staff were made responsible for the integrated delivery of every component of the programme, and a banker with many years of experience in rural development was put in charge.

The origins of SKDRDP

Veerendra Heggade, the present incumbent and holder of the hereditary position, inherited the role in 1968, when he was just 20 years old. He was studying at college at the time. As a descendant of a rich family, he had developed expensive tastes, such as photography, modern cars and architecture, and if events had turned out differently he might have taken on a traditional career, or he might even have entered politics, as his father had attempted to do. Due to the sudden and unexpected death of his father, however, he had to abandon his studies and take on the responsibility of the position of *Dharmadhikari* when he was least expecting it.

Veerendra Heggade's father was very devout, and was also interested in local history. Two years before his death, in 1966, he had started building a giant statue of Bahubali on a hill above the temple. Bahubali is one of the most famous spiritual leaders of the Jains, and the most famous sculpture of Bahubali is in Shravana Belagola, a small town about 100 km from Dharmasthala. The stone sculpture of Bahubali symbolizes renunciation, self-control and subjugation of ego as the steps towards salvation. The naked form of the statue represents complete victory over the earthly desires that hinder man's spiritual ascent towards divinity. Veerendra Heggade's father had organized the carving of a similar statue to the one at Shravana Belagola, out of one piece of granite, but he died before it was completed. When his son took over the position, he naturally had to take on the responsibility of supervising the completion and installation of the statue.

When he ascended the throne of the *Dharmadhikari*, which conferred substantial power on his young shoulders even in modern democratic India, Veerendra Heggade, being a wealthy young man, could have quite easily been tempted by the privileges of his position and become a playboy. As he personally supervised the carving of the statue, however, he underwent a quite dramatic personal transformation.

He took on without question all the rituals that his religious position demanded, but he also retained his youthful openness and inquisitiveness, and his interest in the wider world beyond Dharmasthala. He was at the same time overwhelmed and somewhat worried by the faith which the temple's devotees had in the temples and in the position that he had acquired. He felt somewhat uneasy about their need to improve their livelihoods. Was there a way in which their dependence on charity from the temple might be reduced, without eroding their faith?

At this point, as he completed the installation of the statue of Bahubali, the symbol of ultimate renunciation and sacrifice, Heggade conceived of the idea of an institution which could go beyond charity and could help the devotees of the temple to build sustainable and dignified livelihoods. He rapidly grew into the responsibilities of his office, but he also started to transform the charitable work of the Dharmasthala Temple into a modern rural development institution, which would enable the people to lead dignified lives, without losing their faith in the temple.

Heggade was overwhelmed by the expectations of the followers of the temple, but he disliked their apparent economic and emotional dependence on him and his religious institution. Although the money which was mainly contributed by the poor when they visited the temple was in some way going back to them in charity, it was not systematically used and the grants depended mostly on *ad hoc* responses to individual requests for assistance. It was difficult to track the impact of the temple's charitable donations, which were in some sense given by Veerendra Heggade himself since Dharmasthala was his personal heritage. As a modern young man, with some training in economics, he wanted to know what was happening to the money he was giving away, and to maximize the long-term productive benefits of the donations. He wanted to ensure that they did not merely increase people's dependence on Dharmasthala but instead enabled them to manage without charity in the future.

He decided to start a separate development institution, which would help people to empower themselves and to develop their own independent livelihoods, but would at the same time be closely allied to the Dharmasthala Temple. Heggade conceived of two institutions. First was the Shri Kshetra Dharmasthala Rural Development Project, or SKDRDP, to serve the people in the rural areas around the temple, who Heggade felt really deserved the credit for building Dharmasthala to its present position. This was wholly funded and managed by Heggade himself and the Dharmasthala Temple. Second was the Rural Development and Self Employment Training Institute, or RUDSETI, which was to offer training and livelihood assistance over a wider area. This was suggested and supported by Heggade, but was legally constituted as a joint venture between Canara Bank and Syndicate Bank, the two large national banks which had originated in South Canara district.

The initial plan for SKDRDP was that it should assist the small farmers who had obtained freehold land rights under the Land Reform Act of 1974. Heggade and his colleagues who had started the programme felt that there was nothing they could do for the poorest people, those without any land at all, but that the problem of the small farmers could be solved within five years. For that reason, SKDRDP was set up as a temporary project, rather than being registered as a permanent institution. The immediate need was to provide the farmers with the knowledge as well as the capital they needed in order to make the best use of their holdings. The programme centred on improving the small farmers' land.

Two local management staff were appointed, and two friends of Dr Heggade were asked to be his advisers; he was in effect the project director. A few village-based field officers were selected from the local community by the local people themselves. This work was started in the villages around Belthangady, because this is where the Dharmasthala Temple is located, and where the people are very loyal to the Heggade family and the whole temple community. The farmers were struggling to cultivate their own land due to their lack of simple resources such as agricultural implements, seeds, and fertilizers.

At first the work of SKDRDP was focussed on marginal and small farmers. It was a natural extension of the charitable activities of the temple, and the organization provided every kind of support that was necessary to help the farmers to cultivate their land. They were helped to improve their land, they were given seeds, tools and fertilizers, and were also taught how to use them. The programme even provided all the basic assets required for a household, from the basic food requirements to household utensils. Whole truckloads of rice were purchased from the market and distributed in the villages by SKDRDP.

The field animators or *sevanirathas*, as they came to be called, identified needy families and tried to help them to develop their land and infrastructure through an informal food-for-work programme. The farmers would themselves hire other labourers to help with the work when they were required, and they too were paid by SKDRDP with rice. Every morning all the staff went out with vehicle-loads of rice and cultivation equipment. They worked with small farmers, showing them how to clear their land and plant the new tree crops, and they paid them for their time with rice. The landlords who had employed the people before the 1974 Act used to give them rice for their labour, but this had stopped when the farmers took possession of their own land. Paradoxically, they were worse off than before.

The teams would then return to Dharmasthala in the evening. Mrs Heggade served food to the *sevanirathas* herself while they shared their experiences with each other. Dr Heggade and his close colleagues gained a much closer understanding of what was actually going on in the villages. The fieldwork was carried out with great enthusiasm by this small initial team, who felt that they were working for the temple and Dr Heggade, and were content with very low salaries. After five years, when the time came to end the project, the fieldworkers, and Dr Heggade's advisers convinced him that five years was far too short a period in which to make a lasting change to the habits of many lifetimes.

They also appreciated that one major problem, which wiped out much of whatever they achieved, was alcoholism. Also, they had hardly involved the village women in the process at all, since they had initially assumed that once the organization had worked with the farmers, the lot of their womenfolk would naturally improve. During this period, Mrs Heggade, stayed in the background and played a quietly supportive role, but she gradually took a more active part in the work of the new institution.

In 1991, after much discussion, the legal status of SKDRDP was changed and put on to a more permanent footing. It was formally registered as a charitable society, in recognition of the fact that the task that it had undertaken would occupy many years.

The work continued for some years, since the most profitable crops required five to seven years before they could yield any income. In order to help the farmers to do major jobs that needed more than one person, the staff informally started another intervention, using small groups of farmers who lived near to one another and had similar labour requirements which they could not do alone. They would work as a group, moving from one member's plot to another. By pooling their labour, and their skills, they were able to achieve more than they could individually.

Reappraisal and restructuring

These initial modest interventions for the farmers gradually resulted in increased household incomes. At first the increase was quite small, but it did mean that the farmers had more cash in their hands from time to time. Inevitably, much of this money was spent on alcohol. All the farmers who owned land were men, since the landholdings were in their name, and it was becoming very clear that two important stakeholders, the women and the landless households, were being neglected. As the staff evaluated their work year by year, they recognized that the interventions had not led to any significant change in the lives of people, although there had been some marginal economic improvement.

It was also clear, as the work expanded, that SKDRDP's systems were quite weak. Dr Heggade recruited a retired postmaster as the first full-time director. More emphasis was also put on formalizing the administration and controls to avoid waste and misuse of funds, as the amount of money that was being handled by the programme was slowly increasing. The activities were also extended beyond Belthangady, and this was put under the management of a different director, in order to decentralize the operations.

In the late 1990s, Dr Heggade was becoming increasingly dissatisfied because SKDRDP was not growing as he had hoped, in terms of its programmes or its outreach, and he was not himself able to give it the time it needed. The programme had made some improvements in the area, but these were not substantial and it was probable that they would not survive if SKDRDP's assistance was withdrawn. Basically, it was little more than a continuation of the charitable tradition of the temple.

It was clear that the money from the temple trust would not be sufficient to cover the expansion of the programmes as they were being run, beyond a point that might quite soon be reached. And since SKDRDP was linked to a temple trust, which was known to be quite wealthy and was not seen as being involved in development work, it would be difficult for it to access conventional donor funds.

At this point the idea of microfinance was suggested by some of Dr Heggade's advisers who also had banking experience. Around this time the concept of microfinance self-help groups was rapidly taking shape in other parts of the country, partly in response to similar developments in neighbouring Bangladesh. After lengthy discussions, Dr Heggade was convinced that microfinance groups would enable him to achieve his dream of reaching all the people in the area who needed to improve their position. Some savings and credit activity had started in some parts of Belthangady in the mid 1990s, and this was a way of reaching both the farmers who had small parcels of land, and the landless people who depended on manual labour for their livelihoods. Small amounts of credit could help them to start small non-farm microbusinesses, and would also enable them to access lower cost loans than were available from local moneylenders.

Dr L. Manjunath, a veterinary doctor who had worked for many years with Syndicate Bank, had come to know SKDRDP and its activities when he was manager of the RUDSETI centre at Ujire, a small town near Dharmasthala. He had been one of Dr Heggade's advisers, and was dissatisfied with his work at the bank so he approached Dr Heggade asking how he could help. After some discussions, they both decided that he should leave Syndicate Bank and take over as executive director of SKDRDP.

When Dr Manjunath joined SKDRDP he had very strong backing from Dr Heggade, and he introduced a number of quite radical changes in order to formalize the institution and put it on a more professional basis. The work with individual farmers, with farmers' groups and with general community development outside the Belthangady area had become separated into three different sections, and the first change that Dr Manjunath made was to integrate them. The *Sevanirathas* were clearly designated as the sole representatives of the institution at the village level, responsible for every programme being done in their village, if necessary with the assistance of specialized staff from head office.

Salaries were increased, and a pension scheme and concessionary vehicle loans were introduced. Many of the staff who had worked for SKDRDP for 10 years or more were promoted as the institution expanded into new areas and new opportunities opened up. SKDRDP also started to work closely with government departments in their development programmes for small towns, and in special job and enterprise creation initiatives. There are large numbers of such programmes in Karnataka, as there are throughout India, and their main weakness is often the lack of competent and honest links to the people whom they are intended to benefit. All too often, such programmes are 'hijacked' by politicians or dishonest officials, and they fail to reach the people who need them. SKDRDP's *sevanirathas* provided an effective and unbiased link to the communities where they worked.

The field operations are organized into circles of eight to ten villages. Each village has its own *sevaniratha*, and each circle is under the management of a *melvicharaka,* or supervisor. The circles come under a project office, which is at the level of the sub-district. The technical specialists who support the *sevanirathas* are based in these project offices, and they only visit villages when they are asked to do so by the responsible *sevaniratha*. Every project office has one project officer in charge, with a dairy officer, an agricultural officer, an assistant in charge of insurance programmes and two women's group coordinators, as well as an office manager and support staff.

Each project office is guided by a director at head office, who is usually also responsible for a functional department. There are seven of these: microfinance, health insurance, SIRI (which looks after the various production units which have been promoted by SKDRDP), livelihood promotion, rural development, community development, and self-help groups. Additionally, there are departments for human resources, finance, administration and audit. The auditors are mostly ex-*sevanirathas* who have been promoted because of their particularly good performance, and they are thus very familiar with the day-to-day operations and are able to carry out their auditing duties without diverting the field staff from their work.

All the staff under each project office meet once a month, and each circle has a meeting every week. The executive committee, consisting of the functional directors and project officers meets once a month to take management decisions. This meeting is usually attended by Dr Heggade, the chairman of the board of directors of SKDRDP.

The monthly meetings have a clear sense of hierarchy. The seating is arranged like a classroom. The directors and project officers occupy the dais, the supervisors and auditors sit in the front row and all the *sevanirathas* behind them in the places which are reserved for the staff of each project and circle office. Everyone who speaks has to start with the phrase '*Om Shri Manjunathaya Namah*' [blessings to Lord Manjunatha], and all the proceedings are carried out in Kannada, the language of Karnataka, or in local dialect; no English words are used. This ensures that everyone can understand, and it also makes it impossible to use any development jargon, which can so often conceal the speakers' understanding, not only from their audience but also from themselves.

Any notable successes which individual *sevanirathas* have achieved in their villages are discussed and acknowledged in these meetings, and any serious outstanding issues are discussed, even if they only concern one village. If any loans are seriously in arrears, these too are discussed, and nothing is done behind closed doors. Everyone feels free to speak, and if someone has done particularly well, the achievement is described and applauded. If someone has failed, this too is acknowledged and discussed.

Until the institution was restructured, the bulk of its assistance had been provided on a grant basis, without charge, at the expense of the Dharmasthala Temple Trust. The management of SKDRDP realized that the expansion of their programmes would require more resources than the trust could afford, and they also appreciated that grants were likely to create dependence rather than to empower the recipients. This was what had happened to the people of Belthangady throughout the history of the temple, and it had to be stopped not only in order to ensure the independent survival of SKDRDP but also to assist more people in a genuinely sustainable way.

SKDRDP's programmes

It was therefore formally decided that SKDRDP would move away from charity towards a more empowering approach, and would also to try to use microfinance as a way of involving the women and landless people who had so far been left out. It was also clear that all their efforts would be in vain unless the problem of drunkenness was dealt with once and for all. In order to achieve these goals, the *Pragathi Bandhu, Jananavikasa Kendra* and *Jana Jagruti* programmes took formal shape in the early 1990s.

SKDRP has always used local Kannada language words to name their programmes. These words have Sanskrit origins, and they also have strong religious connotations, which link the programmes very firmly to Dharmasthala. This makes them all the more powerful, since the local communities immediately identify with the programmes. Most NGOs, and most government programmes, use English words and acronyms even when speaking in Hindi or local vernaculars. They say 'IRDP' for the integrated rural development programme, or 'SHG' for self-help groups. Terms of this kind are never used in formal discussions or general conversation by SKDRDP. Nobody uses the words 'microcredit' or 'microfinance', they refer to '*Pragathi Nidhi*'.

A number of these Kannada terms have already been used in this description of SKDRDP and its work, and more will be used in subsequent pages. Exact literal translations of such words are not possible, and it is appropriate at this point to provide an informal 'glossary', which attempts to explain not only the literal meaning of each term but also some of the spiritual meanings which are attached to all these Sanskrit words.

Sevanirathas

Sevaniratha means 'eternally at the service (of the gods)'. The term is used in some temples to describe the people who provide daily services to the God, such as cleaning and cooking. These apparently quite humble tasks are in fact the most honoured among the staff of temples such as Dharmasthala, because they are performed by the front-line staff. For that reason, the most blessed title in the whole institution has been given to the village fieldworkers, because they are without doubt the most crucial link in the SKDRDP's programmes. The term shows quite clearly to everyone that they are the representatives of the institution, and of Dr Heggade himself, the *Dharmadhikari*, and are at the service of the community. It also confers respect on the *sevanirathas* in the communities that they work with, as well as in society at large. Most crucially of all, it gives them self-respect.

Pragathi Nidhi

A *nidhi* is a fund and *pragathi* means growth or development, so the combined word means a fund which enables someone to progress. This is the name given to SKDRDP's microfinance programme, because finance can be provided for just about every conceivable reason to the members of the groups, for production, for consumption or for local infrastructure development. A *nidhi* is not necessarily a monetary fund, and the word also has the connotation of a treasure, someone's most precious resource, and it can be applied to a person's intelligence, to children, to money, or to one's faith in god. It was traditionally not associated with material resources. The word has a feminine connotation, and *nidhi* is a popular name for daughter. Some popular financial companies have taken up the term to promote their schemes for savings, insurance or mutual funds.

Pragathi Bandhu

Bandhu means friends, and *pragathi*, as above, means growth and development. The combined term means friends who help you to grow, develop or progress. This is usually the first intervention in a village by SKDRDP, and involves a small group of farmers getting together to share their labour as described earlier. The *Pragathi Bandhu* programme evolved beyond labour sharing and became the basis of the SKDRDP microfinance programmes, including savings, credit and insurance.

Jnanavikasa Kendra

Jnana means knowledge, *Vikasa* means development and *Kendra* means centre. The whole phrase means a centre for enriching knowledge for development. SKDRDP uses this term, often abbreviated to 'JVK', to describe the women's' groups that it uses to spread awareness in a village. These are groups of up to 50 women who come together every month to discuss anything that is relevant for them to lead better lives. Their discussions include health, incomes, culture and cooking lessons, and they are also involved in the microfinance programme.

Jana Jagruthi

This means 'mass awareness' or 'rising of the people', and is the title which SKDRDP has given for its anti-alcoholism programme. It has become one of the most successful social movements of its kind in Karnataka and indeed in all of India.

Nava Jeevana Samiti

A *samiti* is a group of people who share a common cause. *Nava* means new and *Jeevana* means life. It therefore means a committee of people who are starting a fresh or new life together. SKDRDP uses this term to describe the groups of people who have gone through the alcohol de-addiction camp process of the *Jana Jagruthi*, and who come together in a village every week for a *Bhajan Mandali*. A *Bhajan Mandali* is a religious meeting where a group of people come together to sing hymns in the praise of God and to express their thanks for their good fortune. This is a very popular custom in rural areas of India, although it is known by different terms in different areas. It is one of the most basic ways in which rural people from all walks of life come together, and many very important forms of folk art owe their origin to it. Hindu rituals do not usually include a routine community meeting of this sort, and the *Bhajan Mandali* in some ways mirrors the Friday prayer meetings of Islam and the Sunday church services of most Christian denominations.

In the *Nava Jeevana Samiti* the people come together to express their gratitude to God for liberating them from the vices of alcohol, and it acts in some ways like the wholly secular Alcoholics Anonymous of the USA and elsewhere. The members are also very often members of other *Pragathi Bandhu* or microfinance self-help groups.

Jeevan Dhama

Jeevan Dhama means 'place for life', and the term is used to describe the SKDRDP housing programme, through which credit is provided for building and renovating houses, and houses are also built on a grant basis for destitute families. Over 14,000 houses have been built for destitute families under this programme.

Suraksha

This word means 'safety', in a divine as well as a physical sense, and is used in SKDRDP to describe the health and sanitation programme.

Sampoorna Surakshya

Sampoorna means 'complete', 'all-embracing'. This is the name of the SKDRDP combined insurance scheme and benevolent fund, which takes care of people's emergency needs.

Jnanadeepa

Jnana means 'knowledge', as in *Jnanavikas,* and *Deepa* means a traditional form of candle with a cotton wick which burns vegetable oil, which is often burned before the idols of Gods in Indian temples. These candles had particular significance before electric light was available, since they were the only means whereby rural people could read and study after sunset. Now that electricity is generally available, these candles are mainly used for religious purposes. *Jnanadeepa* refers to the traditional need for light for reading, and to the sense that knowledge is light. It is the title of the SKDRDP education programme, which provides teachers and equipment for primary schools.

Rudra Bhoomi

Rudra primarily means 'anger', but is one of the many names of Shiva, of the Hindu Goddess who shares the temple of the Manjunatha of Dharmasthala. *Bhoomi* means 'land'. *Rudra Bhoomi* is a place where bodies are cremated, according to Hindu custom. Through this programme, SKDRDP finances improvements to the common cremation facilities in villages, since Hindus, like most people, consider people's final resting place to be very sacred.

The *Pragathi Bandhu* groups

As the name indicates, the members of a *Pragathi Bandhu* group are partners in each other's progress. This relates not only to their formal weekly work sharing, and their microfinance activity, but to all their difficulties and emergencies, as well as their pleasures. It is based on the old tradition of labour sharing, when there was no concept of hiring labour for money. People used to work together on their communal farms and it was only in the last century that the concepts were developed of private land and hired labour. The 'tribal' communities, some of whom still live in the higher hill areas above Belthangady, still use various forms of non-monetary labour sharing.

The practice has always been particularly prevalent during the planting and harvesting seasons, and after a *sevaniratha* chanced to observe the practice in a village called Nauru he described it to Dr Heggade and his colleagues in the daily meeting the *sevanirathas* used to have with Dr Heggade at that time. From that time it became the flagship programme for SKDRDP.

The small and marginal farmers started by sharing their labour to cultivate their own fields, which they had previously left fallow while they worked as labourers with the big landholders, since they had no capital to pay for the inputs they needed for their own farming. As time went by, however, the groups have become much more flexible, and they started to work on house construction and also on infrastructure projects for their village communities.

The basic principle has, however, remained the same. A *Pragathi Bandhu* is essentially a group of between five and eight small farmers who own land in the same village or hamlet. They give one day a week to shared labour, working in turn on each others' land or on other tasks as required. They also use the groups for savings and credit, in conjunction with the SKDRDP *Pragathi Nidhi* programme. The member on whose work the group are engaged has to feed his colleagues that day, but no money changes hands. They also collect their weekly savings and loan repayments on that day, and make decisions on any new loan requests.

Whenever SKDRDP enters a village for the first time, it starts by forming *Pragathi Bandhu* groups. The groups are also used as a first point of contact when SKDRDP is considering any new interventions. The maximum size of any group used to be eight members, but this has now been relaxed in a few cases. All the members used to be men, and farmers, and the groups are still dominated by the men, but now women and others who are engaged in petty trade and other non-farm enterprises are admitted. Women usually come in only when they are unmarried, and have lost their fathers, or when they have been widowed or their husbands have migrated elsewhere for work or other reasons. Thus it is not uncommon to have mixed groups, in terms of both gender and profession.

If one member cannot contribute his labour on one day for a good reason, the group can allow him to send someone else from his own family or to replace himself with a paid labourer, whose wages he pays. The workdays are not necessarily rigidly rotated, and the groups work on whatever task most urgently needs to be done. They keep a record of who has benefited and try to even out the work over the year.

The groups are self-selected and self-managed and the *sevanirathas* play only a facilitating role, as they do with all the various types of groups with which SKDRDP works. Most of the members are farmers. Some have up to about five acres of land in the same village or hamlet, but the average land holding is only about two acres. Since every member has to contribute his labour, except on rare occasions when they provide substitutes, better-off people of higher social standing do not get involved.

There are occasional dropouts, such as when a member leaves the area or is unable to contribute his labour. Such dropouts are very rare, and there is therefore usually no need for groups to recruit new entrants.

The JVK Women's Groups

There is a popular saying in Kannada *'Hennondu Kalithare Shaleyondhu Theredhanthe'*, which means 'if one woman learns, it is the same as opening a new school in the area'. For more than a decade, SKDRDP worked only with men, and women were more or less excluded from its programmes. When Mrs Heggade became involved in SKDRDP, she introduced the idea that women should be made equal stakeholders in the development of the community, and the *Jnanavikasa Kendra* (JVK) concept was born.

In a strictly social sense, the women of this part of Karnataka are more liberated than in much of India, and there are very few crimes against women. The gender balance is nevertheless skewed against women, and they are seen as subordinate to their husbands in most respects. They work on their family land, but it is not usually held in their name, and many of them earn some extra income by rolling *beedis*. This is one of the few traditional ways in which women can contribute to household incomes apart from farm labour. The JVKs have enabled many thousands of women such as Pushpavathi (see Box 4.1) to improve on this very inadequate form of income generation.

The JVKs have between 30 and 50 members. The members are generally uneducated, under-employed rural women from the poor sections of the rural villages, including backward castes and tribal people, and women from landless families. The JVKs were initially started for women of over 40 years of age, who came together for social empowerment.

The village *sevaniratha* initiates the group formation process, and in the early stages of a group's formation the women meet every week at a common place in

---

Box 4.1 Pushpavathi

Pushpavathi was born to a very poor family in a village in Belthangady. Her parents were farm labourers, and they lived in a mud hut with their nine children. They struggled to earn enough to have two meals a day. Her memory of childhood is the siblings sharing gunny bags as blankets during winter. Once in a while the girls would each be given Rs.2 to buy bangles; these were the happiest moments of her childhood.

Pushpavati started rolling *beedis* at the age of 11 and then married a man from a neighbouring village. He was a drunkard, and he abused and beat her. She complained to the older people in the village, and to the police, and eventually left her husband and returned home to stay with her mother. By this time, she also had a small son.

She again rolled *beedis*, to support her son, but the village elders and her own family disapproved of her decision to leave her husband, and she could not remain at her parents' house. She was then fortunate enough to be awarded a household plot under a government scheme.

Pushpavathi then joined the Sri Dhurgambika Mahila JVK that had been started by SKDRDP, and she was soon chosen as the president. She saved part of the money she earned through *beedi* rolling and after two years she got a loan of Rs.20,000 (about $400) from the government under the government Aashraya Yojana programme of housing for the poor.

She built her own house with help of her group members, and gained confidence and was able to stand on her own in society.

A SKDRDP staff member suggested that she do something else apart from *beedi* rolling to improve her income. She borrowed Rs.5,000 to start bangle trading. This did well, and she then borrowed Rs.10,000 to start a small shop. She plans in the future to stop *beedi* rolling since she can earn more by spending time in her shop.

the village for up to two hours, to interact with each other and discuss day-to-day issues. The meetings start with a prayer, and proceed to discuss a variety of issues. Specialists from SKDRDP come at regular intervals to conduct training programmes on health, sanitation, leadership, literacy, culture, and even new cooking skills. The women are also taken on exposure visits to other villages to see what has been achieved by other groups.

The initial objective was to inculcate awareness and inspire the women to improve their social position, but as time went by, and when some groups started to be used a forum where the smaller microfinance self help groups could meet to discuss their financial business, some younger women started to join. Nevertheless, the main purpose of the JVKs remained primarily for awareness generation and general discussion, and most younger women still preferred to be the members of self help groups and not of JVKs. There was some overlap between the two types of groups, and some members were in both, but JVKs were still seen primarily as a way of acquiring knowledge, while the self-help groups performed the financial intermediation functions for the SKDRDP *Pragathi nidhi* or microfinance programme.

Later on, as women started to engage in more activities and had less time for meetings, and the microfinance programme developed and grew more important, the two types of groups became more integrated. A self-help group would be formed by 10 or 20 women, and four or five of these groups would come together and form a JVK. The age restriction was dropped, and the older JVKs were sub-divided into four or five self-help groups as they wished. If a woman does not want to be a member of a larger JVK group, for whatever reason, she can join a self-help group which is not part of one of the larger groups.

Many women continued to roll *beedis*, in spite of the low earnings and the health hazards of continued exposure to tobacco leaf, and the JVKs were used as a forum for identifying and promoting alternative employment opportunities. The focus then shifted from microfinance to income generating activities, and some JVKs moved into group enterprises, with assistance from SKDRDP. The original JVK awareness meetings continue, at monthly rather than weekly intervals. The emphasis has thus passed from social empowerment to finance, and then in some cases to group enterprise. The original spiritual emphasis has not been forgotten, however, and the women still start their meetings by singing hymns, and they retain their sense of obligation to God. The groups have retained their strong faith-based solidarity, but this is in no way religiously exclusive.

Alcohol de-addiction

During the early years of SKDRDP's work it became clear that whatever good work the institution did was being wiped out by the menace of alcoholism. It seemed to be an integral part of the culture of the region, and all the farmers' increased incomes were being spent on alcohol. Dr Heggade and his colleagues tried to point out to the village people how foolish this was, but there was no systematic programme to stop it.

Box 4.2 Maimun Nabi

When Maimun Nabi married Abdul in 1975, her life seemed to be going well. Abdul had just moved to Qatar to work as an electrical technician and coastguard. He was well paid, he married off his seven sisters, and he also repaid a loan he had taken to buy a five acre plot in his village. He returned from the Gulf in 1990, with $6000 savings. He cultivated paddy and coconuts, and lived comfortably with Maimum Nabi and their three children.

In the mid 1990s, however, Abdul's father was diagnosed with cancer, and Abdul had to spend all his savings on hospital treatment. His father died nevertheless, and Maimun Nabi had to start rolling *beedis* like the other poorer women in the village in order to support the family. Farm input prices were rising, and paddy cultivation was less remunerative, and then in 2000 Abdul was diagnosed with diabetes. He became very weak and was unable to work. The family had completely to depend on hired labour for paddy cultivation, which made it even less profitable.

Maimun Nabi had in desperation become a member of a network door-to-door marketing group. She failed to earn any more money from it, but when she was out trying to sell she heard that SKDRDP was forming women's savings and credit groups in the village. She joined the JVK in her village and started to save Rs.10 (two cents) a week. By 2002, she was eligible for a loan of Rs.10,000. She had five years to repay it, at Rs.60 a week.

The agricultural officer from SKDRDP showed her how to cultivate jasmine, and she used her loan to plant jasmine in a small part of their unused land. This proved to be the critical turning point for Maimum Nai's livelihood.

The agricultural officer guided her closely for the first six months, and the jasmine started to yield about Rs.60 worth of flowers a week after only four months. This increased gradually and settled at around Rs.1,000 a week after three years. Maimum Nabi sprays and waters the flowers regularly, and she and her two daughters pick the flowers every morning.

In 2005 Maimum Nai borrowed Rs.50,000 and bought a new irrigation pump, two cows, and a digester to produce domestic cooking fuel from cow dung.

The family have also taken a Rs.500,000 ($10,000) loan from Syndicate Bank to build a new house, and Maimun Nabi and Abdul are grateful to Allah for their good fortune.

She and the other 15 Muslim members of their group join the other 27 members in singing the Hindu prayers that start their meetings. She does not take an active part in Hindu rituals, but she does visit the Manjunath Temple in Dharmasthala about twice a year.

At around this time a public anti-alcohol movement started in this area, which was known as the *Jana Jagruthi*. Dr Heggade realized how important his was, and in 1992 he and his staff started to support it. In 1996, the state government banned the sale of alcohol in Belthangady. This was, however, counter-productive, since it was only illegal on paper, and the sales of illicit liquor more than compensated for the ban. Many local people made large profits, and this only fed the market all the more.

It was then realized that a fundamental change was needed. The demand had to be stopped, by working with the people affected by alcoholism. Only then could the supply issue be dealt with. The ban was lifted in 1994, and the whole strategy was changed. SKDRDP became centrally involved, and the concept of de-addiction camps was introduced.

The *Jana Jagruthi* process is based on one week residential camps, which are arranged at regular intervals to motivate people to give up alcohol. The aim is totally to change people's attitudes to liquor. The camps include health education, individual and group-based counselling, and more fundamental faith-based processes to influence the addicts' basic attitudes.

The participants pay Rs.200 ($4) to attend the camp, and they have to stay in the camp for the entire week. The cost is partly subsidized by better-off people in the local villages. An average of 50 people attend each camp, and as all the participants are from the same area; everybody in each village knows who is attending. Their families are also involved, since they have to provide lunch every day for the entire week. This not only saves money, but, much more important, it ensures that each participant's family observes the programme, and they keep in touch with the daily progress of their family member.

The de-addiction programme is closely linked to the other SKDRDP programmes, such as the JVK women's groups, and they are mutually self-supporting:

Box 4.3 Dharanamma

Dharanamma and Channana Gowda of Vacha village near Belthangady have three children. Dharanamma was unable to provide even two meals a day to her children, as her husband was a drunkard and did not bother about the family. She had no education and totally lacked any confidence. She stayed inside her hut, she did not dare to criticize her husband, and took care of the cooking as she was told.

Channana always came home late and abused his wife, but she did not have the courage to complain. Even when their first daughter had to be married, Channana did nothing about it. He was drinking five litres of liquor a day, which he bought on credit from their neighbours. Dharanamma depended on help and loans from her relatives to feed her children, and the family fell deeper and deeper into debt.

In 2000 the SKDRDP *Sevaniratha* heard about Dharanamma's situation and called on her. He saw how helpless she was and encouraged her to join the village *Jnanavikasa Kendra* women's group. She was at first very reluctant, but after some persuasion she joined. At first she did no more than attend and follow the set procedures, as well as making what small savings she could afford. As time went on, she talked to the other members and started to share her problems.

Eventually, she broke down in tears and told her whole story to the group. The other members realized how serious her situation was and reported it to the village federation. One of the senior members was very moved by the story. He visited Dharanamma's home and forced her husband Channana to attend the SKDRDP de-addiction camp. The family could not afford the Rs.200 fee, so the members of Dharanamma's group contributed Rs.5 each to cover it.

Channana was completely transformed in the camp. He started to take proper care of his family, and joined a local *Pragathi Bandhu* group. He started to cultivate the family's small plot of land, and took some small loans to pay for the necessary inputs, and to pay off some of the family's earlier debts. He also earned money from casual labour.

Dharanamma was also a changed person. She made friends in the community, and they found a suitable boy for her daughter. Dharanamma borrowed Rs.45,000 ($900) from her self-help group for the marriage, and Channana became the vice-president of the village federation.

Religion plays an important role in the camps. All the local religious heads attend the programme, and the Christian priests, the Muslim mullahs and the Jain 'Munis' or leaders address the participants. Dr Heggade visits every camp, and religious songs and prayers are an important part of the proceedings.

Once the participants leave the camp, they become members of *Nava Jeevana Samitis* in their respective villages. This is a group of people who have gone through de-addiction camps, and it acts as a support group to try to ensure that those who have forsworn liquor during their de-addiction week do not slip back into the habit once the moral pressure and enthusiasm of the camp is removed. These groups are quite separate from the self-help groups and *Pragathi Bandhu* groups, of which the members may already be members. The *Nava Jeevana Samitis* meet every week; they sing religious songs and then discuss the daily challenges and temptations they experience in their efforts to stay away from alcohol. The local *sevaniratha* facilitates these meetings, and they are held either in one of the members' houses or more often in the local temple. Religion and ritual plays a continuing role in the mutual support process, and the reformed alcoholics play an important part in the extension of the *Jana Jagruthi* programme.

The *Jana Jagruthi* movement has now spread to whole of South Canara district. Four or five camps are held every month, and by late 2006 over 150 camps had been held. Over two-thirds of the participants succeed in staying away from alcohol permanently. This is about twice the success rate which is achieved by such programmes elsewhere in India and abroad.

Secret camps have also been organized, where well-known people from the area have been treated without having their names disclosed, and the success rate has been equally high. A preventive programme known as the *Swasthya Sankalpa*, or pledge for health programme, has also been organized for schools, where young people are warned of the dangers of alcohol and are encouraged not to start drinking.

The organizers of the *Jana Jagruthi* programme are proud that the state's excise collection from alcohol has gone down, and the government revenue collectors have sometimes been known to contact them and ask them to stop the programme; this is the best evidence of its success. The movement has basically changed people's attitudes to liquor, and those who do still drink no longer admit it. They do not want it to be known that they take alcohol, and people no longer serve liquor at parties. The programme has also had a positive impact on the *Pragathi nidhi* microfinance programme, since it improves loan recoveries and enables previously disqualified people such as Sidappa Gowda to take loans.

Community development programmes

From when it started in 1982 until 1990, SKDRDP worked mainly with individual members and their families and only in Belthangady. From 1990 onwards, they extended their working area all over the district, with a primary focus on the

---

Box 4.4 Sidappa Gowda the drunkard

Sidappa Gowda's mother and father both drank heavily, and he followed their example. By the age of 18 he was already an alcoholic, and he was soon drinking a litre of spirits every day, costing about Rs.100. He got married when he was 26. His wife rolled *beedis* and earned just enough to support their three children, and he spent all his wages on liquor and gambling.

He had a strong physique, and the liquor did not affect his ability to work. In 1994 he joined a *Pragathi Bandhu* group, because he wanted to take a loan to improve his small house. The other members of the group refused to allow him to borrow and in 1996 they told him that they would expel him from the group unless he joined the SKDRDP de-addiction programme.

The programme lasted nine days; it consisted of health and information sessions, intensive counselling and prayers and exercises. At the end, all the 42 participants swore an oath to the Lord Manjunatha to stop drinking. Sidappa and another 5 of the 42 participants successfully broke their habit. Sidappa and other reformed drunkards in the area formed an informal 'rebirth' committee, and continued to counsel the failure cases; by the end of the year only one was still drinking. Since he has been cured, Sidappa's life has radically changed. He has borrowed Rs.100,000 to buy two acres of farmland and build a new house, and two of his three children are being trained for good jobs. His eldest son never had this opportunity, however, because his father was still drinking when he left school; he still works as an unskilled garage mechanic.

Sidappa credits his success to the Gods' intervention, and is proud that he is now an active member of the informal de-addiction committee in his village. SKDRDP has cured 7,000 people in its own programmes, and a further 20,000 have been through the informal programmes. This improves SKDRDP's loan recoveries and enables more people to borrow and repay their loans, so the programme and the people both benefit.

---

construction of basic village infrastructure. This community development work depends on the participation of the communities which are involved. If the people in a particular village or town want to improve a public facility, such as a school, a road or a cremation ground, they have to form a committee and offer some initial contribution. They can then apply to SKDRDP, and if the need and the community's contribution are properly verified SKDRDP can provide financial and technical support. The group could be a village committee, a *Gram Panchayat* [the lowest level of the national political structure], or even a government department.

This activity was managed as quite a separate department of SKDRDP until the year 2000, when it was integrated into the main structure of the institution. This programme is focused on three major areas:

- Under *Jnana Deepa,* SKDRDP helps to provide voluntary teachers for primary schools, and also assists with construction and equipment for government and private primary schools. The programme provides a stipend to a local educated young man or woman who then works as a part-time teacher, particularly with the specialized needs of school dropouts. SKDRDP may also assist with the repair and extension of buildings, and can provide furniture, sports equipment, electricity connections, drinking water, playgrounds, toilets and so on.

- Under *Grama Kalyana Yojane,* SKDRDP provides facilities to villages such as day nursery facilities, local roads, bridges, or water supply systems, temple extensions and community halls. They also assist with the initiation and management of local milk cooperative societies, and the staffing of *anganwadi* or children's day care centres.
- Under the *Rudra Bhoomi,* grants are given by SKDRDP for the improvement or construction of facilities for cremation.

Most of SKDRDP's spending under the community development programme has been in collaboration with the village *Panchayats.* It has mainly been done in conjunction with government development programmes, where the budgets are not enough to complete the work or to pay for good quality construction. SKDRDP has also made grants to people in areas affected by personal disasters, or natural calamities such as floods or persistent drought.

Box 4.5 The misfortunes of Tania and Kamala

Tania and Kamala have three sons and one daughter; all four were born blind. There is no history of blindness in their families; they had four children in the hope that one might be sighted, but this was not to be.

The family has one acre of land, where they grow 200 betel nut trees and a few other consumption crops. The trees produce a total of about 20 kg of nuts every year, although one tree alone should produce that amount. Their land is stony and dry, and their well only gives water for six months for domestic use; a deep tube well for irrigation is far beyond their means. Kamala earns around Rs.300 (£6) a month, from *beedi* rolling, and the third son Dinesh helps her to put labels on the packets. Tungappa, the eldest boy, occasionally earns Rs.20 a day shelling betel nuts, and their sister helps her mother in the house. Gangarya, the second son, is mentally handicapped and does nothing.

Tania joined an SKDRDP *Pragathi Bandhu* group, and his wife was also a member of a self-help group. Both had to leave their groups, however. Kamala left after five months because she could not afford the regular weekly savings of Rs.10. Tania stayed in his group for some years, and took and repaid a loan to repair the roof of their house, as well as giving a day's labour every week, but he was then diagnosed with cancer. His brother gave him the necessary Rs.9000 ($180) to get treatment in Bangalore, which arrested the disease, but he could not do hard physical work any more and had to leave the group.

In 1996 the *sevaniratha* who was responsible for their groups arranged for each of the four children to receive a monthly pension of Rs.100 from SKDRDP. This is renewed annually, after the *sevaniratha* has checked that the family is still in need. SKDRDP provides pensions to about 200 similar households, and the expense is considered a part of the institution's operational costs like any other. Tania and Kamala visit the Dharmasthala Temple regularly, and they hope that they may one day be able to get their children married. In the meantime, they are grateful to SKDRDP for its regular support.

CHAPTER 5
Microfinance

Abstract

SKDRDP originally promoted farmers groups as a basis for shared labour, but the members soon started to pool their savings, and to borrow from their accumulated funds. As their financial needs increased, partly because of the new farming techniques they were learning from SKDRDP, the groups started to borrow additional money from banks under the national self-help group programme. The farmers' needs soon outgrew the maximum amounts that the banks were willing to lend. At the same time SKDRDP's management realized that their programme would need additional resources beyond what the Dharmasthala Temple could provide if it was to expand beyond the immediate neighbourhood of Belthangady and reach more people who needed assistance. SKDRDP therefore started to take bulk loans from national commercial banks, backed by the reputation and resources of the temple, and to finance the groups itself. This allowed the groups to borrow far larger sums than the banks allowed, for longer terms The repayments remained at a high level, partly because of the group members' reverence for the temple and for Dr Heggade and his wife, who had herself become deeply involved in the women's programmes.

The origins of SKDRDP's microfinance programme

The *Pragathi Bandhu* groups originated as a way of formalizing labour sharing. The JVK groups were started in order to get women involved and make them equal stakeholders in development of their communities, and *Jana Jagruti* was a group approach to addressing alcoholism. Gradually, the group members of *Pragathi Bandhu,* who were mostly men, and JVK, who were all women, were encouraged to save. They then started internal lending from the group funds to the members, and some of the groups then took loans from their local bank branches to supplement their own savings. This sequence was based on the national self-help group programme which was getting under way at that time.

The *Pragathi nidhi* programme was implemented like any self-help group programme until early in 2000. The focus was on opening bank accounts and taking small one- to two-year loans. Repayment rates to the banks were maintained at 100 per cent, and great emphasis was placed on rigorous discipline; the *sevanirathas* followed up every loan to every group, and no delays were allowed.

In spite of this apparent success, there were some worrying features. From the members' point of view, the rather small loans had very little long-term impact on members' livelihoods. From the institutional viewpoint, SKDRDP was not moving towards sustainability since many of the groups were borrowing direct from their local bank branches. In 2001 and 2002 almost all the groups were borrowing direct from banks, even though SKDRDP had access to the necessary funds to lend to them itself.

SKDRDP's management were ambivalent on whether they should merely act as facilitators for groups to borrow from banks, or as an institution that itself makes loans. The banks were unable to fulfil the entire requirements of the groups but the *sevanirathas* reflected their management's own uncertainty and were not clear whether they should act as facilitators or as lenders. The cohesiveness within SKDRDP groups and between the groups and the project staff was weakening in areas where SKDRDP's *Pragathi nidhi* programme was not being aggressively promoted, and the groups were losing their sense of belonging to the Dharmasthala family. The SKDRDP programmes were all financed from the donations that pilgrims made to Dharmasthala. It was becoming clear in the late 1990s that after two decades the institution's work had hardly moved out beyond Belthangady except in some isolated places where community development initiatives had taken place. Even in home territory the numbers of communities that had been reached, and the impact on them, was substantially lower than might have been hoped.

Senior staff at SKDRDP, who had many years of experience, were also realizing that there were few opportunities for them to utilize their potential since the organization was not expanding its outreach beyond the local area. Both the men's and the women's credit and savings groups which SKDRDP had promoted were moving away from their dependence on Dharmasthala as the banks were now able to lend to them on their own, and this weakened their links with SKDRDP. The bank loans were not always accessible by the poorer villagers, however, and the amounts were insufficient to allow the more ambitious group members to borrow as much as they needed. These problems started to emerge at the same time as Dr Manjunath took over the management of SKDRDP, and there was some debate as to whether to extend the full range of services beyond Belthangady to the rest of the district.

There was also an issue of funding. SKDRDP was completely dependent on donations from the Dharmasthala Trust, and any expansion would require more money, even if it were only to satisfy the growing needs of the existing groups in the Belthangady area. The Dharmasthala Temple Trusts' resources were not unlimited. SKDRDP decided that they could solve this problem, and at the same time retain the loyalty of the savings and credit groups which were moving away to do business with their local bank branches, if SKDRDP itself started to lend money to the groups when they had outgrown their own savings. This might also eventually make SKDRDP fully sustainable, or even profitable.

It was not easy to convince all the trustees that SKDRDP should move away from its role as a donor, and should aim to earn income out of its microcredit operations. This seemed to some of them to be a major step away from what a religious institution ought to be doing. The banker members of the trustees, however, were very enthusiastic, and some of them offered there and then to provide SKDRDP with bulk loans to enable all its members' needs to be satisfied.

Many bankers were at this time moving away from direct loans to self-help groups and were making large loans to the non-government organizations or specialized microfinance institutions which had promoted the groups, for them in turn to onlend to the groups, after taking a margin of profit to cover their costs. SKDRDP, with the backing of the Dharmasthala Temple and its trust, was a much better risk than most of the new institutions to which they were being asked to lend.

It was also proposed at the same time that SKDRDP should extend its entire programme outside Belthangady. They hoped in due course to overcome the funding constraint and it would be more effective and manageable if all its programmes were implemented in every region, rather than restricting the wider areas to community development initiatives, which by their very nature were dependent on grants and would never be sustainable for SKDRDP.

Raising bank finance

Dr Heggade had been interacting with bankers from the area on this issue for some time, and in particular with senior managers of the three prominent banks which had originally been established in South Canara, that is Syndicate Bank, Canara Bank and Corporation Bank. Direct microfinance offered the only effective way to expand, as there was a limit to the money the temple could either be give as charity or lend out as loans. It would also have been very difficult for SKDRDP to obtain grants from other donors, since it was known to be affiliated to a wealthy temple institution.

After lengthy discussions the trustees finally agreed to the two major changes: SKDRDP would itself engage in microfinance, not only as a group promotion institution but as a lender, and the full portfolio of development activities would be rolled out to all areas together, including microfinance.

At this point SKDRDP also became more outward looking in other respects; they started actively partnering with government and other institutions' schemes for welfare and for enterprise development. The Small Industries Development Bank of India offered both loans and foreign donor grant funding for capacity building, and the Infosys Foundation also started to support the *Rudra Bhoomi* cremation place programme.

The staff were full of enthusiasm under their new leadership Once this critical decision had been taken, SKDRDP expanded very fast, first within South Canara district and then into the other neighbouring districts of Udipi and North Canara. They also started work in some urban areas, and started a charity-based community development programme covering the whole state, focusing mainly on education, rural infrastructure and crematoriums. The *Pragathi nidhi* programme was modified to focus on microfinance, the women's JVK groups were subdivided into microfinance self help groups, and they were all encouraged to engage in livelihood generation programmes, often in collaboration with government schemes.

SKDRDP also designed and introduced a comprehensive insurance scheme, which is probably the most effective microinsurance programme in India. The organization expanded very rapidly, both in the range if its activities and in its geographical coverage. Starting with their first intervention in agriculture, where the *sevanirathas* had only worked with farmers, SKDRDP is today implementing programmes which cover almost every facet of life that affects the communities in the area, including health and sanitation, education, housing, livelihoods and microfinance. They have moved from an exclusive focus on small-scale and marginal farmers to working with community members of all backgrounds, including women, landless people, and young men and women.

In January 2003 the Belthangady branch of State Bank of India took the first step to make the expansion possible, by making a bulk loan of $3 million to SKDRDP, so that the groups could borrow from SKDRDP rather than going to their local bank branches, and the savings and credit programme was formalized under the title of *Pragathi nidhi*. This was an enormous loan for a small town branch of the bank, and was the forerunner of further loans for a total of $6 million. More remarkably still, the loan was unsecured, and at a very low rate of interest. The local bank manager and his colleagues who approved the loan felt that it was in some ways a loan to the God of Dharmasthala, and was secured by Him. They were followed by a number of other banks, whose managers realized that SKDRP was an excellent risk. By 2006 SKDRDP was borrowing over $30 million, from ten different banks.

The power of groups

SKDRDP's staff believe that its groups, which are similar to self-help groups, provide a base from which families below the poverty line can be empowered through the strength of their unity. The *Pragathi Bandhu* and JVK groups share activities such as labour, joint training, and group enterprises for income generation in agriculture and other non-farm activities. SKDRDP provides a full range of livelihood assistance to these groups, with microfinance as the basis of its success.

The cost of promoting and guiding a group comes to around Rs.6,000 over a period of some three years, or about $8 per member at an average group size of 15 members. SKDRDP makes a margin of about 4 per cent on its loans, being the difference between the interest it pays to Syndicate Bank and other lenders, and the rate of between 10 and 12 per cent which it charges to the self-help groups. The actual rates differ from time to time according to variations in interest rates at the national level, but the 'spread' remains at about 4 per cent. The group promotion cost per member is about the same as the annual interest margin of 4 per cent on a loan of Rs.10,000, and most self-help group members, like Madiga Harijana (see Box 5.1), take several loans for far more than this amount. The group formation cost is more than recovered.

Box 5.1 Madiga Harijana

Madiga Harijana is one of eight children born to Soma Harijana and Badvethi, a 'scheduled caste' family in Belal village in Belthangady. The family were very poor, and had little to eat, but all of them, both men and women, used to drink liquor whenever they could. Madiga Harijana himself says *'Kudiyodu Namma Parampare'* [drinking is hereditary for us]. He was the only one in the family to stay at school until he was 13 years old, and when he left school he found he could earn about $1 a day. He spent most of his earnings on liquor, and seemed likely to end up in the same situation as his father.

In 1992, Madiga's elder brothers took over their joint family house and he along with his wife and two children had to leave home, with no assets of their own. He had nowhere to live, no land to cultivate, and at the same time he had to maintain a family of four, and he was still drinking. After a few months' total destitution he was allotted a place on the SKDRDP Dharmasthala Trusts' *Jeevanadhama* project for housing the homeless, which provided a 50 per cent subsidy on the total cost of a house. The local SKDRDP *sevaniratha* tried to persuade him to join a *Pragathi Bandhu* labour sharing group, but he was afraid that they would force him to give up drinking and he refused. The *sevaniratha* persisted, however, supported by other people in the village, and he eventually joined the Southegadde *Pragathi Bandhu* group.

The family was wholly dependent on daily wages for food. His fellow group members understood his situation and they persuaded him to acquire the legal rights to a three-quarter acre plot of government forest land which he was illegally occupying. He took a loan of Rs.3,000 ($60) or to bribe the local government official to alter its legal status to private farming land, which was registered in his name under a government land redistribution scheme. The group further supported him with free labour to make the land suitable for agriculture, and he started cultivating paddy and lentils. In 1998 he borrowed a further Rs.5,000 from the group to plant 50 rubber tree seedlings.

He was still drinking at this time, although not as heavily as before, and in 1999 the group persuaded Madiga to attend a SKDRDP *Jana Jagruthi* de-addiction camp. He completed this successfully and stopped drinking once and for all. In the same year he constructed a toilet in his house, then in 2001 he borrowed Rs.25,000 ($500) to dig a well. In 2002 he installed solar lighting in his house, in 2003 he borrowed Rs.27,000 to buy cattle and a further Rs.25,000 to purchase gold for his first daughter's marriage. In 2005 he borrowed a further Rs.25,000 to get his younger twin daughters married.

Madiga Harijana now has a good house, with rubber and cashew trees on his land, and a small herd of cattle. He still earns daily wages, and his wife rolls *beedis*, and between them they earn about Rs.40,000 a year. Api, his wife, who is a JVK member, is an elected member of the village *panchayat*.

SKDRDP's microfinance loans are not restricted to 'approved income generation projects' like those from some banks. The *sevaniratha*s and their management have learned that poor people have a whole range of financial needs, and SKDRDP loans can be used for every conceivable purpose: for consumption, for income generation for farming or non-farm activities, and for housing, toilets, electricity installation, gas digester plants, and so on. Many banks and other microfinance institutions require that their loans are used only for approved 'productive' purposes, but SKDRDP treats its groups as members of the Dharmasthala community and trusts them to use their loans as they think fit. The loans are funded from group members' savings as well as from SKDRDP or the bulk bank loans it has secured, and members are provided with training on how to use their loans as well as the necessary input supply and marketing links they need.

After a group has been formed, the local *sevaniratha* trains its members how to conduct their meetings, how to keep their accounts, and how to manage their lending activity in the best interest of the group and of its individual members. Once the group can manage itself, the *sevaniratha* becomes their auditor and facilitator.

The *Pragathi Bandhu* groups, JVKs and self-help groups in every village organize themselves into one or two federations depending on the total number of groups in the village; usually 25 groups form a federation. A village will usually have about 500 households, so a typical village might have 50 or 60 groups. The federations have representatives from each group, and an executive committee and an audit committee. They guide and assist the groups, with the assistance of the *sevanirathas*. The leadership and committee members of the groups and the federations are rotated every two years. In addition to monitoring the microfinance programmes the federations also identify the needs of their villages and organize various community tasks.

There is a further grouping of the federations at the sub-district level, which liaises with government departments and with SKDRDP management when necessary. The federations are run by the members of their constituent groups, on a voluntary basis. They play an important role in decisions on issues such as interest rates. SKDRDP is in many ways a traditional hierarchic institution, with Dr Heggade at its head, but the clients, or group members, do have a substantial voice in major policy decisions. Unlike many NGOs which promote self-help groups, however, SKDRDP does not allow the groups to make their own decisions on interest rates rules or other critical issues; once a common policy has been agreed, in consultation with the federations, all the groups have to abide by it.

The groups' financial transactions are all carried out in front of a photograph of Dr Heggade, the Lord Manjunath, or in front of the Bible for Christians or the Qur'an for Muslims. The first loan to a group is usually disbursed in the presence of a village elder or other respected person, and the cheques are all signed by Dr Heggade and by Mrs Heggade. Before the recipient takes the cheque, a special religious ceremony is held, offering it to God.

Although it is not a formal part of their job, most of the *sevanirathas* organize religious ceremonies in their villages. One of the favourites is the *Saryanarayana Puja*, which is symbolic of peace and reconciliation and brings unity and harmony to the villages and the community. These are held once or up to four times a year, and the *sevanirathas* also organize *Pujas*, or rituals, associated with other Gods. SKDRDP does not cover the cost of these; the money is collected from the group members or the richer people in the village. The *sevanirathas* also organize weekly *Nava Jeevana Samiti* meetings where *Bhajana Mandalis*

Box 5.2 Koragappa and the SHG Federation

Koragappa is president of the Belthangady group federation. There are about 4,400 self-help groups and *Pragathi Bandhu* groups in the federation, which belong to 146 village level groups. The federation does not carry out any financial tasks; its role is to advise and supervise the groups, and to act as a communication link between SKDRDP and the groups.

The federation meets four times a year, but Koragappa has to have frequent meetings with SKDRDP and with various village and group representatives in order to settle disputes and discuss future policy and new services such as insurance. He reckons that he spends about two days a week on federation business during his two-year term, but he says he 'loves' SKDRDP and is happy to give up the time. He was asked to be president of the federation by the members of the *Pragathi Bandhu* groups and the SHGs, with some advice from SKDRDP, and he is proud that he can help the institution in this way.

One of the most important functions of the federation is to agree with SKDRDP what rate of interest the groups should pay for their loans, and to lay down the rates which members should pay the groups. Most banks and NGOs which lend to groups allow the groups to decide on their own interest rates, but Dr Heggade and SKDRDP feel that the members should be protected from extortionate rates, even when they are charged by their own groups.

In 2006 it was agreed that SKDRDP should charge the groups 11 per cent a year on a daily reducing balance basis. The groups charged their members on a 'flat' basis of 9 per cent for loans under three years and 12 per cent for over three years. This amounts effectively to 12 per cent and 13 per cent on a declining balance basis; the average cost of funds for SKDRDP was about 8 per cent, so this set of rates enabled SKDRDP to cover its costs, the groups could earn a small surplus and the members themselves could borrow at rates well under their only alternative which was the local moneylenders. The groups distribute their profits to their members on an agreed basis, which is decided by the federation.

Koragappa is himself a member of a *Pragathi Bandhu* group; he finds it very useful when he is cultivating his two acre farm. His wife is a member of a *Jana Vikas Kendra* group. Between 1993 and 2006 Koragappa took loans for a total of Rs.140000 ($2800) from his group, to finance his farming and to modernize his house. His group recently distributed the surplus it had accumulated over the previous five years; the total sum amounted to Rs.27,000.

[sacred songs] are often sung. These are primarily religious and are usually held in a temple. The *sevanirathas* also actively organize and participate in any special *Bhajana Mandalis* which take place, in celebration of any particular events of importance to the village. The *sevanirathas* say that organizing *Pujas* is one of their favourite activities.

Financial results

Table 5.1 shows the financial impact of this radical change in strategy. In the eight years from 1999, the value of loans outstanding to the groups from SKDRDP expanded by about 70 times, to a total of over $45 million. Expenses increased

Table 5.1 SKDRDP's loan portfolio, expenses and grants, in millions of rupees

	2006– 7	2005– 6	2004– 5	2003– 4	2002– 3	2001– 2	2000– 1	1999– 2000
Loans outstanding	2277.6	1086.7	491.9	380.1	119.1	27.6	34.0	32.7
Earnings	175.51	65.7	99.8	91	9.3	3.8	4.1	5
Expenses	170.01	82.26	137.7	125.0	34.8	29.5	29.1	26.6
Grant	N/A	16.56	37.9	34.0	25.5	25.7	25.0	21.6
Percentage of grant to expenses	N/A	25%	27.5%	27.2%	73.2%	87.3%	85.8%	81.2%
Percentage of grant to loans outstanding	N/A	1.52%	7.7%	8.9%	21.4%	93.1%	73.5%	66%

Source: audited statements of SKDRDP
Note: Rs.1 million = *c*. $20,000

by only seven times, to some $3.5 million, and SKDRDP's earnings from its financial intermediation rose from about $100,000 to over $3.5 million. The grant from Dr Heggade's Temple Trust increased until 2004/5, but by 2007 it was no longer necessary.

Management estimated that SKDRDP's microfinance programme would be able to cover all its costs, and to end its dependence on Dr Heggade's generosity, when each *sevaniratha* was covering 50 groups, with an average of Rs.100,000 ($2,000), in outstanding loans per group. This target had already been surpassed by many *sevanirathas* and the programme has achieved overall operational sustainability. It is not intended that the costs of all Dharmasthala's development activities will be covered from microfinance earnings, but microfinance should not require long-term subsidy.

The proportion of grant to expenses was the highest in 2001/2 when SKDRDP started to expand to other areas in South Canara and to other districts. This period was also the time when SKDRDP most heavily depended on grants. Like any enterprise, it was necessary to spend and invest before reaping the rewards, and Dr Heggade and his colleagues were confident enough of their eventual success to take the risk. The grants came from the Dharmasthala Temple Trust, which is effectively Dr Heggade's family's money.

Dr Heggade is both a leader and a manager. He is a devout Jain, but is also a good businessman. The Jains are known for their business acumen. His advisers, and particularly the bankers among them and the new management, have played a major role in the transformation of SKDRDP from a grant-making welfare institution into a potentially sustainable and even profitable development finance institution. In the process, the outreach and thus the reputation and influence of Dharmasthala and of Dr Heggade himself have been greatly extended. He has been awarded an honorary doctorate of the British Royal College of Physicians, in recognition of the Dharmasthala Temple's medical charitable work, and he has also received the coveted Padmabhushan award from the President of India.

The transformation has involved many more changes in addition to obtaining loan finance from banks. SKDRDP has intensified its group-building activity, in order to generate more groups and thus to expand the scale of its financial business. The restriction on taking more than one member from one family has been relaxed, particularly for people from socially and economically backward families. For the purposes of SKDRD group membership, each nuclear family is treated as an independent family, irrespective of where they live.

The membership criteria have been relaxed, and anyone with a landholding of less than five acres can become a member of a group. This may admit some slightly better-off people than before, but since additional loans mean additional revenue for the whole institution, this is not felt to be a problem. It is also important that all the farmers on a given watershed can become group members, since SKDRDP is giving more attention to assisting and training farmers to protect their water sources, and this is difficult if some farmers on the watershed are not members.

Similarly, anyone irrespective of their marital status or their age is now allowed to become a group member. As a result of these changes it is now possible for nearly all the families in a village to join a SKDRDP groups, and many new groups have been formed in a short period of time. This was not difficult, since the *sevanirathas* had been living and working in many of the villages for almost 20 years. The poverty focus was definitely diluted, and there are now people with very different sizes of land-holdings in one group. This may have weakened their homogeneity and cohesion, but their loyalty to the Dharmasthala was generally such as to overcome any tendencies for the groups to split. Landless people are still not usually admitted to *Pragathi Bandhu* groups, because they have no land on which the group's labour could be employed, but there have been some exceptions, and landless people are actively recruited into self-help groups.

Loans can also be given to more than one member of a joint family at the same time, so long as they are in different groups and have different income sources, and members are formally allowed to take loans on behalf of other family members' behalf, even if the latter are not group members, in order to enable them to start or expand their income generating activities. Loans are now also allowed to be taken for 'non-productive' purposes, such as home improvements, marriages and education. This had often been done before, but now it is formally approved. It is no longer necessary for members to conceal the real purposes of their loans, and this has improved the relationships within the groups and between groups and their *sevanirathas* and other SKDRDP staff.

The credit limit has been expanded from four times up to 40 times the groups' savings, or a maximum of $2,000 per member, whichever is less. This was a very revolutionary move, since the limit of four times had been established by the

National Bank for Agriculture and Rural Development, the government's initiator and promoter of the self-help group movement. So large a multiple would have seemed most unwise to any commercial banker.

SKDRDP also liberalized the method of calculating borrowers' repayment capacity, taking into account all the income sources of the individual and her or his family, and not only the income expected to arise from the enterprise for which the loan was intended. The maximum loan term has also been extended to 10 years for long-term investments such as house construction.

When SKDRDP started its group credit activity, groups had to have been saving and internal borrowing for two years before they could take a loan from outside. This was later reduced to nine months, and then to six months or even to three months, if it was recommended by the group's *sevaniratha* and the federation to which it belonged. The earlier, more restrictive regulations had been one of the reasons why groups preferred to borrow from banks, rather than from SKDRDP, but the newly liberalized system was much more generous than any bank could offer. This made an important contribution to the rapid growth of the portfolio, and there was no apparent reduction in the repayment rates. The same banks whose own branches had to follow the more restrictive national system were happy to allow SKDRDP to break all the rules that they themselves followed. The high personal status of Dr Heggade, and the bankers' knowledge of the underlying material and spiritual wealth of the temple, contributed to their willingness to do this, even though their loans to SKDRDP were unsecured.

The groups can access funds from three different sources. They can take loans direct from their local banks, they can borrow from SKDRDP, and they have their members' own regular weekly savings. They have also in the past sometimes received a share of the surplus earned by their local branch SKDRDP on the *Pragathi Nidhi* programme, as a bonus, and this amounted to several hundred rupees per member for some groups. The Belthangady and nearby Karkala branches did this in the early days of the programme, when they were lending zero-cost funds which had been donated by Dr Heggade. More recently, however, as the programme came to rely on interest bearing bulk loans from banks, SKDRDP's profits were reduced and indeed eliminated, so that the programme continues to rely on grants from the Dharmasthala Temple Trust. When it becomes sustainable, however, as is forecast for 2008, it is planned that a share of each branch's profits will once more be distributed as a dividend to the groups it serves, based on the level of their business. This is a further reason for groups to maximize their business with SKDRDP rather than borrowing from banks.

The group members do not take any regular interest on their savings, so the small profit that they make from internal lending becomes an additional source of funds. The groups maintain a single account with their local bank into which all their funds, including loan repayments, are deposited and from which all loans are disbursed. Members who leave their groups for any reason can withdraw their savings along with 3 per cent annual interest, so long as they have cleared any outstanding loans.

There are detailed rules and regulations covering all aspects of group management, such as the annual interest charges, which depend on the duration of loans, the repayment schedules and any security. The members pay their savings and repayments to their groups every week, but the groups repay their loans to SKDRDP on a monthly basis. Unlike most of the two million or more self-help groups elsewhere in India, the groups promoted by SKDRDP do not make their own decisions on weekly savings amounts, interest charges and so on. These decisions are all made centrally, albeit with some input from the federations, and the groups do not appear to regret their lack of autonomy. They believe the rules are fair, but they also have the sanctity associated with Dharmasthala and Dr Heggade.

Because many of the loans are for quite long terms, and repayments are made weekly, the instalments are very small, even for quite large loans. The weekly repayment on a ten-year loan for Rs.10,000 is only Rs.33 (just over six cents), for instance. Collateral is required for loans of over Rs.50,000, and whatever assets that are bought with the loan are in any case considered as security. The banks make similar security demands for larger loans, but the people are reluctant to give them their land title deeds, whereas they are very happy to entrust their most precious assets to SKDRDP because it is so closely identified with the deity of Dharmasthala.

The average cost of funds to SKDRDP is around 8 per cent, and the groups pay about 11 per cent to SKDRDP. A one-time additional administration fee of 1 per cent was introduced in June 2005 in order to cover more of SKDRDP's costs. This 'spread' of 3 or 4 per cent, as previously mentioned, covers most of the running costs of SKDRDP. The groups themselves charge 9 per cent interest on the annual outstanding balance for loans which are to be repaid in less than three years, and 12 per cent on the annual outstanding balance for loans with a tenure of more than three years. These rates are calculated on the annual balances rather than on the declining balance basis which is used to calculate the interest charged by SKDRDP on its loans to the groups, so that their effective rate is somewhat higher. This allows the groups a small margin with which they can build their own capital. The groups' costs of funds vary according to the proportions of their own savings, their accumulated surplus, loans from SKDRDP and loans from banks in their pool of money. Groups have to deposit two months repayment instalments in their accounts before their loans are released. This gives some leeway within which the *sevanirathas* or federations can follow up any problems. These apparently quite onerous conditions are accepted without question by the groups.

There are four basic types of loans, and the total lent to any one individual member, or to his or her family if other family members are in different groups, cannot exceed Rs.100,000 ($2,000).

The first and most common type of loans are known as revolving fund loans, because they are taken from SKDRDP for three years or more but are often circulated much faster within the groups. These loans make up almost 40 per cent of all advances, and are primarily used for repaying more expensive loans from local moneylenders, for medical expenses, for education, for marriage, and for buying 'luxury' items such as a radio or gold ornaments. Groups can borrow this type of loan up to 10 times their savings, and individuals are allowed to borrow a maximum of about $500, or 10 times their own savings, whichever is less.

The second major type of loan is for productive activities, for farming or non-farm enterprises. Groups can take loans of this type for up to 20 times their savings, and individuals can take up to about $650, or 20 times their savings, whichever is less. About 15 per cent of groups' loans are used for such purposes.

The third category of loans are for infrastructure, for houses, land or land development, for irrigation pumps or electricity connections. Here again, a group can take a loan for up to 20 times their savings, and individuals can take a maximum of about $2,000, or 20 times their savings, whichever is less. Slightly over a third of all loans are taken for infrastructure investments of this kind, and these loans are becoming increasingly important as the proportion of smaller consumption loans goes down.

Finally, some groups may want to finance group enterprises, such as the snacks manufacturing business which is described later. They can borrow up to 30 times their savings for such purposes, but the total borrowings of any group must not exceed 40 times their savings. Only just over 10 per cent of loans are taken for group enterprises, since most families want to build their own private or household businesses rather than joining group or cooperative businesses.

The *Pragathi Bandhu* group programme is SKDRDP's oldest initiative, but in later years, as people's need for shared labour decreased and they wanted to take loans for both farm and non-farm ventures, the numbers of members of self-help groups overtook those in the original labour sharing groups. Many of the *Jnanavikas Kendra* women's groups have also broken up into smaller women's self-help groups, and most of the surviving JVKs consist of the minority of women who want to maintain their group social activities but do not want the financial services offered by self-help groups. It is possible that they too will eventually break into self-help groups.

Because of the rapid growth of women's self help groups, loans to women have grown to make up over two-thirds of SKDRDP's total disbursements. In

Table 5.2 Group and member numbers, March 2007

Type of group	Pragathi Bandhu	Jnanavikas Kendra	Self-help groups	Urban development groups	Total
Number of groups	14,517	1,675	27,684	2,194	47,656
Number of members	85,913	18,602	331,270	27,980	463,765
Average group size	6	12	12	13	10

2001, the amount lent to women was negligible. The average loan amounts taken by men through the *Pragathi Bandhu* groups are still almost twice that of the loans to members of self-help groups, however, because they borrow for investments in infrastructure or agriculture, while the women take small consumption loans or small shares of larger loans for group enterprises.

The *Pragathi Bandhu* groups have generated nearly 14 million shared labour days, worth almost $20 million at the unskilled daily wage rate in the state. But 65 per cent of all SKDRDP's group members are now women, and the average group size has increased from 6.5 to 10 people as the emphasis shifted to women's self-help groups as opposed to the earlier focus on men's *Pragathi Bandhu* groups.

These figures make SKDRDP into one of the largest community development institutions in all of India. In spite of its strong Jain and Hindu links, the percentage of Muslims and Christians in the groups is about the same as for the population as a whole in South Canara.

The rate of growth has also increased dramatically, and in the year ending March 2006 more groups were formed and more people were enrolled than in SKDRDP's entire previous history of 25 years. This has been achieved partly by a deliberate policy of increased coverage of existing areas, partly by relaxing the criteria for membership as discussed earlier, and partly by reaching out to new areas.

The growth in outreach has been very dramatic. Table 5.3 compares the scale of activity in 2001 and in 2007.

The number of staff has increased substantially, but they have also achieved far greater levels of efficiency. In 2001 there were 120 members for every staff member, but by 2007 this figure had increased by almost three times, to 405 members per SKDRDP employee. The proportion of 'front line' *sevanirathas* to higher level supervisory and head office staff also went up, so that by 2007 three-quarters of the staff were based in the villages, working directly with group members.

The financial growth has been equally rapid. Table 5.4 gives some basic financial indicators during the period from 2001 to 2007. As it shows, the annual disbursements grew by nearly 20 times and the loans outstanding by over 30 times during these five years.

Table 5.3 Outreach

	2007	2001
Branches	18	2
SKDRDP staff	1,145	229
Sevanirathas	865	81
Villages and towns reached	1,924	169
Total groups	47,656	4,251
Total households	328,000	27,432
Total active borrowers	494,152	21,787
Number of loans outstanding	282,738	26,118

Table 5.4 SKDRDP and its groups: financial indicators for years ending 31 March, in millions of rupees

Indicators	2007	2006	2005	2004	2003	2002	2001
Disbursements from SKDRDP to groups	1620 ($32.4 million)	730.62 ($16 million)	170.3 ($3.7 million)	303.3 ($6.7 million)	98.7 ($2.2 million)	12 ($250,000)	2.7 ($60,000)
Disbursements from banks to groups	0	0	57.2 ($1.27 million)	0	0	39.08 ($850,000)	34.2 ($755,000)
Loans outstanding from groups to SKDRDP and banks	2325 ($46.5 million)	1086.76 ($24 million)	491.9 ($10.93 million)	380.1 ($8.4 million)	119.1 ($2.6 million)	27.6 ($6.1 million)	34.0 ($750,000)
Total group savings	804.3 ($16.09 million)	475.7 ($10.5 million)	283 ($6.3 million)	180.4 ($4 million)	119.9 ($2.6 million)	73.3 ($1.6 million)	54.6 ($1.2 million)

These figures show how SKDRDP's lending to groups has replaced bank loans, apart from a brief period in 2005 when SKDRDP was operating jointly with Corporation Bank. The interest rates have been similar, and some banks are willing to lend to self-help group at lower rates than SKDRDP could afford, given that it has itself to take bulk loans from the banks from which to lend in smaller amounts to groups. Most groups, however, as the figures show, prefer to borrow from SKDRDP because their terms are more liberal and because the non-financial assistance they receive from SKDRDP enables them to invest larger sums more productively. They also have a strong sense of loyalty to Lord Manjunatha. Interest costs are not the only determinant of their choice of finance.

The groups' own savings, and their accumulated surpluses, have also grown substantially, and they make up almost one-third of their total funds. Experience elsewhere shows that in a growing local economy people's needs for finance grow faster than their own resources, so that they borrow more rather than less from outside. Credit is not a one-off injection that enables poor people to become independent of further loans, but is a permanent and growing accompaniment of prosperity.

The figures in Table 5.4 for group savings do not include their accumulated surpluses, and these amount to around $5 million more which is available for the groups to circulate among their members.

SKDRDP has deliberately adopted a policy of increasing the proportion of loans which are for relatively large amounts. This is partly because group members need larger sums as they become better-off and their need for immediate small sums goes down. It also reduces SKDRDP's own transaction costs, since the administrative expenses involved in processing a loan for Rs.5,000 are about the same as for one of three or four times that amount. Loans to groups of over Rs.15,000 (about $330) increased from around 33 per cent of all loans in the year 2000 to over 90 per cent of loans by 2007. Loans below this amount are no longer to be permitted from 2007 onwards. This does not of course mean that group members cannot take very small loans from their groups; the new rule applies only to loans from SKDRDP to the groups.

In a further effort to reduce operating costs and to give the groups greater flexibility, SKDRDP has steadily increased the duration and the size of its loans to groups. This has made it more possible for group members to take loans for longer terms, to use for projects such as housing, or investments in land improvement and irrigation. At the level of members' loans from groups, by 2005 over one-quarter of the individual group members had loans of over Rs.25,000 ($550), and under one-third had loans of less than Rs.10,000 ($220) In India as a whole, most bank loans to groups themselves are around Rs.10,000, which demonstrates how much more prosperous the people of South Canara have become, partly as a result of SKDRDP's interventions since the early 1980s.

SKDRDP has consistently achieved 100 per cent repayment from all its groups over the years. The groups' repayments are all made from their savings accounts, which act as a buffer against any defaults within the groups themselves, and the requirement that two months' instalments should be deposited before loans are disbursed also prevents arrears. The three level checking system, using the *sevanirathas*, the federation auditors and the internal auditors from SKDRDP's head office, checks that any defaults are quickly observed and corrected, but the groups themselves ensure that repayment delays by any one member do not feed through into arrears by the group to SKDRDP. The case of Narayan Gowda (see Box 5.3) shows how the groups intermediate between SKDRDP and the individual members in a positive way.

Most borrowers are also very aware of the fact that their groups have in a very real sense been promoted by the God of Dharmasthala. The funds which they have borrowed from SKDRDP are kept in the same bank account as their accumulated savings and surpluses and any loans from the bank, although they are of course accounted for separately, so all the groups' money has a certain sanctity. Defaulters are cheating God, not just a bank. In 2006 one family came to pray at the temple and then walked across the compound to the SKDRDP office. They handed a small payment to SKDRDP, which, they said, had been owed by their grandfather and had not been repaid when he died some years before. They said that the God had told them to repay it.

Box 5.3 Narayan Gowda the defaulter

Narayan Gowda has no farmland of his own; he works for other farmers at around Rs.65 per day, and his wife earns about Rs.20 (40 cents) a day,, rolling *beedis*. Somehow, they earn enough to sustain themselves and their two children. He is a member of a *Pragathi Bandhu* group, and he took two overlapping loans, of Rs.15,000 and Rs.10,000 to build a better house on his small piece of homestead land.

He was repaying this at Rs.180 week, but then both his children fell sick. He borrowed Rs.600 from a friend to cover the medical costs, and in order to repay this and, he hoped, to improve his income, he took a job as a watchman in a nearby town for Rs.2,400 a month. He had to spend Rs.40 a day on travel, and he missed four weekly group meetings and shared group work, and fell into arrears of Rs.720 (about $15).

The other group members agreed to cover his arrears temporarily from their savings, but they sent a message to him saying that he should return home, rejoin the group and make up his arrears. They also pointed out that his earnings from his new job were about the same as he got from labour work after he had paid his travel costs, and his new job was in any case not a permanent one. They threatened that they would come and force him to come home if he did not come on his own.

Narayan Gowda was convinced. He gave up the new job and returned home, and repaid his loan arrears as well as his friends' loan after two months. The whole group was very pleased, because their neighbour had rejoined the group and they had also maintained their 100 per cent repayment record with SKDRDP.

Microinsurance

The goal of SKDRDP's range of group-and community-based programmes is to help thousands of families to improve their standard of living to a decent and sustainable level. In spite of all the successful mobilization of groups and communities, improvements to education and health services and provision of loans and support for group enterprises, one major problem remained. The households were still highly vulnerable to unexpected shocks, which could quickly undo all their progress.

The major potential shock was ill health, which could deprive a family of its main source of income overnight, and could also involve heavy expenses. Even anticipated health issues, such as births or deaths, involved heavy expenditure. A family's savings and other assets, which had been accumulated for productive purposes, could rapidly be absorbed in living and medical costs, and the family might also have to borrow from friends or local moneylenders. This cycle could quickly put a family back to the precarious condition from which they had only recently escaped. This personal and family risk was also a risk for SKDRDP, since people who were hit by disasters of this kind could not repay their loans, and might also need further grant support from Dharmasthala. It made good business sense to try to address the whole issue of vulnerability.

Dr Manjunath and his colleagues worked with United India Insurance, a public sector insurance company, and designed a comprehensive scheme which they called *Sampoorna Suraksha*. This means 'all-embracing protection', with strong implications of divinity. Many microfinance institutions in India were at this time starting to offer insurance cover to their customers, often on a compulsory basis in order to protect their loans by covering the risks of default. The SKRDP scheme was unique in that it covered not only hospital and other medical costs but also a full range of other risks, including maternity expenses, loss of earnings during convalescence, funeral expenses, losses arising from floods and other natural calamities, damage to housing and standing crops, and general accidents.

The annual premium is Rs.190 (just under $4) for the first member of a family, and Rs.115 for every additional member of the same family. Out of this premium, 65 per cent is paid to the insurance company, and this company then reimburses the costs of treatment carried out by members of a chain of hospitals which has close connections with Dharmasthala. The payment provides a maximum family cover for medical costs of Rs.5,000 (about $110) per person. This sum can be drawn on for any medical risk that is covered by the policy. If one family member in a family of five, for instance, requires hospital treatment, the policy will cover the cost up to the limit of Rs.25,000.

The remaining 35 per cent of the premium is paid into a benevolent fund which is administered by SKDRDP. Rs.5,000 is paid from this fund within 24 hours in case of the death of a family's main breadwinner, and in case of accidental death this is increased to Rs.20,000. Generous payments are also made from the benevolent fund in the case of full or partial disability, and for maternity expenses. If the main breadwinner is ill and cannot work, a Rs.50 ($1) daily allowance is paid for up to 30 days, even if he or she is staying at home and does not have to be treated in hospital. If an insured family's home is damaged by a natural calamity, Rs.1,000 can be paid for repairs. All these payments are made from the benevolent fund.

Every family has to renew its membership every year by paying the specified premium amounts. These can be collected along with the members' weekly savings, or if they need to they can take loans from their groups to pay the premium. *Sampoorna Suraksha* is marketed as a mutual security and support fund, since everyone is paying in order to help those who meet with problems. Dr Heggade is closely associated with this programme, and promotes it whenever he addresses people in the area. As with all SKDRDP's programmes, there is a personal element in this support, and there is some implication that families who are members of *Sampoorna Suraksha* are also under the personal protection of Dr Heggade and the deity.

Unlike many microfinance insurance schemes, *Sampoorna Suraksha* is optional. Eligibility is restricted to SKDRDP's group members and their families, and the staff of SKDRDP and other institutions in the Dharmasthala 'family'. By 2007 nearly all the members of SKDRDP's various groups had subscribed. Table 5.5 shows how rapidly it has been taken up and also shows the premium income and the value of settled claims.

Table 5.5 *Sampoorna Suraksha*

	Families covered	Lives covered	Premium collected	Claims settled	Network hospitals
2004–5	54,000	186,000	Rs.15.4 million ($310,000)	Rs.35.4 million ($710,000)	76
2005–6	77,000	196,000	Rs.28.2 million ($564,000)	Rs.32.8 million ($656,000)	41
2006–7	146,000	400,000	Rs.57.43 ($1.15 million)	Rs.66.24 ($1.32 million)	48
2007–8	368,002	892,492	Rs.106.90 ($2.14 million)	Rs.23.05 ($460,000)	80

Note: settlements up to 31 August 2007 from 1 April 2007 are included.

Table 5.5 shows that there was a substantial loss in the first year of *Sampoorna Suraksha*. The United India Insurance Company abandoned the programme during this first year, and SKDRDP was forced itself to cover the initial loss of Rs.10 million ($200,000), in order to maintain the credibility of the product. The ICICI Lombard insurance company, a private sector joint venture between an Indian bank and a British insurance company, was persuaded to replace the previous collaborators. The premiums were increased by about 50 per cent, but nearly all the first year's subscribers renewed their policies and the losses were reduced to Rs.4 million in the second year. For SKDRDP the insurance programme earned a modest surplus of Rs.5 million for 2006/7 from the benevolent fund created by it. However, the insurance company anticipates that the programme would cover its costs during the current year 2007/8.

The forecasts used in the original design of the programme were clearly at fault, but there were also some cases of fraud, where staff at some of the listed hospitals colluded with members to make false claims. These hospitals were removed from the list of approved hospitals to which insured members could go when they were sick, and a system of pre-authorization was introduced for non-urgent cases. A dedicated *Sampoorna Surakshya* assistant was also posted to every SKDRDP field office, who is responsible for verifying all claims. He also visits everyone who is being treated in hospital, and this is regarded by members' families as a valuable form of emotional support, since the assistant is seen as a representative of Dharmasthala.

The generous savings multiples which SKDRDP allows the *Pragathi nidhi* members means that they can climb up the loan 'ladder' as their needs evolve, and the insurance programme protects the members against the worst financial effects of ill health; this mitigates the members' problem but also reduces the risk of loan losses for the programme.

Box 5.4 Kurappa the returned migrant

Kurappa left school at the age of 12 to work in a small teashop in this village. He then moved up to restaurant work, and moved away from Koyyuru, his home village, first to Belthangady town, then to Mangalore, and thence to Bangalore, Hyderabad and Mumbai. He moved from one restaurant to another, and between jobs he kept himself going as a mobile hawker. In 1992 he got married to a girl from his own village, and ended up working in a beer bar in Mumbai.

In 1996 Kurappa decided to come back to his village, as he had been away for 20 years. His family had very little land, and his three brothers were using it in any case, so he started a teashop. He ran this for three years on a very modest scale, but he was not able to expand the business because he had to spend everything he earned on keeping his family. He was wondering whether to go back to Mumbai again, but his elder brother took a loan for him through his SKDRDP *Pragathi Bandhu* group.

His brother had been a member of the group since it started in 1982, and when the programme was liberalized and expanded it became possible to take multiple loans for the use of other family members, so long as the total outstanding was below Rs.100,000 (about $2,200). The elder brother already had an outstanding loan, but the group agreed to lend him Rs.10,000 for Kurappa, to expand his tea shop. He took three more loans, the last being for Rs.35,000, and was able to build his shop into a substantial business as well as to construct a separate house for himself and his family.

Kurappa took a self-employment training course at RUDSETI in 2000, and learned some very good lessons on how to run a business. His shop now stocks almost everything anyone in the village needs, and he also leases space in his shop to a tailor, who is a member of another *Pragathi Bandhu* group. Kurappa also sells the products of some of the group workshops which have been set up by SKDRDP, and he is proud that the other two nearby shops have lost business due to competition from his shop.

In 2006 Kurappa himself joined a *Pragathi Bandhu* group, and in addition to the Rs.35,000 loan he took through his brother for his house, he has borrowed a further Rs.10,000 ($200) to get an electricity connection to his shop. He achieves a turnover of between a Rs.1,000 and Rs.1,500 a day in his shop. He is often too busy in the shop to contribute his weekly labour to the group, so he hires another labourer for Rs.65 a day to work in his place.

Kurappa was one of the first in his village to subscribe to the *Sampoorna Surakshya*, and he was soon able to benefit from it. His wife became ill and had to be hospitalized for a week; Kurappa did not have to pay anything for this, and from then on he encouraged everyone to enrol. Kurappa was also elected to the audit committee of one of the SHG federations in the village, and in addition to everything else he still runs the teashop that he started with, in the same premises.

CHAPTER 6
Livelihoods

Abstract

The small-scale farmers in southern Karnataka need finance, but they also need livelihoods. The SKDRDP field staff help every group member to prepare a simple but detailed farm plan, with the assistance and advice of the fellow group members, and SKDRDP also promotes or itself operates nurseries to cultivate the thousands of saplings which are needed to make best use of the steeply sloping land that is most suitable for tree crops. Many of the poorest people served by SDRDP own no land at all, and must look for other ways to earn their living. Some of the most vulnerable and disadvantaged people still receive charity from SKDRDP, but the institution aims to assist as many people as possible to secure sustainable livelihoods. Landless people are assisted to access government subsidies, and SKDRDP has promoted a number of successful group enterprises. They have set up a central facility to help with marketing and raw material purchases, and this is becoming a profitable business in its own right.

Microfinance is not enough

SKDRDP's mission is to enable all the inhabitants of people of the region where it works to be self-reliant and live in harmony with each other. This involves the physical environment as well as the people themselves, since they depend on the land and water, as well as their own skills. SKDRDP therefore works with small and marginal farmers to adopt sustainable farming practices and to build rural infrastructure.

Everyone is treated the same for the purposes of microfinance, irrespective of their landholdings, but the farmers who own less than a hectare of land are the main targets of the livelihoods programme. They can obtain credit through their *Pragathi Bandhu* groups, but loans alone are not enough to get them out of poverty.

The small farmers, who are usually members of *Pragathi Bandhu* groups, are helped to prepare five-year farm plans to develop their smallholdings into high yielding commercial farming businesses. The local conditions are suitable for cash crops such as betel nut, rubber, cashew, vanilla, and coconut, and all these have long gestation periods. The smaller farmers had not been able to convert their land to these profitable tree crops because they did not have the necessary finance, and as a result they never learned how to plan and manage the conversion process.

The farmers are assisted to prepare individual farm plans, in consultation with their fellow group members and their *sevaniratha*, which include the full details and timing of every improvement that is necessary. This includes fencing, irrigation wells, water management works such as dams and terraces, planting trees and short-duration crops, and also the creation of household assets such as a toilet, improved housing, electricity and so on. The family maintains a special book which includes all the details of what is to be done, and by when, and they formally review their progress every year, as well as discussing the details regularly with their fellow group members and the *sevaniratha*. The farmers do not regard these plans as an intrusion into their private affairs since they are worked out together with their colleagues, and they also have some sanctity through being approved by the representative of Dr Heggade.

More than 60,000 families have prepared and implemented these farm plans, and this has created a big demand for tree seedlings. SKDRDP has therefore financed selected farmers in each village to start nurseries to provide the necessary planting material to the farmers. SKDRDP also has it own central nurseries and also buys material from other seed producers and from government sources in order to take advantage of subsidized prices and other schemes. The farmers can use their groups to borrow the money they need to pay for irrigation equipment such as sprinklers and pumps, and to dig wells.

A total of almost seven million rubber, coconut, betel nut and cashew saplings have been distributed to the farmers, and about 13,000 families have been helped to cultivate paddy and vegetables over 5,000 acres. These families, and several thousand others, have invested in irrigation pumps, water management systems and fencing. SKDRDP also encourages and trains farmers to take up organic farming, through training and financing the purchase of natural worm-based composting material. They can also sell any surplus organic manure they generate through SKDRDP's marketing outlets.

The farmers are encouraged to use renewable energy sources such as gas from manure and solar energy. SKDRDP claims to have the largest concentration of solar home lighting systems in one small geographical area anywhere in the world. Over 3,000 such systems have been installed in Belthangady alone. Some of these have been supplied through SKDRDP, and others by private companies. SKDRDP have also installed a small hydroelectric generator on a river in a hilly area of Belthangady. The 32 tribal families contributed half the total cost by their labour, and they now have reliable low-cost electricity in their homes.

Unlike many NGOs, SKDRDP works closely with government departments, and the *sevanirathas* ensure that all the official programmes are properly delivered in their villages. SKDRDP's specialized staff provide a link between the farmers and research centres, and they have also taken up watershed management programmes in collaboration with the government of Karnataka.

SKDRDP works very closely with the government's extension services. Until 2001 this collaboration was generally informal, and was based on the special interest or goodwill of an individual member of the government's agriculture staff. In 2001, SKDRDP appointed a specialist well-qualified agricultural officer to each project office. The *sevanirathas* also attend regular agriculture training

Box 6.1 Southegadde *Pragathi Bandhu* group

Southegadde is a small hamlet in Belthangady, which in 1970 had just eight families. They lived in miserable mud huts, without any drinking water supply, electricity, or toilets. Seven of the eight family heads were habitual drunkards. They could earn easy money for part of the year by working for a contractor illegally cutting forest trees. This earned them 10 times more than casual farm work, and they spent all the money on liquor. At other times, the men worked as tenants for the local landlord, while their wives and children rolled *beedis* to support themselves.

The eight families were given ownership of the land in 1974 under the land reform programme, but it was all totally barren and they had no tools with which to clear and cultivate it since the landlords had taken all the equipment away when they left. The men were no better off in spite of being owners of the land, and they continued to earn casual wages, and to drink.

The number of families increased to 13, but their economic position became worse every year. A few cultivated rain-fed paddy and pulses once a year, when the rain allowed. They could not possibly plant any more productive crops, because there was no way in which they could finance the gestation period of five years or more. They had become used to using whatever money they earned to buy alcohol, on a day-to-day basis, and there seemed to be no way they could change.

The newly appointed SKDRDP *sevaniratha* came to the hamlet in 1982. At that time, the emphasis was on charitable donations, so he arranged for the two poorest families to be given some basic household items such as mats, glasses, plates, blankets, a photo of the God in Dharmasthala, a lamp, some farm tools, and a few seedlings of rubber, betel nut and cashew trees. Most of the seedlings were neglected and died, and these gifts did not seem to make any long-tem difference to the families. The other 11 households did not benefit at all.

In 1987, the food for work programme was introduced. SKDRDP paid all the eight farmers with rice to clear and level their land, and to build check dams and pits for water storage. Some of the farmers wanted to do more, so they took expensive loans from local moneylenders to buy more farm tools. They were nervous about taking these loans, however, because they knew that they would lose their land if they failed to repay. The farmers were also given new roofing tiles for their huts, but in spite of all these interventions not very much changed.

In 1993 the *sevaniratha* persuaded nine of the Southegadde farmers to start a *Pragathi Bandhu* group. They had to meet every week, to prepare five-year plans for their land, and to contribute one day's free labour every week to each other. At the beginning there were many disagreements, since some members wanted to drink or gamble rather than work on each other's land, but the *sevaniratha* persisted and they slowly started to stick to the rules. They were also persuaded to save Rs.10 (20 cents) each every week, and by 1995 the group was able to take a small loan from the local cooperative bank. The members took small loans for farm tools, fertilizer and seedlings.

The drunkards in the group were persuaded to attend a *Jana Jagruthi* de-addiction camp in 1999, and all of them were cured. Yogish Gowda, who used to be one of the worst drunkards, has also persuaded 30 others to drop the habit.

SKDRDP organized training courses for the group, and as their funds increased they were able to get larger loans. They invested in long-term assets such as irrigation pumps, wells, hybrid cattle and orchards. In the 11 years between 1995 and 2006 the nine members of the group took 183 loans for about Rs.1.2 million (about $24,000).

Some of the individual loans were for over $2,000, and the average was for about $1,000. The loans were used for housing, education, marriages, medical expenses and a wide range of farm activities.

All the farmers' landholdings are now fully productive. SKDRDP has been able to help them to access various government subsidies, for solar lighting, toilets, manure gas plants, and electricity. All the farmers now have good houses with toilets and solar lighting.

programmes. They recognize when any problem is beyond their competence and seek advice from the appropriate agricultural officer, and they in turn are in regular contact with the government departments. SKDRDP helps government to make contacts with farmers, and has organized over 600 training events for its group members in collaboration with the government staff.

Group businesses

In addition to promoting and financing individual livelihood activities, SKDRDP has promoted a number of group activities by financing them, by training the members and also by assisting with their management. These have included jointly owned power tillers, retail shops, crop processing businesses, joint land leasing and cultivation, vegetable vending, and milk production and marketing. Many other income generating activities have also been set up, including milk processing, vanilla, banana, ginger, vegetable and jasmine flower cultivation, detergents, incense stick rolling, beekeeping, and tailoring. Almost 39,000 families from over 3,000 groups have been helped to start businesses of this kind.

The SKDRDP approach in all these activities is similar. The groups are helped to get the fixed assets they need, usually from one or more of the many government programmes which are available but are often under-utilized or misused because of lack of information. They can then access working capital through their group systems, and SKDRDP provides training and helps them to buy raw materials and to sell the final products. The *Sevanirathas*, and the other specialist staff continue to help them as necessary until the groups are able to manage the businesses themselves.

In 2003, SKDRDP started to work with a new government self-employment programme called *Swarnjayanti Gram Swarozgar Yojana* (SGSY), the Golden Jubilee Village self-employment programme. This is designed to help self-help group members who are below the official poverty line to start their own businesses, individually or in groups. The government provides a subsidy of 30 per cent of the total investment required for the chosen business, up to a maximum of Rs7,500 ($150) per person. Somewhat higher subsidies are available for low caste and tribal people, and for the disabled. The subsidies are also higher for group businesses, going up to half the investment, to a total of Rs.10,000 per member. The government also provides a grant to NGOs which help to implement this programme, and SKDRDP was chosen to fulfil this role in South Canara district during 2003 and 2004.

SKDRDP identifies the groups which have poor people who are qualified for this programme among their membership, and then helps them to choose a business. Two or three groups may join together if the business is too large for one group. The SKDRDP staff then help the group to start the business by guiding them in buying the necessary equipment and materials and finding suitable locations. This quite often requires a temporary loan from SKDRDP to tide the groups over until the SGSY subsidy is released, since the government system is very slow. In spite of all the problems associated with working with the government, SKDRDP has been able to form some 300 groups in about 35 activities, and many of these have been reasonably successful.

These groups are encouraged to evolve into independent entities. They may need to buy supplies and to market their products through SKDRDP's own facilities, but SKDRDP is treated as a service provider to the groups, not as the owner or manager. All the profits or losses accrue to the groups, and if they make a profit some part of it is distributed to the members as a dividend, in addition to their wages. This has already happened in the case of one of the groups which makes folders and bags as described in Box 6.2.

During 2001 there was a big publicity campaign about the dangers of smoking hand-rolled cigarettes, or *beedis*, and *beedi* rolling, which had always been women's traditional way of earning extra money, was seriously hit. SKDRDP promoted a number of women's group businesses in order to provide some replacement earnings, and many groups of women started working in a variety of different enterprises. They could often make their chosen products quite successfully, but they usually failed to sell them, and SKDRDP had to take over. They hired some people to sell some items door-to-door, and some staff took stalls at local markets, but the results were not satisfactory and it became clear that the groups had to be supported in a more organized way.

It was not too difficult to standardize the quality and the costs of the quite simple products which most of the groups made, but buying the raw materials and marketing the finished products was not easy. There were many competitive products on the local market, and SKDRDP was unable to deal with so many different products and markets on an *ad hoc* basis.

Group enterprises, like any other business, have to make a profit if they are to survive, and this seemed to be very difficult under the umbrella of SKDRDP. After much discussion, SKDRDP set up a separate entity to promote and support its members' group enterprises. It was called *Shri Dharmasthala SIRI Gramodyoga Samsthe* [Dharmasthala village business], and was set up as a not-for-profit company, specifically to provide supply and marketing services to the businesses which SKDRDP's groups had set up.

SIRI is the name of a famous local woman who fought against social injustice, who is worshipped as a god in South Canara, and the word also means 'sprouting' or 'germination' in Tulu, the local language in the region. In Kannada, the official language of Karnataka, it means 'wealth'.

By 2006 more than 10,000 women were engaged in around 2,000 group businesses producing more than 75 different items, including soap and

---

Box 6.2 The women's plastic folder workshop

Thirteen young women have set up the *Sri Lakshmi Jnanavikasa Swa Sahaya Gumpu* plastic folder workshop at Gerugatte village.

In 2002, a group of eight women first showed some interest in setting up a folder business, and their *sevaniratha* encouraged them to enrol in a training course at the nearby RUDSETI centre. They learned how to make plastic folders, and also how to run a business. After they had been trained their group fund was insufficient to enable them to borrow enough money to start the business, so SKDRDP encouraged them by providing them with everything they needed. This included a small workshop, two stitching machines, hand tools and raw material. The members acted like paid employees of SKDRDP; they came every day to the workshop, stitched the bags that SKDRDP had asked for, received their wages and went home. The finished bags were taken by SKDRDP and sold through various channels, and the women played no part in management. The inevitable losses were covered by SKDRDP.

This was obviously not sustainable in the long term, and it was clear that the women had the ability to run the business on their own. They had accumulated some savings in their group fund out of their wages, and SKDRDP helped them to get a loan of $4,000 from the local branch of Corporation Bank. The women added new products to their range, they bought two more machines, and recruited five new members. In August 2003 SKDRDP helped the group to get a subsidized loan though the government's SGSY programme. They were able to repay their loan from Corporation Bank, to buy four more machines and to move into a new building of their own which they paid for with a their SGSY grant.

The group continues to depend on SKDRDP for its raw materials and marketing, and the finished goods are priced by SKDRDP depending on market conditions. The payments to the group varies accordingly. SKDRDP continued to cover any losses, but the profits remained with the group.

Some of the original members left as they got married, and new members joined. The older members trained them on the job. The group made a small profit in 2005, and all the members, including the ones who had left, received a share based on the piecework wages they had earned.

---

detergents, pickles, spices and chips, ready-made garments, plastic bags and organic fertilizers and disposable leaf plates. The enterprises are labour intensive, since the aim is to employ as many people as possible. Table 6.1 shows the sales turnover achieved by SIRI in 2006/7.

Table 6.1 SIRI's sales turnover in 2006/7

Enterprise	Sales
Food items	Rs.17.42 million ($350,000)
Incense sticks	Rs.31.2 million ($620,000)
Garments	Rs.7.4 million ($150,000)
Plastic bags and folders	Rs.1.9 million ($40,000)
Others	Rs.10.28 million ($210,000)
Total	Rs.68 million ($1.36 million)

Each of the 2,000 groups has contributed Rs.1,000 ($20) towards the share capital of SIRI, and the Small Industries Development Bank of India, which is very active in microfinance, has collaborated with the SGSY programme management to provide low-cost long-term loans to finance its operations. The SGSY programme has also financed all the buildings that are needed for collecting, stocking and sending out the wide range of raw materials and finished goods that SIRI handles.

SIRI is based in Belthangady town, several kilometres away from the SKDRDP office and the Dharmasthala Temple. The company encourages and trains SKDRDP's group members to start up individual and group enterprises, it helps them to get finance from its own or other commercial sources or from government schemes when these are available, and it finds raw material suppliers and buys from them in bulk so that groups can buy them at lower prices than they would have had to pay in the market. Most importantly, SIRI acts as the marketing arm for the 2,000 groups. It helps them with designs and quality control, it buys their products, and it has developed a common brand and advertises and promotes it through various channels. SIRI also helps the groups with their accounts and their local sales tax arrangements.

SIRI has appointed sales representatives to cover the local region, and has set up special SIRI shops in some villages and nearby towns. Dealers have been identified in more distant cities, and local sales are made by door-to-door sales agents or from sales vans. The business made a small profit in 2007 and it is expected that from 2008 onwards a portion of its profit can be distributed to the shareholder groups and used for welfare purposes such as the purchase of school uniforms for children whose parents cannot afford them.

CHAPTER 7
The *sevanirathas*

Abstract

The sevanirathas *are the 'face' of SKDRDP and its main representatives in the communities it serves. They make up 90 per cent of the total staff numbers, and half of them are women. Because of the rapid rate of expansion there are many opportunties for promotion; the majority of the senior management of the organization started work in the field as* sevanirathas. *The* sevanirathas *are well paid, but their work is very demanding, and requires total commitment. Every aspect of their personal is well as their professional life is bound by the values of the temple and of Dr and Mrs Heggade, both of whom take a great personal interest in their development and personal problems and opportunities*

The role of the *sevanirathas*

The *sevanirathas* are the frontline staff of SKDRDP. Originally, there were three separate programme staff in each village or group of villages, but they then became the sole representatives of the organization in a village, responsible for all its programmes.

The *sevanirathas* have been trained in the all the basic aspects of SKDRDP's entire programme; health, education, microfinance, agriculture, non-farm business, insurance and group training methods and promotion. They are carefully chosen from the local youth, and so long as they have satisfactorily passed the Year 10 or Year 12 school-leaving qualification the main focus is on their apparent attitudes and motivation.

SKDRDP recruits nearly all its staff at the basic *sevaniratha* level, unless specific technical skills are needed. Because SKDRDP is well known in the area, large numbers of young people apply without the need for any advertisement. There are in any case very few employment opportunities in the area, and the position of *sevaniratha* is generally held in great respect because they help the community and because of the association with the *Dharmadikari*, and it is therefore a much sought after job. Most of the applicants are in any case referred to SKDRDP by older staff or group members' families. They are usually in their early twenties, and most have been working on the land, as well as hoping for better employment, for some years.

The applicants for the *sevaniratha* position go through a formal process of selection and induction. SKDRDP invites about three times as many applicants as there are positions to complete a written test. This consists mainly of questions about village life, along with some simple general knowledge. Those who do well on this are then interviewed. The candidates are judged on their apparent motivation and attitudes, and, very importantly, on their background. Applicants from rural farming families, and from the families of group members, or even group members themselves, are given preference.

About 5–10 per cent drop out at this stage, and the remainder spend eight to ten days in the field on their own with an older *sevaniratha*. The applicants can see for themselves what the work involves, and can assist in a small way. Many drop out voluntarily. The remainder go through three days of classroom training, where they are introduced to the basic concepts of rural development work, including communication skills, both oral and written, and group building. Candidates who score over 50 per cent in a short test following this training are offered provisional appointments as *sevanirathas*, depending on the number of vacancies which are available.

The selected candidates are then employed on probation for three months, still working with an experienced *sevaniratha*, during which they are paid an allowance of Rs.2,000 (about $40) a month. If they have worked well, they are confirmed and put on the regular pay scale of about Rs.2,800 (about $60) a month. This is a very good salary for an unskilled young person in a rural area, anywhere in India. After about four more months, they newly recruited *sevanirathas* attend a further one-week training programme on a specific subject, and they attend further such programmes every six months. Special training programmes are sometimes organized to address particular weaknesses in their skills.

SKDRDP invests very heavily in its newly appointed *sevanirathas* once they have been with the organization for about three months. In addition to their salaries, they are provided with free housing, a loan for a motorcycle along with the cost of its fuel and maintenance, household equipment, a gas cooking stove and subscriptions to professional magazines to keep abreast of current developments. SKDRDP also contributes to their pension fund and provides maternity leave on full pay to women staff; these benefits are very unusual in development work.

The new recruits can advance very quickly because the organization is expanding so fast. Their performance is evaluated every three months, and within two years a *sevaniratha* can be promoted to a supervisor. Those who do unusually well can advance even faster, and gain more responsibility than others. Jobs which need special technical skills are only rarely advertised because SKDRDP prefers to grow its own staff, who share its culture and have learned their skills on the job.

Some of the first *sevanirathas* have now become directors of SKDRDP, or functional or district heads. All the members of the executive committee, which consists of the directors and project officers, apart from Dr Manjunath, the executive director, and the two women, have risen from the level of *sevaniratha*. Bodhapa Gowda, the director of human resources, left school in 1974. He left his village near Belthangady and took a job as a cashier in a small hotel in the north of Karnataka. He came back in 1978 to work as a clerk in the local government office, and in 1984 he heard that Dr Heggade was looking for field staff for his new development organization. He applied for a job immediately, and was promoted steadily, and in 1990 he became a senior *sevaniratha*. He advanced to supervisor in 1993, project officer in 1996 and finally became director of human resources in 2005.

When Gowda joined SKDRDP in 1984 there were less than 10 staff and they would all meet Dr Heggade every evening and discuss the day's experiences in villages where they went to distribute food and utensils with him. By 1992 there were 60 staff and by 2006 there were 1,200.

SKDRDP appointed its first women staff in 1992, when it started the JVK women's group programme. From that time onwards, preference has been given to women, so that now half of the total staff are women. The higher positions are still dominated by men, and there are only two women in the executive committee out of a total of 15 members. Neither of them has come through all the levels of SKDRDP; one joined as a director and the other as a supervisor.

The staff are all local except for a small number of subject specialists, and none of them come from further than Bangalore, which is about eight hours away by bus. Most of the staff also come from quite humble backgrounds, from rural farming families, and very few have been educated beyond their local village schools. Many did not complete even primary education, because their families needed them to earn money.

Many have been members of SKDRDP groups, or are relatives of members, including some sons and daughters. Some started working with SKDRDP programme as part-time teachers in the *Jnanadeepa* programme, and moved across to become *sevanirathas*, and the majority have a good idea as to what the job of a *sevaniratha* involves before they apply to join.

The *sevanirathas* constitute more than 90 per cent of SKDRDP's staff. They are well paid, and the rural location and the generous facilities provided by SKDRP means that they have to spend very little money on themselves. They also appreciate the chance to work not very far away from their own villages.

They do, however, have to adhere to SKDRDP's rules and values. The *sevanirathas* are never posted in their own villages, to avoid any charges of favouritism. They have to reside in the village where they are posted and cannot live in their own villages, even if they are quite near. This is quite common practice in government and private businesses in India, in order to avoid family pressures and favouritism. They are not allowed even to visit their family homes except on their one day off per week or when they are on leave. Even the use of mobile phones is discouraged, because it increases their expenditure, and these are only allowed when the *sevaniratha* is promoted to be a supervisor. They are transferred to a different village at least every two years.

A *sevaniratha* is expected always to be a role model and an ideal citizen in the eyes of the villagers, in his or her personal life as well as professionally. They are not allowed to smoke or to drink alcohol, and everything is done to ensure that the *sevanirathas* remain strictly professional in all their dealings with the village people. They are forbidden to have anything other than strictly professional relationships with other young men or young women. If anything of this kind

Box 7.1 Pushpa, a *sevaniratha*

When Pushpa completed Year 10 , she had to leave school. Her father used to spend all his income on liquor. Pushpa and her mother rolled *beedis* to support the family.

Her school teachers had supported her by her giving books and whatever else she needed because she was good at sports and strengthened the school's reputation. She was the secretary of the village girls' group, and she wanted to join the police or the army. But her mother wanted her to stay at home, and would not let her go.

In 1993 her mother joined her village JVK group. Pushpa watched the meetings, and the SKDRDP supervisor came to know her. She could see that the young girl was very bright, even though she had had to leave school early, and she encouraged Pushpa to apply for a job with SKDRDP.

She was appointed as a junior coordinator whose job was to look after one JVK. Her salary was Rs.200 (about $5) a month, and it soon went up to Rs.600. In 2000 she was given responsibility for four JVK groups, and her salary went up to Rs.900. In 2001 she was promoted to be a *sevaniratha*, and her salary was increased to Rs.1,900, and by 2006 she was earning Rs.2,800 in the same job.

Pushpa has been transferred three times after being promoted as a *sevaniratha*. She manages 50 groups; 22 *Pragathi Bandhu* labour-sharing groups, two of which are women's groups, 25 self-help groups, of which 14 are women's groups, and three larger JVK women's groups. All these groups have weekly meetings, and the two self-help group federations also meet once a month. Pushpa has to visit seven groups a day on average to check their record books and accounts, and she also has to assess their progress and identify their training needs.

In addition she attends a *Bhajan Mandali* song meeting every week which is organized by the *Nava Jeevana* group of ex-alcoholics. This is the programme Pushpa enjoys the most. She believes that her greatest achievement is to have played some part in curing some alcoholics, and she regards those who relapse in spite of the treatment as her personal failures.

Pushpa does not enjoy supervising the women's groups who make products for SIRI, since it is hard to enforce the necessary quality standards and to tell the women that they will not be paid for sub-standard products. She also finds it difficult to explain the intricacies of the *Sampoorna Surakshya* insurance programmes to all the members, most of whom have never even heard of the concept of insurance before.

She has been to seven or eight training courses during her career with SKDRDP, on documentation, accounting, gas digester plants, microfinance, and small business, and she hopes that she will be promoted to the level of a JVK supervisor, covering an even larger number of groups.

Pushpa was married in 2002, to Balakrishna, an accounts manager in a transport firm nearby, who earns about Rs.5,000 ($100) a month. They have a 3-year-old girl who stays with her grandmother, because Pushpa's hectic schedule as a *sevaniratha* does not allow her to take care of her child. She sees her daughter for a day every alternate week, as she has to be with her husband's family on her other weekly day off.

Pushpa is very religious. She prays to God every day and visits the Dharmasthala Temple once a month. She also fasts on the fourth day of every month. Her religious faith was greatly strengthened after her father was miraculously cured of an undiagnosed disease which he had contracted as a result of worshipping Daiva, the spirit of a departed person. Worship of this kind is quite common in South Canara and the Dharmasthala Temple has some images of these spirits. Pushpa and her family prayed for him to be cured, and their prayers were answered. In spite of her strong religious beliefs, however, Pushpa is convinced that there is no place for charity in SKDRDP. People have to be guided to help themselves, and SKDRDP itself must be sustainable in order to maintain its rapid pace of expansion.

Pushpa's main inspiration comes from Dr Heggade, and in particular his personal simplicity. She remembers in detail every occasion when he has talked to her. She is very glad that her mother overruled her many years ago, and she feels she has done much better than her three friends who joined the police and others who are housewives, and still have to roll *beedis* for a living.

occurs, a formal marriage is arranged at once. There is also a strict dress code. *sevanirathas* are not allowed to wear T-shirts or jeans; the men have to wear shirts and formal trousers and the women have to wear saris when they are in the field. They can only wear *salwar kamis* in the office, and shirts and trousers are strictly forbidden for the women at any time. If any *sevaniratha* breaks the rules, he or she is advised to change; if they continue to disobey, strong action is taken.

The *sevanirathas* are not allowed to associate with the village youth unless they are discussing business, and they are provided with kitchen utensils and cooking facilities to cook their own food. They are not allowed to take their meals outside except in exceptional circumstances.

The senior staff of SKDRDP set an example for them through their own simple lifestyles. They also spend time with the *sevanirathas* at regular intervals. If they have any personal problems they are taken care of immediately. If the problem is a financial one, for instance, the *sevaniratha* can have an immediate personal loan. Their salaries and travel claims are paid promptly. This is unusual for many NGOs in India. The children of SKDRDP's staff are given priority places in all the schools and colleges linked to Dharmasthala. This is a major benefit since all these institutions are of a high standard and there is a demand for places.

In the early days Dr Heggade used to spend time with the SKDRDP staff every day. This is no longer possible, but Dr Heggade and his wife make a point of seeing every staff member at least once every three months. They discuss personal problems as well as professional issues, and when he is travelling in the area Dr Heggade makes a point of calling on the families of the *sevaniratha*s when he can. If any member of staff is ill, he sends them a message, and arranges for their medical bills to be paid if this is necessary. This may seem to be normal old-fashioned personnel management, but all the money that is spent comes from Dr Heggade's own pocket. For many of the staff, and their families, he is a divine figure.

When the JVKs started, Mrs Heggade also used regularly to meet the staff and to help with appointment interviews. She sends gifts for the marriages of their children. She advises them to save regularly. She is perceived by the staff almost as a mother.

The village people in their turn respect their *sevanirathas* in the same way, since they are seen as representatives of Dharmasthala. The villagers help and support the *sevanirathas* in all their work, particularly the female staff, and when a *sevaniratha*, especially a woman, is to get married, there is no shortage of suitors. They are well-respected by everybody in the community.

The *sevanirathas* are generally very religious people. Most of those who apply have some inclinations in that direction before they join, but it is very much strengthened by the culture of SKDRDP and the expectations of their colleagues and their clients. Almost all of them have a photograph of Lord Manjunatha and Dr Heggade in their homes, and they pray to the God every day before they start work. They visit the temple at Dharmasthala whenever they have time, and they go to their local temple regularly. They organize worship and temple celebrations, as well as cleaning up the public spaces in their villages, because they believe this makes for unity in the community. All the village people, including Muslims and Christians, contribute their time voluntarily to this, although they do not take part in the actual rituals.

The *sevanirathas* identify completely with Dr Heggade; their commitment and loyalty to him is absolute. They feel that he treats them like an extension of his own family, and if they have any problem, they can always fall back on him for help. The job itself is also very satisfying, it fulfils their basic needs and provides many opportunities for personal growth and development. The *sevaniratha* is responsible for the development of the villages in almost every aspect, and their work includes many things apart from facilitating microfinance groups.

The work that the majority of *sevanirathas* most enjoy is alcohol de-addiction, motivating women in their JVK groups, and organising religious ceremonies in the village. They almost become village leaders.

The *sevanirathas* are thus very motivated and their morale is high. The rate of staff turnover is very low throughout SKDRDP. During the five years between 2001 and 2006, during which the staff numbers grew from 229 to 1,120, only 100 people left. Most of those were women who left because they got married, and a few others moved to jobs in the government, which are not as well paid but are totally secure. The whole area is developing very fast, however, like much of southern India. SKDRDP has contributed significantly to this, but as people become more prosperous they may not be willing to devote themselves so completely to the institution. Very few of the *sevanirathas* would like their children to do the same job.

A day in the life of Sivaram Pujary, a *sevaniratha*

The alarm bell rings at 5:30 a.m. on Saturday. The *sevaniratha* wakes up, washes himself and his clothes, and prays to his picture of Lord Manjunath for about 10 minutes. He then takes his breakfast and cooks his lunch. At 7:30 a.m. he attends a self-help group's weekly meeting, and checks the records, and by 11:30 a.m. he has attended four more group meetings and been through the same routine.

Box 7.2 Savitha d'Souza, project officer

Savitha has a degree in social work. She started work in a missionary organization promoted by the Church of South India, whose objective was to provide vocational training to young people. She worked there for about nine months, but she found it to be an unsatisfactory institution. The Father who ran it used to recruit 10- to 12-year-old children from poor families and used them as unpaid labour to run the whole farm, without any training. He stayed 50 kilometres away in Mangalore and left everything to her. The children learned nothing, the farm was badly run, and the place seemed to have no purpose.

At this point Savitha happened to hear that SKDRDP was looking for women to help organize its JVK groups in Karkala, the town in South Canara from which she came. She applied, was interviewed by Mrs Heggade and got the job. She had in the meantime got married and she had a child shortly after she had joined. She was then asked to go to Udupi, a town some distance to the North of Belthangady, to head the new project office where SKDRDP was starting its urban programme.

Savitha was rather nervous about taking on a new job when she had only just had her first child, but her husband and the SKRDP management gave her every support so she agreed. At first she travelled from Karkala to Udupi every day, but after a year, although it is quite unusual in rural India for a husband to shift in response to his wife's job, the whole family shifted to Udupi. Her mother, who was working as a housemaid in the Gulf, came back and lived with them.

The Udupi programme has expanded under Savitha's leadership, and now also works in the surrounding rural areas. Savitha has won over the local MP, who used to oppose SKDRDP's programmes, and is now a vigorous supporter. Savitha is only 27 years old, she is the youngest project officer, and the only woman project officer. She may be asked to become the youngest director, but she is not sure whether she will be able to give the job the time it requires.

When Savitha first joined SKDRDP, she used to be very reluctant to write or say '*Om Manjunathaya Namah*', as everybody else did when starting a document or a talk. As a devout Roman Catholic, she felt it was wrong. She is deeply religious and goes to church regularly. She has now started to visit the temple at Dharmasthala, whenever she comes to the SKDRDP head office. She has no hesitation in prefixing her statements and reports with the blessing '*Om Manjunathaya Namah*', because she has come to appreciate the all-embracing love which emanates from Dharmasthala and from Dr and Mrs Heggade, its leaders.

Savitha is herself totally loyal and committed to SKDRDP, but she feels that it will in the future be very difficult to recruit young people with the same sense of commitment, since young people's attitudes are changing so fast. As people get better education they become more confident and even arrogant and impatient. Professionalism is good, but it is often a substitute for loyalty to one institution. She has also observed how the village people are changing. They are more educated, they desire to go beyond the satisfaction of their basic needs and want a better life. These changes are in part the result of SKDRDP's own success in bringing development to the area, but Savitha believes that fundamental changes will be necessary if the organization is to continue to survive and be effective.

It is *Sharada Puja* festival day in Karnataka. Sharada is the goddess of intelligence, and her festival is celebrated in every village with great enthusiasm. This year in a nearby village they are having a particularly big celebration with big tents and lavish decoration. The *Pragathi Bandhu* group there is organizing the whole affair, and all the local *sevanirathas* and supervisors have been asked to help. He visits this festival for a quarter of an hour, to make sure that all is well, and he then visits yet another village for which he is responsible. He attends three more self-help group meeting and a *Pragathi Bandhu* meeting, before visiting that village's *Sharada Puja*, which the school has organized.

He has a late lunch at his house at about 3 p.m., and then attends a women's JVK meeting at the first village, where they are also celebrating the *Sharada Puja*. The members are in a party mood because of the festival, so they do not get through the business which he had hoped they would cover.

After the JVK meeting, there is another *Pragathi Bandhu* meeting in the same village, and by the time that is over, it is time to go to the alcoholics support meeting which is being held at the local Vinayaka Temple. There he attends the *Bhajana Mandali* singing session, which goes on for almost an hour and a half. He takes his small holy meal there, and then goes back to the big festival, where the image of the deity has to be immersed in a nearby river. A big procession along with entertainment has been arranged, and he meets all the local *sevanirathas* and their supervisor there. This goes on until about 10 p.m.

By that time it is too late to cook dinner, and most of the local hotels are closed. He searches in the dark on his motorbike for about 5 km, and he finally finds a very basic hotel which is open. Most of the food is finished, but the owner knows him well and respects him what he does for the area, so she cooks him a simple meal of *dosas*, or pancakes, with a basic curry.

He gets back to his lodging at about 11 p.m. He has to write up his daily report and his weekly report to his supervisor. He also has to complete the special report on the case of a widow who received Rs. 25,000 from the *Sampoorna Surakshya* insurance programme after her husband, who drove an auto-rickshaw, was killed in an accident. He has to deal with two villages, not one, and to write up special cases, because he is well educated and had performed well as a *sevaniratha*. The reward for doing well is to be asked to do more.

The *sevaniratha* for whom this is a normal busy day is Sivaram Pujary. He had a post-graduate degree in history and sociology, but when his parents were killed in a road accident in 2000 he had to look for a job immediately. He got a short-term contract job as a lecturer in a local College at Rs.1,500 ($30) a month, but in 2003 he had to get his only sister married. He spent Rs.150,000 on her dowry, which he raised by selling part of the small landholding he had inherited from his parents, and he gave the rest of the land to her as well.

Sivaram was very intelligent, and he passed two stages of the state administrative services exam. But then he was asked for a bribe of Rs.100,000 to get through the last stage. He did not have that much money, and when it became clear that his position as a lecturer was unlikely ever to be confirmed he started to look for other opportunities. His cousin, who was the president of a village federation, told him about SKDRDP.

SKDRDP happened to be going through the recruitment process on the same day that Sivaram went to Dharmasthala to enquire for an opening. He was asked there and then to go through the recruitment process; he qualified, went through the probationary village stay and training, and was asked to join SKDRDP immediately.

It rained all day on 21 June 2005, Sivaram's very first day as a *sevaniratha*. His first task was to recover an outstanding loan of Rs.300,000 ($6,000). It took seven months of rigorous follow-up to get the money back. In the process he reactivated the dormant self-help group in the village, and he used to remind the people that the money was not theirs, nor his, but it belonged to the God Manjunatha. Abdul Khadri, a leading Muslim villager, helped him to persuade all the defaulters to repay their loans.

When Sivaram joined, 36 of the 43 groups in the village were of C and D grades, but when he left the village a year later, he had added 11 more groups and all the 54 groups were rated A or B, except for one, which was a C grade.

His fondest memories are not about loan recoveries. He organized the 50th anniversary celebrations of the village school, with a massive tree plantation exercise and a special training programme in environmental management. He has also organized health and eyesight camps in the village, and a veterinary camp for the diary animals.

In view of his achievements, he was transferred to Aladangady, and is now responsible for two villages with a total of 86 groups.

CHAPTER 8
Two cases of success

Abstract

Moneppa Gowda's father was a marginal landless farm labourer and sharecropper on four acres of leased land, but could not afford to cultivate it, and when he died the family was destitute. Moneppa then joined an SKDRDP shared labour group, and was given a $150 grant to enable him to cultivate some land. He gradually improved his position, and started to take loans from his group. He eventually took and repaid a total of fourteen loans. He started a small dairy and a jasmine flower plantation, and plans to rebuild his house. He ascribes his success to the divine personality of Dr Heggade. The Sree Nidhi Panakaje *is a group of 21 formerly destitute women who have set up and now manage a snacks-making business with the assistance of SKDRDP. The organization helped them to obtain a government subsidy to cover the cost of their small factory and the machinery, and they now plan to take a substantial loan to buy an improved packaging machine. They start work every day with prayers to the divinity of Dharmasthala.*

Moneppa Gowda, a successful household

Moneppa Gowda's house is on the outskirts of Puthila village, on the road from Dharmasthala to Bantwada. The surrounding forest is thick with peepal, banyan, tamarind and jackfruit trees, and the house is surrounded by betel nut, coconut and cashew. A clear mountain stream flows through his four acre farm.

Moneppa is 47 years old and looks much younger than his age. He lives with his mother, his wife and their three children. His mother celebrated her 100th birthday in 2006. When she was younger, she used to be a herbalist and dispensed local potions and powders to all the sick people in the village. She suffered from diabetes for some years, but Moneppa claims that she has now cured herself. She has lost her sight and her teeth but she is alert and moves around on her own, taking an active interest in everything that goes on.

Moneppa's wife Bhavani is 43 years old. The oldest boy is 21 years old. He took a course in diesel engines at a local college and works for Hyundai Motors at Bangalore as an apprentice mechanic. Many other young people from Puthila village have migrated to Mumbai and Bangalore in search of jobs, but few of them are as young as Moneppa's son, and very few of them are employed in companies like Hyundai. Their only daughter is training as a teacher, and their two younger sons are still at school. They also help their father on the farm.

Moneppa's father was a landless labourer and sharecropper. He took a lease on a four acre farm but lacked the capital to cultivate it so he returned one acre to the landlord. He planted a hardy low-yielding local variety of paddy, which earned very little, and in any case much of what he harvested went to the landlord as rent. All he owned was his tiny homestead plot, with his small hut, 10 coconut and 18 betel nut trees. He wanted to plant more perennial tree crops, such as betel nut, which need less labour and give much better returns, and for which his land was very suitable, but he could not afford to plant them because of their long gestation period and the high investment that was needed.

He was in many ways typical of the farming community around Belthangady. Life was a constant struggle for the whole family; they frequently had to go hungry, and Moneppa remembers that when he was a child his family could not afford an umbrella. He used to go to school with an improvised umbrella made from coconut leaves, and his friends used to laugh at him. His father died in 1981, after a lifetime of hard but unrewarding work. Moneppa was 21 years old at that time and, as the only son, he had to take on the whole burden of running the family.

After his father died the family went through even worse troubles. When his mother had to go to hospital shortly after his father's death, they could not afford any medicine for her, they rarely had enough rice to eat, and were reduced to eating the green leaves which grew wild in the village.

Like the whole of the Belthangady area, Puthila is very hilly, and the land has to be levelled to improve its productivity. It rains heavily from June to September, but irrigation is needed for the rest of the year. When SKDRDP started their work in the area, they realized that the farmers would have to be given food to tide them over the period before their crops started to yield any return. Moneppa and many other small farmers in Puthila village benefited from this. He received a total of 400 kg of rice, which was worth about Rs.4,000, to pay him for clearing a pond, fencing his field and deepening his well.

In addition to giving the farmers rice to meet their labour cost, SKDRDP also gave them good quality seeds and saplings, and subsidized the cost of the farm tools which were necessary for good cultivation. Moneppa was given material for coconut, betel nut, cashew nut and vegetables, and he was also given irrigation pipes and a sprayer.

Between 1982 and 1991 Moneppa received 15 subsidy payments, to a total value of Rs.7,000 (about $150). Many other poor farmers in his village received as much or even more. The SKDRDP subsidies helped him to move up from subsistence farming. He used to grow rain fed paddy, which yielded barely a 1,000 kg per acre, but after he had deepened his well and installed an irrigation pump he started to grow irrigated paddy. The village *sevaniratha* explained that SKDRDP required farmers to produce a written plan for the development of their land as a condition of getting loans, and showed him how to cultivate the new varieties. He trebled his paddy yield to 3,000 kg per acre.

The *sevaniratha* also convinced Moneppa that high-value perennial crops were more profitable than paddy. When his land was levelled and irrigated he started to replace paddy with 200 betel nut seedlings every year. All this helped Moneppa to improve his income substantially, and in 1994 he bought one more acre of land for Rs.60,000. His total holding reached four acres, whose total value was about Rs.2.5 million (over $25,000), after Moneppa had irrigated and planted them.

Although Moneppa benefited immensely from the SKDRDP programme, he felt quite guilty that he had received so much from the Dharmasthala Temple Trust. He knew that the money had mainly been donated by poor devotees, and he felt that he should somehow repay the money. He did not like being dependent on charity. He therefore welcomed SKDRDP's change of policy, when they switched from giving grants and subsidies to promoting self-reliance through labour sharing and self-help groups. He also felt that not all the families who were assisted SKDRDP really benefited. Many of them squandered their income on liquor and wasteful expenditure such as ostentatious marriages, rather than investing in their own future.

SKDRDP started the *Pragathi Bandhu* programme in his area in 1994, and Moneppa persuaded four farmers in his neighbourhood to form a group with him. He included his two brothers-in-law and two other neighbours in the group. Three of the members are high caste Gowdas, as is Moneppa, while one is a Billawa, a lower caste. About 25 per cent of the farmers in Puthila are Billawas, and less than 10 per cent are Gowdas, but caste is not allowed to be an issue in *Pragathi Bandhu* membership.

The group members' land holdings ranged from one and a half to two acres, and Moneppa was the biggest landholder. The caste and land differences were not a problem, and they all worked together harmoniously. The members have remained close friends for 12 years. At one point one of the members became an alcoholic and left the group. The others stood by him and supported him when he attended a SKDRDP de-addiction camp, and he was able to rejoin the group in 2002. They meet every Tuesday for labour sharing, and Moneppa has only once missed a meeting. He had to go Mangalore on business, but he paid a labourer Rs.75 ($1.50) to replace him for the day. Moneppa does not plan ever to leave the group, although he is now so much better off than when he joined. He hopes the group will continue for generations to come.

In 1997 his wife and eight other women founded a self-help group, with assistance from SKDRDP, and she has been a member ever since. She did not take any loans from her group until 2006, because her husband was able to borrow enough for the whole family from his *Pragathi Bandhu* group. She used her first loan to buy a pair of gold earrings.

Moneppa gradually built up his assets, year by year, and he made good use of loans from his group. Between 1996 and 2006 he took 14 loans. The smallest loan was to pay the *Sampoorna Suraksha* health insurance premium for his family, and the largest was to construct a bore well. He used other loans for a pump set and a cross-bred cow, to build a cow shed, to buy fertilizer and to cultivate bananas, as well to pay for his children's schooling.

In 1997 and again in 1998 Moneppa borrowed Rs.5,000 ($125) to pay off loans he had taken from the local Primary Agriculture Cooperative Society. The society's loans cost 12 per cent per annum, whereas the SKDRDP loan to his group cost only 10 per cent. He realized that it was better to move to the cheaper source of funds, and he also felt some loyalty to SKDRDP. The group added a margin on its cost, in order to add to its own surplus funds, so that Moneppa actually paid rather more than 12 per cent. The margin belonged to the group, however, of which he was a part-owner, so he gained indirectly from it.

Altogether, the five members borrowed Rs.600,000 from the group between 1996 and 2006. Moneppa owed about Rs.75,000 in 2006 and was repaying about Rs.350 ($7) a week to the group. SKDRDP also offers housing loans to group members, and Moneppa wants to build a modern house for his family. He wants first to concentrate on his farm, however, because he knows that the main reason that he has always been able to repay his loans on time is because they have all been invested in activities which produce a regular income.

Moneppa owns two Jersey cows and three Holsteins. He borrowed Rs.9,000 to buy one of them, and bought the others with his savings. The five cows give around 30 litres of milk every day, for about 300 days a year. They are kept in a specially constructed shed, and Moneppa carries the milk every day to a chilling plant two kilometres from his home and sells it for about 10 cents a litre.

Moneppa also installed a manure digester in his field for about $280. He paid about 70 per cent of the cost from his savings, and the balance was paid by a state government subsidy which was arranged by SKDRDP. The plant generates enough cooking gas for all his family's cooking needs, and it also saves the money and time taken to get LPG bottles from the town. The slurry from the plant is excellent compost, and the five cows produce enough dung and urine to keep it going all year.

He also has a solar dryer for his betel nuts, which cost about $30, and he earns about $50 a year from half an acre of bananas. They also have a small plot of jasmine flowers, which is a labour-intensive, low–volume but high-value crop. This earns an annual net income of Rs.8,000 (about $160). These high returns are only possible because Moneppa does not hire any outside labour. He and his wife pluck the flowers and thread them into small garlands and then take them to the market before 7 a.m.

A very old carved stone lies half-embedded in the ground under a tree by the corner of the jasmine field. It is a holy place, and the family pray to it for favours, such as a good marriage for their daughter, and they repay it with small offerings when their wishes are granted.

Moneppa also has 50 coconut trees along the boundaries of his fields, which earn about Rs.12,000 a year. His most profitable crop, however, is betel nut. He has 1,500 betel trees. They do not yield any nuts until they are six years old, which is why poor farmers without any savings or loan facilities are unable to plant them even if they have suitable land. One thousand of these trees can earn about Rs.60,000 a year, and by 2008 the trees should be earning about Rs.90,000. The total income from his farm will then be about Rs.130,000 ($2,600) a year, which would have been an impossible dream twenty years ago.

Moneppa has worked hard to build his livelihood, but he believes that much of the credit for his success is due to the *sevanirathas*. They are regularly trained by SKDRDP, and they in turn pass on what they have learned to the members of the *Pragathi Bandhu* groups.

Moneppa has worshipped at Dharmasthala all his life and used to visit the shrine of Lord Manjunatha whenever he could, but before he joined the SKDRDP group he did not feel he had any connection with Dr Heggade himself. He knew that he was the hereditary owner and manager of the Dharmasthala Temple, but that was all. The SKDRDP's outreach programmes have made him feel much closer to Dr Heggade. Moneppa says that the people in Puthila village now respect Dr Heggade more as a wise and generous person than as the holy *Dharmadikari*. People treat him as the representative of Lord Manjunatha, but in a far more personal way than before.

Dr Heggade in his turn does not want to be seen as a source of charity. The early grant scheme showed that the way to help poor people was not to give grants but to help them to help themselves. The *Pragathi Bandhu* groups make people feel that SKDRDP, and through it Dr Heggade himself, are their partners, rather than a God.

SKDRDP is not the only development organization working in the area. There is also a large state-level NGO called Navodaya, and a whole range of government development offices. Moneppa has never had any contact with the NGO. Each of its field staff apparently has to cover eight or ten villages, whereas one SKDRDP *sevaniratha* is responsible for only one village. He also prefers to access government schemes through SKDRDP rather than working direct with the government personnel, who are very impersonal when compared to the SKDRDP staff.

Moneppa is not the only successful farmer in Puthila village. The other four members of his group and many other farmers have benefited in the same way. Moneppa feels that the food for work programme, the *Pragathi Bandhu* group and its shared labour system and his loans have all been vital to their success. But he believes that none of this would have been possible without the direction and guidance of Dr Heggade, which itself arises from the divinity of his position and his closeness to God.

According to Moneppa, India's independence in 1947 did not make any difference to people like him. The first independence that mattered to him came in 1974 when the land tenancy act was passed and his family became the owners of three acres of land, so that they were no longer landless labourers. But his family was unable to make any real use of this land until the second independence, which was SKDRDP. Their grants and extension work enabled him to improve his farm and to earn more income.

The third independence was the *Pragathi Bandhu* group, through which he could take loans for as much as Rs.100,000 ($2,000) at low interest rates. His fourth independence, he believes, will be when he builds a modern house and when all his children are properly educated.

Moneppa installed a telephone in 2002, and this is also a form of independence. He speaks regularly to his son in Bangalore, and to his other relatives who have telephones. It also gives his family a sense of security. Puthila is quite a remote place, and both the doctor and the vet are 15 km away, but now they are only one phone call away.

Moneppa has great personal respect for Dr Heggade. A big photograph of him and his wife hang in his house, along with pictures of gods and goddesses. There is also a photograph of his *Pragathi Bandhu* group and Dr Heggade standing with them. Moneppa believes in honesty and hard work. He has a deep faith in Lord Manjunatha and claims his strength comes from his daily prayers. He has always been a religious person, ever since he was a child, but he grew spiritually after coming into contact with SKDRDP and their employees. He is deeply impressed by SKDRDP's development programmes and their spiritual values, and by the selfless service of the *sevanirathas*. As he became more religious, Moneppa started to take more interest in the local temple in his village, and served as president of his village *Bhajan Mandali* meeting for two years.

Every member of Moneppa's family shares in the household work and they believe in the dignity of labour. Akkoo, his 100-year-old mother, knows that the whole family is there to look after her, and Moneppa and his wife respect and cooperate with one another, but his wife makes her own decisions.

Dr Heggade and the SKDRDP have played a major role in the transformation of Moneppa's life. He has wiped out all traces of his past poverty, but he still has a balanced outlook on life and appreciates his good fortune. Moneppa has seen many families in his village ruined due to drinking. He was so impressed with the *sevanirathas'* preaching against drinking and their work in the de-addiction camps that he vowed to Lord Manjunatha that he would never fall a prey to drunkenness. True to his vow, he has never touched a drop of liquor since.

Sree Nidhi Panakaje, the Women's Snacks Group

Sree Nidhi Panakaje in Sonanduru village in South Canara district is a food factory, producing a variety of south Indian snacks. It is unique in many respects. It is owned by a group of self-help group women, who are poor and have never been in business before. The factory has a turnover of about Rs.4 million ($80,000) a year, and it is managed by a group of 21 women who are barely educated. The most remarkable feature is that they all work harmoniously together under one roof.

In 2001 the *sevaniratha* of Sonanduru village convened a meeting to discuss the possibilities for group enterprise. All the members of the self-help groups and *Pragathi Bandhu* groups from Sonanduru and two neighbouring villages attended. The *sevaniratha*, along with his supervisor, explained the advantages of group enterprises, and they described some of the economic activities which could be undertaken on a group basis. They encouraged the participants to select an activity and to start such an enterprise.

The members of five of the self-help groups whose members were at the meeting expressed an interest in starting a group snack production business. They wanted to enhance their incomes, and they felt that they could use their existing skills as cooks at home. The five groups had been started between 1992 and 2000. They had a total of 61 members, and they were all very attached to their groups. Not a single member had dropped out over the eight years. Two had died and three others had moved away after marriage, but otherwise every woman had remained in her group.

All the 56 members of the five groups were from backward castes. They came from marginal farmers' families, who owned less than two acres of land, and the little land they owned was degraded and not irrigated. Because they could earn so little from farming, 35 of the 56 women helped their families by rolling *beedies*.

Beedi rolling used to be a popular activity for poor women in South Canara district. They could work sitting down, at home, with flexible working hours, and it did not require any investment. It is however quite difficult, and very tedious, and a women has to work for many hours every day to earn even Rs.600 ($12) a month. The income is very low, but the work is also very unhealthy. *Beedi* rollers suffer from neck and back pain, stomach problems, eye strain and bronchitis. The anti-tobacco movement has also cut the demand for *beedis*. It used to be a fairly reliable supplementary source of income but the demand was declining quite rapidly, which was a severe blow for hundreds of thousands of poor families in South Canara district, including the members of the five groups.

Since the formation of the groups, the members had been saving Rs.10 (20 cents) each every week. They were also paying their premiums for the *Sampoorna Suraksha* health insurance scheme. They took frequent small loans, mainly for consumption purposes, such as buying medicines, marriages, and repaying personal loans. A few of the more enterprising members had taken small loans for income generating activities, such as buying cattle, or vegetable trading. The women felt more secure because they knew that they could get money when they needed it, but their income had not significantly increased. They had not been able to engage in any substantial income generation activities.

Their income from *beedis* was going down, and they were looking for other work. The Sonanduru meeting on group enterprises gave them many ideas, and after a lot of discussion among themselves, they decided to start a snack production business. They had the necessary skill, the investment was quite small, and the risk was minimal.

They started their business at the house of one of the members. They made a very small range of locally familiar snacks, such as 'mixture', which is made of rolled rice, cornflakes, peanuts, and lentils fried and mixed together with spices, and *murukku,* made from chickpea flour and spices, shaped like spaghetti and fried, and fruit and vegetable pickles. Each self-help group specialized in one item. They bought their raw materials to their common place, and then made the snacks independently in their respective villages. The members sold the snacks themselves in their own villages, by going from house to house. Many of their customers were the members of other SKDRDP groups in the neighbouring villages; the snacks were of good quality and low cost, but they also liked to support their fellow members.

The business operated on a basic level. The women did not have anywhere to store the raw materials or the finished products, so they had to make small quantities and sell them before they could make any more. They could only buy very small quantities of raw material, so their costs were high, and the profit margin was low. The business was seasonal, and they earned only $6 or $8 a month each. But they persisted because they had no better alternative.

The *sevaniratha* and the areas supervisor were impressed by their enthusiasm and persistence, and encouraged them to expand their operations by acquiring a factory building. The SKDRDP officials suggested that that they might raise a bank loan, and they told them about the liberal subsidy which was available under the central government's SGSY scheme for lower-caste people.

The women were initially very doubtful. As it was, they could work at home at their own convenience, whereas if they had a factory, they would have to commute every day outside their village and keep to strict timings. They also wondered how they could be away from their families for a full day: who would take care of their children and their old parents-in-law and how their household work would be done? Their biggest worry was what would happen if the enterprise failed and they had to close down the factory. It would be extremely difficult to repay their loan. They also worried whether they would be all be able to work harmoniously in a large group, as they came from different smaller local groups of close neighbours and friends. *Beedi* rolling and making snacks at home seemed to be much safer and more convenient.

On the other hand, the women were very excited at the idea of having their own building, and a number of them were very enterprising. The *sevaniratha* encouraged them to take the plunge, and they finally decided to go for their own factory premises.

SKDRDP had good contacts with banks and government officials, and the formalities of getting a bank loan with the government subsidy were rapidly completed. The Belthangady branch of Syndicate Bank sanctioned a loan for Rs.859,0000 (about $17,000), including a subsidy of Rs.200,000 to be repaid over five years with an interest rate of 9 per cent. The monthly repayment was fixed at Rs.12,250 ($245), since the principal was reduced by the amount of the subsidy.

There was one condition. The government subsidy was intended only for families whose monthly incomes were below the official poverty line of Rs.1,000 (about $20) income per month. Only 34 of the 56 members of the five groups had the necessary 'BPL' (below poverty line) cards. Because of this problem, nine of the members withdrew, but 13 members who were not qualified agreed to stay and to be responsible for a slightly higher proportion of the loan repayments. The 47 women went ahead with their plan. The bank sanctioned the loan to all the five self-help groups, without any collateral. The subsidy was sufficient guarantee, and the bank manager was also convinced that the business would succeed because SKDRDP was involved.

The first step was to build the factory in Sonanduru village in 2003, for $9,500. The balance of the loan was spent on kitchen tools, stoves, weighing machines and other equipment, along with raw material for two cycles of production. The SKDRDP SIRI staff managed the whole process without involving the members. The building is an impressive structure of 2,900 square feet, with a long veranda connecting all the rooms, a large kitchen, the collection centre where the finished products are weighed and packed, the raw materials store and a small office. It has a reliable water and power supply.

Soon after the factory started to operate, there was trouble. Many of the members found it hard to get to the factory every day. Some had to walk nearly 3 km each way, and the parents of those who were not married were worried about their daughters' safety. Others had taken up other activities such as rolling incense sticks and did not join, and some did not like the work and dropped out. One member left because she was hired by SKDRDP as a *sevaniratha* and in the end only 21 women remained. Generally, it was the older women who left; the younger women were more enthusiastic and continued to work in the factory.

SIRI provided the raw material and recipes for different products, but the members ignored what they had been taught because they thought that they knew how to cook. They used the same rough measurements as they had earlier when they were producing on a smaller scale. They fried the snacks for too long, or for not long enough, and they did not control the temperature of the oil properly. The snacks were tasteless and looked unappetizing and could not be sold. The women did not know how to organize their work systematically. The plan which SIRI had drawn up for the women was based on daily production of 20 kg of snacks per member, but they could only make 4–5 kg of product a day each. It cost Rs.40 per kg instead of Rs.25, and the unit made heavy losses.

The SIRI coordinator realized that something had to be done. He identified and trained the members who had some aptitude for the more difficult tasks, such as kneading and frying the dough. He also arranged for some of the women to be trained in time management and interpersonal skills; the cost of this was covered by the government SGSY office which had provided the subsidy for the building.

After three years of constant supervision from SIRI, the productivity of the workers increased gradually to 20 kg a day, as had been originally planned. SIRI carries our regular market surveys and identifies new products, and by 2006 the factory was making 25 different varieties. Demand continued to increase, and production rose from 3 tons to 10 tons a month.

SIRI purchases bulk supplies of raw material at very competitive prices and keeps stocks in its own premises from which the women can draw what they need. The members are satisfied with the quality and price, and they do not have to deal with the suppliers. SIRI also checks the quality before the products are packed and deals with all the sales and marketing. SIRI has a network of dealers, of which two are in Belthangady. They visit the factory three times a week to place their orders and to collect the products which they had ordered earlier.

In 2005/6 the factory had a turnover of Rs.4.2 million (about $84,000). The women spent well over half of this on the raw materials, and they also had to make the monthly loan repayments of Rs.12,250. Finally, they paid their own wages. The wages were different according to the level of skill that was needed, but the difference between the highest and lowest paid was not more than Rs.10 a day, and the average was about Rs.50 ($1) a day. If a member was absent, she was not paid.

They try to make the workload as equitable as possible. Those who live farthest away are allowed to arrive half an hour after the others and to leave half an hour before them. The women who live in Sonanduru village do not mind working an hour longer than the others, because the factory is so near to their homes. The wages are low, but the women enjoy the work much more than *beedi* rolling or making snacks at home, because it gives them a chance to work in a group. They feel that being employed is more dignified than working at home, and it is also more interesting. The members are thrilled that by 2008 the bank loan will be fully repaid, and they will own the building and all the other assets. Their wages will also increase because the loan repayments will no longer have to be deducted from the monthly surplus.

The women also learned how to work together effectively. At the start they frequently quarrelled about issues like attendance, punctuality and productivity, and they used frequently to appeal to the SIRI coordinator to solve even their most petty problems. After some training in interpersonal relations, the members began to manage their affairs on their own. They sorted out most problems themselves, and if something could not be resolved, they would solve it at one of their weekly meeting, which were also attended by the *sevaniratha* and the SIRI coordinator.

The SIRI coordinator was well aware that it was vital that one of the women should take over the management of the group. Quite early on he saw that Vasantha, who was only 19 years old when the unit started, had the capacity to take on the task. She had been the record keeper for her self-help group, and although she was from a poor family and had only completed seven years of school she had the potential to be a leader.

After she had attended a simple management course the members followed the SIRI coordinator's recommendation and unanimously agreed that she should be the manager of the factory. She was responsible for keeping all the records, for sending out invoices and orders, and for maintaining the members' attendance register. She also helps out with packing the products when she has time, and she is very happy to take on these extra responsibilities without getting any additional remuneration.

At their weekly meetings the members discuss what they have achieved during the previous week and the targets for the following week. They have an additional business meeting once a month to discuss finance and other commercial matters, and they have all these meetings an hour before the normal starting time of 9 a.m. so that they will not lose any production.

The factory has been gradually improved since it started. New stoves have been built, and new packing and cutting machines have been bought. The members also want to buy an automatic packing machine for $10,000 so that their products will be able to compete with the well-known national brands, but they realize that they will have to wait until they have paid off their present loan before they can apply for another. They also plan to buy a computer to replace their manual accounting system, and to get an internet connection in order to contact dealers and explore the market.

All the members are devotees of Lord Manjunatha. They start work by singing a prayer which sanctifies their work as service to God, and they sing how by working together as one unit and seeing each other as one family, they will bring joy, peace and prosperity into their lives. They also deeply revere Dr Heggade and his wife. They see him as an earthly representative of Lord Manjunatha, and they believe that whatever he says comes from God.

They are grateful for the attention the divine couple give to their factory, and they are happy to do as Mrs Heggade has asked them, to work properly, to learn everything they need to know and to become fully independent. She occasionally visits the factory, and she advises the workers to value their work and to view it as an offering to God. She also reminds them to keep the factory clean and orderly, and to maintain strict personal hygiene, by wearing caps, gloves and aprons as they work. The members all join in the monthly JVK meetings which Mrs Heggade started. They learn about sanitation, hygiene, good relationships, nutrition, education, health care and personal grooming. This new knowledge further enhances their self-respect, and they share everything they learn with their family members and their neighbours.

Young village women in India are generally shy and are often socially oppressed. They rarely dare to speak to strangers, and they are sometimes badly treated by their husband's families with whom they live. As the members of the snacks factory have learned to work together harmoniously, they have also become far more outgoing and confident. They also say that they are able to be more effective at home as well. They have learned how to present their views clearly without offending their husbands and their in-laws, and their relationships at home have greatly improved since they started working in the factory.

When the factory started, the women's families expected them to do all their household chores, in addition to working at the factory. Some of the older women were close to giving up the factory work, because they were so exhausted. The interpersonal skills training and the experience of working together has given them the confidence to convince their family members to share their household work.

Their earnings have also helped them and their families. One member paid off a Rs25,000 ($500) loan she had taken for her daughter's marriage, and she was also able to buy a few luxuries for herself for the first time in her life, and to help her son to open a shop in the village. Out of the 21 women 10 are unmarried, and they are pleased that their earnings will be used for their marriage expenses, and will thus reduce the burden on their parents.

The factory proves that even uneducated poor women can become successful entrepreneurs if they have some support and encouragement. The spiritual influence of the Heggades on the group is no less important than the material help given by SKDRDP and SIRI. The group's losses are still being absorbed by SKDRDP, but once the bank loan has been repaid, it will be a profitable business.

CHAPTER 9
The results of SKDRDP's work

Abstract

The SKDRDP groups are different from most of the millions of self-help groups in India, in that they were started for shared labour, not for savings and credit, and they have continued to carry out many different functions. These are linked by their members' concern for improving their livelihoods in the broadest sense, including their spiritual reverence for the Dharmasthala Temple and its governing dynasty. The groups have as many male members as women, which is also unusual, and they use their savings and credit for personal and consumption purposes as well as for income generation.They perceive their loans as being God's money, and the repayment performance reflects this belief. The Heggades have also set up a number of cultural and educational institutions, as part of their concern for the holistic development of the area. SKDRDP faces many challenges. As it expands and reaches communities further from the temple, its spiritual influence may weaken. Greater size in itself requires more formalized systems and professionalization which may dilute the personal sense of respect for the Heggade dynasty, which is in some sense the glue whch holds together the institution and the communities it serves.

The impact on the community

SKDRDP started primarily as a charitable activity to help marginal and small farmers to cultivate their fallow land. It now encourages and supports all kinds of income-generating activities and livelihoods with finance and a range of other supporting services. SKDRDP is a banker, a supply and marketing intermediator or 'middleman', as well as a manager of rural affairs.

The programme started with groups, for small farmers, poor women and reformed alcoholics. These groups have been mobilized and many have been converted into self-help groups, becoming part of the fast-growing national movement but still retaining the special features associated with their origin. Most such groups elsewhere in India have been started as financial intermediators, by NGOs, by banks and sometimes by their members themselves. Some of them have evolved beyond this, to a whole range of community activities.

The early SKDRDP groups were started for other purposes and moved later into financial intermediation. This has probably made them stronger and has certainly increased their loyalty to SKDRDP and Dharmasthala. SKDRDP has effectively evolved its own model of microfinance, breaking most of the conventional rules, and without compromising its basic goals of supporting life and livelihoods.

The quantitative results are impressive. In March 2006 SKDRDP was working with 34,301 groups. The total number of groups formed over the 20 years was 35,321; more than half of them were formed during 2005, when the rate of expansion accelerated. Just over 1,000 groups have dropped out. This dropout rate of under 3 per cent is far below the rate of 10 per cent that is normal over a much shorter period of five years (EDA Rural Systems/APMAS, 2006). About 348,000 members are involved. A small minority of these are from the same families, but there are almost certainly well over one million people in the households which have members who are members of SKDRDP groups.

The average group has about 10 members; this is lower than the national average of around 13, but is explained by the large numbers of *Pragathi Bandhu* labour-sharing groups, which tend to be smaller than groups which are formed for financial intermediation since they are made up of small farmers with neighbouring plots.

The financial results are no less impressive. The members have accumulated Rs.475 million ($10 million) of savings, and in March 2006 the loans outstanding stood at Rs.1,087 million ($24 million). The loan defaults have been very low, and less than 1 per cent of the loans have been waived. About two-thirds of the 348,000 group members had outstanding loans in March 2006. This high rate of borrowing suggests that the groups and their members still had large numbers of investment opportunities.

The *Pragathi Bandhu* groups were the first and have probably been the most successful interventions by SKDRDP. Their members have shared more than 10 million days worth of work over the last 25 years, worth Rs.777 million (about $17 million dollars if a labour day is valued at the average going rate of Rs.77 or about $1.70).

About seven million saplings have been distributed and over 50,000 acres of land have been made into small and very productive tree plantations. Before SKDRDP started work in the area, the same farmers who now farm these plantations survived mostly from casual farm labour. They lacked the ability to invest in plantation crops. More than 20,000 families have constructed irrigation wells, and about 17,000 families have bought irrigation pumps. Almost 8,000 small farm reservoirs have been constructed in the same period.

SKDRDP has helped around 20,000 families to build their own homes, through loans and partial subsidies, and about 1,000 destitute families have been given grants to build their homes. Thousands of families have obtained government subsidies for solar lighting systems and gas digester plants through SKDRDP's interventions, and SKDRDP also runs education and health awareness programmes to help people to move towards development in a total sense.

SKDRDP has worked in the region for 25 years, and its work has moved from simple charity through in-kind donations to a range of potentially sustainable programmes working for integrated rural development in an area with a population of several million people. Having started with agriculture, SKDRDP now covers every aspect of life in the communities it works with: health and sanitation, alcohol de-addiction, education, livelihoods, microfinance with savings and insurance and housing. It has also made a significant if immeasurable contribution to the social empowerment of the previously marginalized people of the region.

The situation of the small farmers was bad when SKDRDP started work, but there were some mitigating features which have made it easier to achieve good results. The land holdings are very small, and the land is undulating and needs extensive work before it can produce at the optimum level. It is however potentially very fertile, and there is heavy rainfall. Farming requires heavy initial investment but once this has been done it is less risky than in many other parts of India. Partly because of the difficult conditions, the people of South Canara have always been enterprising, and although the traditional pattern of land ownership was very inequitable, within the village communities themselves there was never a high level of social or economic inequity.

The concept of labour sharing has always been fundamental to SKDRDP's approach, and this enabled the wage labourers who had recently become landowners in theory actually to become landowners in practice. There are now more women's groups than men's, but the concept of farmers sharing labour is central to SKDRDP's success. This is still the unique feature of the whole undertaking and is the principal entry point for most of SKDRDP's programmes. The men still start their proceedings with prayers as they have from the beginning.

The shared labour has helped thousands of small farmers to level and fence their land, to dig wells, and to construct new buildings. It has stimulated progress and promoted social unity by encouraging collaboration. Community conflict and antagonism has been reduced. Self-help groups in India, and all forms of microfinance groups everywhere, are usually dominated by women. Men's groups, where they exist at all, are few in number, and they almost always have poorer records of saving and loan recovery than women's groups. The *Pragathi Bandhu* groups of SKDRDP are the only male-dominated self-help groups in India.

This success has not been achieved at the expense of women's groups. It took almost 10 years for SKDRDP's management to realize that it had neglected the most important stakeholders in community development, but in 1996 the mistake was recognized and by 2006 two-thirds of SKDRDP's loan portfolio was with women. The women have now gained confidence and self-respect. The JVK women's groups have helped their members to start many different forms of farm and non-farm businesses, and *beedi* rolling is less popular, although it is not entirely eliminated. It is no longer the main source of income for the thousands of women who are now working in individual or group businesses promoted by SKDRDP.

The microfinance programme has been designed to reflect members' needs. From the beginning there has been a demand for larger, longer-term and lower-cost loans than are normal in microfinance, where short, small, high-interest loans are usually the norm. This was necessary because farmers needed such facilities in order to make the best use of their newly acquired land.

Credit is also available from the start for every conceivable purpose, and members do not have to pretend that loans are for 'productive' purposes when what they really need is money for consumption, school fees, medical expenses or family events such as marriage. The programme is in many ways more systematic and standardized than elsewhere. Groups all charge the same rates of interest, unlike most self-help groups where the members are free to charge what they think fit.

The *sevanirathas* focus on helping the group members to generate sustainable livelihoods. Strong discipline is maintained, partly because of continuous follow-up by the *sevanirathas*, auditors and others, but also because of the strong sense of shared values and loyalty to Dharmasthala and the person of Dr Heggade. The staff of many microfinance institutions have to spend most of their time dealing with repayments, but the SKDRDP staff can spend more time on identifying and assisting with livelihoods opportunities. This in turn means that they are seen by the groups as advisers and friends rather than loan recovery agents, which further strengthens the bond between the members, their groups, the *sevanirathas* and SKDRDP.

As the demand for farm credit reached a plateau in the areas where SKDRDP had started, the emphasis was shifted to group enterprises to be run by women. These are being effectively supported by SIRI, and the strategy has so far been to have groups working on a wide range of products. They are produced or processed by the women's groups, with supply and marketing links through SIRI, so that both men and women are able to be profitably and independently occupied.

SKDRDP is itself moving slowly towards sustainability, through its microfinance programme and SIRI, and it may in the long-term become a viable business in itself, without need for subsidy from Dharmasthala or elsewhere. The wealth of the temple will then be available to initiate other development activities, within the same area or beyond. This a very long-term goal, but is not unreasonable given the progress it has achieved in its first 25 years.

The key strength of SKDRDP, however, lies in its links to Dr Veerendra Heggade, the *Dharmadhikari* of the Dharmasthala Temple. The Heggade family has been in charge of the religious institution for over seven hundred years, and both Dr Heggade and his wife are heavily personally involved in SKDRDP's work. This spiritual link is not incidental but is central to every aspect of SKDRDP's operations.

Dr Veerendra Heggade is heir to a dynasty of some 20 generations, but he himself started SKDRDP and it development activities as recently as 1982. He has also initiated a wide range of other work, and has set up schools, colleges and hospitals throughout the region which have no formal links to SKDRDP. Dharmasthala is also engaged in other work, such as archaeology, preservation and cultural promotion. Much of the physical development of the temple compound is also quite recent, and Dharmasthala has only become well-known outside its own neighbourhood during this Heggade's time. Earlier, it was one more temple, under a local dynastic leader somewhat better known than many others because of its Jain-inspired polytheism.

Dr Heggade's father was a typical wealthy patriarchal figure. Like many such people he had political ambitions, but he lacked a local following and was unsuccessful when he stood for election to parliament. Many similar temple trusts in India have been taken over by the government because of misuse, alleged or otherwise, and a case was brought against the former Heggade in an attempt to take over the Dharmasthala properties. It was still pending when he died, and was later defeated by his son.

When Veerendra Heggade succeeded to his father's position he realized that both the temple and his family were losing their popularity. His father had initiated the project to install the statue of Bahubali on the hill above the temple, and by seeing this through to completion his son was able to preserve the dynastic continuity and to reinforce the reputation of Dharmasthala.

Dr Heggade's work can be see as a result of divine intervention, or as an effective strategy to reverse the decline in his family's and the temple's reputation, or as the result of his genuine concern for the welfare of the people of the surrounding area. All three influences are no doubt involved, and it is pointless to try to disentangle them. The results are there for all to see.

Dr Heggade is a master strategist, and a good leader as well as a good manager, which is a rare combination. He could see that while SKDRDP initially had to depend on the Dharmasthala Temple Trust, not only financially but also in terms of local goodwill, the situation would later be reversed so that SKDRDP would become a source of strength both for his family and for Dharmasthala as a whole.

Dharmasthala is a Hindu shrine, and the Heggades are Jains. Most of the better-off people in the area are also Jains, who might have felt threatened by a typically socially activist development NGO. Dharmasthala, like most religious institutions in India and elsewhere, is very much a part of the existing social structure, and none of SKDRDP's programmes have ever appeared to be attacking the local hierarchy. Dr Heggade has thus ensured that the Jains support the village interventions. As a result of this strategy, SKDRDP has strengthened the reputation and influence of the family and Dharmasthala, even at a time when many religious institutions are being threatened by the growing secularization of society.

SKDRDP does not promote any particular religion, or indeed religion as such, at all. It promotes values. Since the installation of the Bahubali statue, a deeply religious act, the emphasis of Dr Heggade's work has moved to spirituality, and to values. He denounced drinking and smoking, and emphasized simple living, health and hygiene. John Wesley, the founder of Methodism, said that cleanliness was next to godliness, and Dharmasthala demonstrates a similar belief. Even the toilets are spotless, which cannot always be said of Indian public places, particularly religious ones.

In addition to SKDRDP, Dr Heggade set up the Santhi Vana Trust, which promotes value-based living and naturopathy, ayurveda and yoga. He also established the Dharmothana Trust to restore temples and places of historic value, as well as a number of educational institutions, including one for orphaned children. In the field of medicine, he has set up colleges for naturopathy and ayurveda, as well as a conventional medical school, which can of course be a money-making venture as well as an expression of values.

At the level of his own family Dr Heggade demonstrates the virtues of simplicity. He lives a spartan life, apart from his occasional enjoyment of the collection of vintage cars which he inherited from his father. He insisted that his only daughter should study in a local school. This was not easy, since his brother's children study in Bangalore.

He is very much supported in this by his wife, who has emerged from her role as a conventional housewife to play a major part in SKDRDP. She deserves much of the credit for the JVK women's group programme, and for the expanding role of women in SKDRDP's work. It might even be said that the only programmes with any claim to be socially radical are those involving women, which Mrs Heggade has so vigorously promoted.

In addition to their strategic view, their spiritual support and their promotion of certain values, the personal wealth of the Heggades and their institution has of course also been vital to SKDRDP's success. In addition to its initial support, and its continuing subsidy, the Dharmasthala Temple Trust has been able to cover the cost of initiatives such as SIRI, which inevitably make heavy losses for some years before they break even, and to bear unexpected costs like the Rs.10 million ($200,000) losses of the first year of *Sampoorna Suraksha*, the SKDRDP's insurance venture.

Fundamentally, and although it is not covering all its costs, SKDRDP has moved out of its charity mode. Most of the earlier charity programmes have been discontinued, except for grants to the totally destitute such as Tania and Kamala and their blind children. The insurance programme, for instance, which has a generous benevolent fund component, is expected to make a profit in its third year.

Until 2001 all the costs of SKDRDP's development programmes came from the Dharmasthala Temple Trust. Since that time, funds have been acquired from government schemes and from financial institutions. Here again, the reputation and sanctity of the Heggades and their institution have opened many doors. The three other trustees also enjoy very good standing in the area: one is a prominent economist, another a very senior ex-banker and the third is a well-known educationist.

SKDRDP has organizational values which have contributed significantly to its success in the region. These are closely associated with religion, and the need to take a high moral stand in one's everyday dealings. Everyone in the area, of whatever faith, respects the Dharmasthala shrine, and fears God, whoever they believe God to be. In a very real sense, they believe that SKDRDP's money is God's money. The tradition of associating loan disbursements with a religious ritual, and the fact that cheques carry the signature of God's representative, whom many of the people regard as a demi-God, means that wilful default or misuse is at a minimum. In the same way, the decision makers in the major banks which have lent large sums to SKDRDP feel that their loans are in some way guaranteed by God, even though they are technically unsecured. After all, who would demand collateral from God?

Respect for divinity has effectively been combined with respect and unity within families and within communities. Labour-sharing and de-addiction treatment are essentially group based, and these have contributed to SKDRDP's success in mobilizing men in a way that few other development institutions anywhere have been able to do. The field staff are treated in what many would consider to be a patronizing and old-fashioned way, in that any relationships among the staff or between staff and clients which go beyond official or collegial ties are forbidden. This leads to some staff turnover, but the local junior staff generally have rather poor formal qualifications and have few other options for employment with similar remuneration.

More positively, the job of a *sevaniratha* requires an almost monastic level of loyalty and commitment. They feel themselves to be very much more than junior field staff of a development institution. SKDRDP in turn has great faith in its local staff, and is very loyal to them. Older and senior staff are treated with particular respect, and are whenever possible given preference in promotion. The staff are grateful for their jobs, and for this support, and they feel themselves to be contributing to a higher cause.

The religious values are continually reinforced by Dr Heggade and his wife. They are in no sense titular figureheads, but are continuously involved in and seen to be involved in management. This behaviour is mirrored by other senior staff, so that all the staff identify completely with the *Dharmadhikari*, who is the head of the organization.

Future challenges

SKDRDP's success is clearly very closely related to its links to the Heggades and to Dharmasthala, and these are essentially local in character. The programmes have been successfully expanded beyond the immediate neighbourhood of Dharmasthala in Belthangady, within South Canara district and to a lesser extent beyond it. It remains to be seen how durable the programme will be in places which are more distant from Belthangady, particularly if it goes to quite different parts of India as has been envisaged. As SKDRDP expands to other areas where its help is still needed, and thus moves away from the source of its inspiration, will the religious influence on both its staff and its clients become weaker? This question will only be able to be answered by experience.

Many other religious institutions have successfully extended their influence far beyond their place of origin, even to other countries and other continents, but it will clearly require major changes to secure the same loyalty and respect from village people who have had no personal contact with Dharmasthala. Nevertheless, SKDRDP has thus far expanded organically, through gradually extending the frontier of its involvement rather than 'jumping' to more distant locations where funding or other support might be available, and this expansion may continue successfully. It has already been necessary to modify some details of the programme to fit in with practices that already existed in the new areas. In some places, for instance, SKDRDP has had to confine group membership to only one member of each family, as opposed to the more liberal policy adopted in its 'home' area.

The rapid expansion is also putting strains on SKDRDP's staff. The senior staff team are one of the major strengths of the organization. They joined at the beginning of the activity and are now in their late forties and occupying most of the senior positions. More senior staff are needed, and people with less experience and less understanding of the very special organizational culture of the institution are now joining and are being promoted quite fast. SKDRDP still keeps to its policy of recruiting local people at the entry level and then promoting them to higher responsibilities based on their experience and performance, but it is not clear that this can be continued.

A small number of professionals who have had experience in other organizations with different cultures have already been recruited. They are working in specialist departments, such as training and marketing, but problems have already started to appear and some have left because they could not 'fit in'. This difficulty can only become more serious as SKDRDP continues to expand.

There are also some issues related to the actual work of SKDRDP. In the older areas, such as Belthangady, the initial task of helping the small farmers to develop their new plots has been completed. SKDRDP has changed its emphasis to agro-processing and non-farm activities, and to the growth of women's group enterprises. This is a more challenging field than small farm development, since it involves marketing in competition with well-known brands, and there have been few examples anywhere of successful group-owned manufacturing businesses. SKDRDP is taking on a major challenge, and SIRI is being required to develop supply and marketing expertise in a bewildering variety of product lines, which have been introduced because they employ large numbers of relatively unskilled operatives, not because of market demand. If it succeeds, it will be a unique achievement.

It will also be difficult to sustain the group activities and their members' interest and involvement, and at the same time to make SIRI profitable. There is a basic inconsistency between the essentially charitable nature of the temple and its traditions, and the business culture which will have to be adopted if the microfinance operation and SIRI are to stand on their own feet. The large numbers of pilgrims who come to the temple constitute a captive market for groups' products, and the SIRI brand carries some influence since it is associated with Dharmasthala, but production will grow beyond these narrow markets. This may represent SKDRDP's major future challenge. Labour-intensive production is good for the village women's welfare, but it may not be competitive, and products which can more economically be made by machine may have to be dropped. Sales of hand-made incense sticks may be possible because of their religious association, but this cannot be applied to every product.

SKDRDP has evolved from a charity and aspires to achieve sustainability in its local development work. It has already successfully changed course during its lifetime, and thus far the experience has shown that is possible to combine the backing and detailed involvement of a religious trust with professional development management.

There are said to be five types of capital which people need in order to achieve sustainable livelihoods: financial, human, natural, physical and social. The SKDRDP experience supports the view put forward recently by Robert Fogel (2002) and others that is may be useful to distinguish a sixth kind, spiritual capital. The spiritual capital provided by the Heggade family and the Dharmasthala Temple has complemented and strengthened all the other types of capital in the region, in particular the social capital in the villages where SKDRDP has worked, and it is hard to imagine how the programme would have succeeded without this. This has in turn strengthened the spiritual capital of the *Dharmadhikari*; it has thus far been a 'win-win' intervention for the community as well as the family. Time will tell whether this will continue to be possible in the future, particularly if SKDRDP's work is extended to areas where Dharmasthala has no influence.

Numerous questions remain. Southern India as a whole is developing rapidly, and the villages where SKDRDP has worked have not been left behind. There are more employment opportunities than ever before, and people's aspirations are changing. Mangalore has become a big industrial centre in its own right, and Bangalore has become one of the fastest-growing cities in the world. These changes will have a major impact on SKDRDP's client population and on its staff. Most of the village people no longer need the basic services that were so effective in 1982, and the brightest and more enterprising young men and women can find work elsewhere; they need not suffer the privations of employment of a *sevaniratha*.

SKDRDP is essentially a traditional community-based institution, inspired by a local God, and relying on a local institution and locally recruited staff, to serve local people. Its competence is home-grown rather than professional, and Dr Heggade has whenever possible resisted the employment of development 'professionals'. They are more expensive than people who have risen from the ranks of the *sevanirathas*, but, even more importantly, they are loyal to their profession, not to an institution or still less to one man, even a semi-divine man.

There is also the critical issue of leadership. Many development NGOs fail because they are too dependent on the one charismatic leader who sets them up who is the focus of loyalty of both the staff and their clients. Dr Heggade is such a person, but it remains to be seen whether SKDRDP can survive in a world of impersonal and professional relationships.

In the meantime, these uncertainties in no way diminish the achievements of SKDRDP since 1982. Every rural development institution, and every local religious institution, can learn from SKDRDP how faith and development management can be combined, and a religious body can successfully address the social and economic needs of a community in the larger agenda of poverty eradication.

References

EDA Rural Systems/APMAS (2006) *Self Help Groups in India, A study of the lights and shades*, Delhi.

Fogel, R. (2002) *The Fourth Great Awakening*, University of Chicago Press, Chicago.

CHAPTER 10
What explains SKDRDP's success?

Abstract

SKDRDP is one of India's largest and fastest growing development NGOs, reaching almost 400,000 people. It breaks many of the generally accepted rules of microfinance and development, such as lending to men as well as women, mixing welfare and development and business services with finance and continuing to provide charitable donations to desperately needy people as well as credit to those who can make good use of it. This appears to be the result of a judicious mingling of good management and spiritual leadership. This is facilitated by Hindusim, which emphasizes the spiritual nature of everything rather than separating faith from physical things, and by the Jain religion of the temple and the Heggade family, which is essentially pantheist. Dr Heggades provides charismatic leadership, but this emanates from the tradition and strength of his family as well as from himself and his wife.

Breaking the rules

SKDRDP has some 400,000 clients and is the largest NGO-based microfinance and rural development institution in India. It is also one of the fastest growing in financial terms. In the two years up to March 2006 the value of loans outstanding to its groups, and their members' savings, approximately tripled. Microfinance of all kinds is growing very rapidly in India, but very few of the specialized institutions or the banks can claim similar growth rates. This has been achieved without sacrificing quality, and repayments from the groups to SKDRDP continue to be maintained at 100 per cent.

This record is all the more remarkable in that SKDRDP breaks most of the 'rules' which have come to be associated with good practice in microfinance, in India and worldwide. It is generally believed that microfinance institutions should not mix charity with credit, they should only lend in proportion to clients' demonstrated ability to save, they should focus on women borrowers and they should focus strictly on financial services, leaving other activities such as livelihood promotion and business development to other agencies.

SKDRDP does provide charity, such as the stipends to the children of Tania and Kamala. It lends up to 40 times self-help group members' savings, in contrast to the four or sometimes six times multiple offered by commercial banks. It lends to as many men as women, and it provides a whole range of financial and non-financial services, including the very intensive business support provided through SIRI.

SKDRDP has also made mistakes, which might have been expected to damage a more conventional institution. The premium for the *Sampoorna Surakshya* insurance scheme was seriously underestimated, and had to be increased by 50 per cent. Nevertheless, clients still believed in it and it grew into one of India's most comprehensive and successful microinsurance schemes. SKDRDP's loans are significantly more expensive than loans from local banks, and the imposition of a 1 per cent up-front processing fee further increased the cost. Self-help groups elsewhere have quite often shifted their business to local banks from the NGOs which promoted them because of lower rates of interest. SKDRDP's clients appear to be more forgiving and more loyal than those of secular institutions.

In spite of breaking so many rules, and some serious errors, SKDRDP is successful; why is this so, and how can other faith-based and secular institutions learn from it?

Involvement in practical development assistance such as is provided by SKDRDP is not necessarily consistent with Hindu beliefs. The ideal personal condition is considered by many traditional Hindus to be total withdrawal from the world. Like Buddhists, Sikhs and Jains, adherents of the other so-called Dharmaic religions which share a belief in the process of reincarnation, they believe that one should aim at self-realization, absorption into God, or nirvana. Progress towards this state can be accelerated by meditation, and by withdrawing oneself from the world. Someone who has reached this level of development is untouched by what others do, and he himself is concerned only to do no harm, to withdraw into the infinite, and not to be concerned by or influence what is happening around him. This ideal condition is also quite different from the idea of 'doing good'. It is about not doing harm, rather than proactively doing good. Perfection is reached by passive withdrawal, not by active intervention.

A more positive interpretation of the notion of 'karma' and reincarnation is that one attains virtue by generosity and sacrifice, by doing to others as one would wish to be done to oneself. This injunction is common to most religions, and can also be applied by development institutions, banks and microfinance institutions (Langsun Mate, 2006). The work of SKDRDP, and Veerendra Heggade's motivation in setting it up, is clearly informed by this interpretation.

It would be wrong to ascribe all SKDRDP's success to its religious links. Good strategic management has also played an important part, and two important timing decisions were crucial. SKDRDP was one of the first institutions to take up the formation of self-help groups in a major way in the 1990s when the movement was at an early stage. Subsequently, in the early years of the present century, management recognized that the best route to financial sustainability, for SKDRDP's existing activities and for future expansion, lay in direct financial intermediation.

The strategy of moving towards 'sustainability', in spite of the backing of the Dharmasthala Temple Trust, is in marked contrast to the strategy of most similar religious institutions in India, which receive regular inflows of donations from visiting pilgrims. The Sathya Sai Trust, for example, which was set up by the internationally celebrated Sai Baba in 1972, has donated over $150 million for drinking water projects in rural Andhra Pradesh and in Chennai (Madras). Doctors from all over the world donate their time to the numerous hospitals and health care activities which are maintained by the trust, and large numbers of young volunteers work for the trust to help people in rural villages to improve their farming methods and livelihoods.

None of these activities, however, is 'sustainable' in the sense of being financially self-supporting, and their very merit can be said to lie in the fact that they depend on voluntarily donated money and time. SKDRDP was initially financed from pilgrims' donations, and is still to an extent dependent on financial support from the Dharmasthala Temple Trust, but there is a clear plan to cover all the local costs from earnings, primarily from interest on loans, within the next few years. This policy involves a very clear break from the tradition of charitable giving which plays such an important part in most faith-based institutions.

Many institutions owe their success to one 'charismatic' leader, whose vision and energy drives the whole enterprise. This can also be a serious problem, when the activities grow beyond the scope of one person's management ability, or when the leader has for whatever reason to relinquish control. Veerendra Heggade enjoys such a position by virtue of his own ability, but also, and even more importantly, because he occupies a religious position which has been held by his family for some 600 years. His charisma is both personal and historical.

The divinity factor

SKDRDP has itself been formally separated from the Dharmasthala Temple, and is an independent development institution. SIRI, the marketing and enterprise promotion arm, is also legally separate company, and it is likely that the financial operations will in the near future also be separately incorporated as a non-bank finance company. This will it is hoped become self-supporting, but it will not mean that Dharmasthala will cease to engage in charitable development activities. Legally formalized separation does not of course cut off these activities from each other or from Dharmasthala and its leader, and many of these institutions' clients probably believe that all the services they receive come directly from Dharmasthala. The activities are legally independent and professionally managed, but their essential spirit and inspiration emanate from and are informed by the spiritual centre; this balance between professional management and spiritual inspiration seems to lie at the roots of their success.

The spiritual influence is of course not confined to top management, and the field activities and direct transactions with clients are if anything more closely linked to the religious aspects of Dharmasthala than their head offices or management. This spiritual aspect is reflected in many dimensions.

The field programmes themselves are to a large extent defined by the values of Dharmasthala. Temperance and elimination of alcoholism have always been closely linked to religious institutions, as in the non-conformist Christian churches' programmes in 19th century England or the Muslim prohibition of consumption of alcohol. Drunkenness is undoubtedly a major reason for the perpetuation of poverty in many poor communities, not only in India, and the high success rate of SKDRDP's *Jana Jagruthi* programme when compared to similar programmes elsewhere in India obviously owes something to its spiritual component.

Similarly, the association with Dharmasthala undoubtedly contributes to the high quality of the loan portfolio, and in particular to the uniquely good performance of male borrowers. Loan cheques are signed by the *Dharmadikari*, who is a divine figure in many borrowers' minds, and loan disbursement is carried out as if it was a religious ceremony rather than a financial transaction. God and Mammon are inextricably linked. This is easier in Indian society than it would be elsewhere, because there are no clear boundaries between spiritual and temporal affairs, but it is only possible because of the close links between SKDRDP and Dharmasthala.

The *sevanirathas* are employed by SKDRDP, but their daily routine and lifestyle, and the strict rules of conduct which govern them, seem in some ways closer to the life of a nun, a monk or a priest than a conventional social worker. They must keep themselves socially separate from their client communities, they must live away from home, they must pray regularly and must in general live like members of a religious order rather than as employees whose life outside working hours is their own. Jobs of any kind are scarce in rural India, so young people can be expected to apply even when conditions are quite rigorous. There is nevertheless some element of self-selection, and the applicants for jobs as *sevanirathas* tend to be people with a religious inclination; it would be difficult for anyone else to maintain the lifestyle that is demanded.

This same element of discipline is evident in other respects, such as in the conduct of meetings. NGOs are often informal in their operations, but SKDRDP is quite strongly hierarchical. Veerendra Heggade clearly and naturally stands at the top of all the institutions, whether formally or otherwise, but relationships within them are more formal than is usual in NGOs, although the institutional climate is very different from that of government institutions where respect is more closely related to rank and less to ability.

Many NGOs campaign vigorously against dowry, and microfinance institutions try, although often without success, to prevent their clients from using their loans for this purpose. SKDRDP does not take any position on this, either because dowry is felt to be a traditional social custom which should not be disturbed, or is so strong that any attempt to discourage it would erode SKDRDP's goodwill in the area, or because management recognize that finance is fungible, and that their clients will indirectly spend their credit on dowry, irrespective of any injunctions from SKDRDP.

The SKDRDP groups are also much less free to manage their own affairs than most self-help groups which are promoted by NGOs or even by banks. Their interest rates are set not by their members as is usual elsewhere, but by their federation, which is closely supervised by SKDRDP itself. Their loan products are also designed and regulated by SKDRDP, and the groups are regularly visited and supervised by their respective *sevanirathas*. This approach is not as 'empowering' as that adopted by other institutions, and it also requires intensive and thus expensive supervision by the *sevanirathas*. However, it does simplify the group members' own management task, since they do not have to make many of the decisions which other groups make, and it fits into the overall hierarchical structure of the institution; 'empowerment' is not necessarily consistent with success.

SKDRDP and the whole Dharmsthala family of activities and institutions are very much of local origin. Most such institutions are actually promoted by outsiders, who may or may not do their best to withdraw and leave the management (or mismanagement) of the institution to the local people. Dharmsthala is very much rooted in the immediate area of the temple, and has been so rooted for nearly eight centuries. SKDRDP has not been 'developed' by an outside NGO or by foreign donors or government. It is wholly the product of a local initiative.

It is nevertheless not a democratic grass roots people's initiative. It has its origins in the traditional welfare interventions of a temple and its local ruling family. Such families, whether or not they also have religious associations, commonly build schools, alms houses for the elderly and other facilities for local people, but SKDRDP has taken the major and unusual step of moving from local welfare to sustainable livelihood development. The long-term effect will almost certainly be to strengthen the community's allegiance to Dharmasthala.

The experience of SKDRDP suggests that a faith-based development institution can be remarkably successful even if it does not follow established best practices. Religion can play a very positive role in staff motivation, and in client and community motivation and loyalty. It is possible to combine the strengths of a religious institution with the need for highly professional development management and operations. In particular, a religious base can make it more feasible to maintain discipline and commitment among clients and staff, and to forge mutually beneficial links with other institutions. It remains to be seen whether and to what extent SKDRDP can expand its operations beyond its own regional locality, and how its links to Dharmasthala and the Heggade family dynasty will influence its future, both in its present area of operations and beyond.

Dharmasthala is essentially a pantheist institution, managed by a Jain family and revered mainly by Hindus. Most of SKDRDP's clients are Hindus, and the temple rituals, as well as the regular religious practices which are so central to SKDRDP's work, are in the Hindu tradition. We have used it to demonstrate how faith can interact with development in one particular community. We shall now briefly examine the development practices of the world's two other major religions, Christianity and Islam, together with short cases of a number of faith-based institutions which arise out of these religions, in India and elsewhere, in order to see whether their experience is similar or not to that of SKDRDP, and whether they can point the way to further practical lessons for both faith-based and secular development organizations.

CHAPTER 11
Islamic development practice

Abstract

Most Muslims live in poor countries rather than in donor countries, most of whose populations are at least nominally Christian. There are more Christian development NGOs than Muslim ones. Most colonial powers were also Christian, and religious conversion was often associated with colonialism. In a number of countries, therefore, and particularly in Africa, Muslim development NGOs originated as defenders of oppressed co-religionists. Islam is a prescriptive faith, and Muslims are enjoined to donate a particular part of their wealth to poorer people, particularly to fellow Muslims. In some Muslim communities, also, women do not play a major part in management. There are also specifically Muslim financial systems, so that Muslim microfinance is very different from its secular equivalent. A number of very effective and quite liberal Muslim development institutions have nevertheless emerged in Africa and elsewere, and have played a major part in the regeneration of Bosnia, in promoting intercommunity goodwill in India and also in microfinance in eastern India. Akhuwat, a microfinance institution based in Lahore in Pakistan, has demonstrated that voluntarism and social capital can be effectively mobilized to provide credit to large numbers of poor people, including many non-Muslims, under a totally different interpretation of sustainability.

The special circumstances of Islam

As may have been clear from the earlier comparative analysis of 'BINGOs', most of the more visible and larger faith-based development NGOs, and most of their smaller local counterparts in poorer countries, are Christian. There are obvious reasons for this. Most foreign aid is from 'the West', the old imperialists of Europe and their younger successors in North America. And most Western 'developed' countries are at least nominally Christian.

The majority of the world's Muslims live in 'developing countries', such as Indonesia, Pakistan, India, Bangladesh and Egypt, which are recipients rather than donors of aid. There are of course a small number of very wealthy Muslim nations and individuals in the Middle East, which are major donors and contribute a higher proportion of their national wealth to poorer countries than 'the West'. Much of this aid is to governments, however, and to purely religious institutions, and there are fewer explicitly Muslim development NGOs than Christian ones.

There is naturally therefore less published material on whatever might be the specifically Muslim approach to development assistance, but a recent description of Muslim NGO development work in Malawi affords useful insights (Nabila Saddiq, 2006).

Muslims came to Malawi well before the arrival of Christianity in the mid 19th century, through Arab traders, but Muslim NGOs have until recently occupied an inferior position in Malawi, since Christian missionaries arrived at the same time as British rule, and Christianity became the organized expatriate and by default the local religion in Malawi. The *Muslim Association of Malawi* was founded in 1942 by Indian traders, and it set up *madrasah* schools for religious education. Otherwise, there was no Muslim NGO development activity.

The missionary organizations used their links with the colonial government to provide vital services as a means of converting Muslims and others to Christianity. The Education Ordinance of 1927 allowed Muslims into Christian schools supported by the government, but stipulated that Christian religious instruction must be given at the schools. This resulted in many conversions of Muslims to Christianity as well as leaving the Muslim population much less educated than their Christian counterparts.

This discrimination was an important element in the development of Islamic NGOs in Malawi. The Muslims set up education and relief projects in the 1970s following independence, financed by the international Muslim community and by Indian Muslim businessmen in Malawi. South African Indian Muslims also took a keen interest in Malawi and tried to organize Black and Asian Muslims to represent and work for their faith. Some Kuwaiti and Saudi institutions were also concerned about conversions from Islam to Christianity, and they financed a number of mosques around the country.

Most Muslim NGOs at this time were focussed on religious education and preaching, in an attempt to halt conversions to Christianity. This concern continues today, but some are becoming engaged in secular education, health care and microfinance projects. The perceived threat from missionary organizations remains a significant consideration, however, and the Muslim community and foreign donors have made significant financial commitments for *madrasahs* and mosques, which do not address the immediate development needs of the community.

There is some disagreement as to the numbers of Muslims in Malawi, and the estimates range between 10 and 40 per cent of the total population. The competition for converts and efforts to retain Muslim members have contributed to a concentration of resources away from other human development needs, and the rivalry between the faiths also raises questions about the ability of Christian and Muslim FBOs to work together on development issues.

Unlike their Christian counterparts, most Muslim NGOs have no formal relationship with a local place of worship, and they reach out directly to the community. They may use the mosque as a facility, but its leaders play no official role in the NGO by virtue of their religious position. Islam is not as hierarchical in its organization as Christianity, and Muslim NGOs are totally independent from the local imams and their congregations.

Charity is one of the five fundamental pillars of Islam and is compulsory for all Muslims. The main form of charity is zakat, which is an annual contribution of 2.5 per cent of the value of one's assets exceeding a minimum of about $1,750 in 2006. Zakat can be given to people in eight categories of need, which includes the destitute, people without livelihoods and those who are in debt.

Zakat is the largest source of funding for Islamic development institutions in most places, but it does involve some problems. It tends to be seasonal, since most Muslims prefer to pay zakat during Ramadan, for food relief, as this is considered a more worthy time to donate. Development organizations require steady funding throughout the year, and famines do not always coincide with Ramadan. It is also common to spend zakat on the construction of mosques and Muslim teaching. This contributes of course to spiritual development, but can divert funds from purposes which some at least would regard as more urgent.

Many Muslims believe that development work should cover not only economic needs but spiritual needs as well. Religious education is sometimes seen as being more urgent then economic assistance, since some Muslims, like some Christians, believe that once people start to understand and follow Islam, they will immediately be on the path to renewal in all aspects of their lives.

Many Islamic NGOs identify themselves strongly with their faith and regard this as the primary motive for their work. This is not universal, however. The Gift of the Givers Foundation, for instance, a South African development NGO, is inspired by Sufism which is an Islamic tradition focusing on spirituality and mysticism. They state:

'We actively seek to build bridges between people of different cultures and religions, engendering goodwill, harmonious coexistence, tolerance and mutual respect in keeping with the divine injunction.'
(Gift of the Givers, website)

Many of the difficulties with zakat arise as a result of simplistic interpretations of the rules rather than from the rules themselves. Some liberal Muslims argue that the long-term purpose of zakat is to help zakat receivers to become zakat payers, which is a neat way of describing sustainability. This may be a minority view, however, and visible humanitarian relief, or even ostentatious construction, is a more popular use of zakat, as it is of most Christian charity. The lines of beggars outside many churches, and mosques, testify to the desire of individuals give direct to beneficiaries, even if in so doing they perpetuate their dependence on charity. The fixed relationship between zakat and wealth is also a disincentive to formal donations to development institutions, since some wealthy donors may not be willing to show what their donations are as this enables others to calculate their net wealth.

Muslims are also enjoined not to trumpet their donations. Although some lavish mosques, like many places of worship of other religions, are in part intended to demonstrate the generosity of their donors, many Muslims attempt to conceal their generosity. This makes it difficult for recipient NGOs to record their zakat income in a transparent way. There is also some debate as to whether zakat can be used to cover the administrative costs of organizations, or whether it must all be spent on actual donations to the poor. This in itself inhibits the development and growth of Muslim NGOs. Not all Muslim charity has to be given as zakat, and there are other additional voluntary forms of donation. Necessarily, however, the very substantial zakat levy on personal wealth constitutes the majority of Muslim giving.

Zakat funding should benefit Muslim beneficiaries, and this naturally makes it easier to give individual grants and more difficult to work in mixed communities. One way in which some Muslim NGOs have dealt with this is by having separate zakat and non-zakat accounts for donors, but this complicates administration and inclines NGOs towards relief, where individual beneficiaries can be more easily identified than in development work which is almost always directed toward whole communities.

Most Muslim NGOs are managed by men, except for those which work specifically on women's issues. Their lack of female staff may affect their ability to work with women. In Malawi, Muslim NGOs engaged in relief work issued announcements about food distribution in mosques, where the women were not present. This meant that women heads of households or those whose men folk were away, who were often the poorest, did not get to hear about the distribution. Many Muslim development NGOs are conscious of women's development and they run literacy and other training projects for women. There is a tendency, however, for women to be taught home-based skills such as sewing and home economics, rather than skills which will get them out of their homes and into the wider community.

Many Muslim women, however, feel inspired and encouraged by the explicitly religious approach of Muslim development institutions from whose services they have benefited, and women in Malawi said that the religious instruction they had received from a Muslim NGO had given them the status and confidence that they belonged to something worthwhile, As a result they walked many miles to attend meetings despite domestic and work commitments. As in so many issues, however, there is a wide range of experiences. The more traditional African Muslim societies such as Nigeria and Sudan may take a very different view, and western notions of gender and development may be viewed, as in Nigeria, as 'a means for the west to wipe out the values and beliefs of Muslim Societies' (Adamu, 1999). There are some specifically racial issues in the management of Muslim NGOs in Africa arising from the fact that many of the NGO leaders are not Africans but are representatives of the immigrant Asian trading communities, which are regarded in many countries as even more exploitative than the European colonists under whose rule they first came to Africa.

Wealthy Asian traders started many of these NGOs, and are responsible for much of their funding, so it is natural that they dominate their management, as they do the management of their own businesses. This can cause some animosity between African and Asian Muslims, since the control over NGOs whose work is mainly directed towards the Africans continues to be in the hands of Asians.

Local offices of some bigger Western international NGOs, both Christian and secular, are making increasing efforts to 'Africanize' their senior staff, but this is not happening in the same way in the smaller locally funded and managed Muslim institutions. Their leadership style also tends to be paternalistic, as it is in Asian-owned businesses; this is in contrast to the practices of other institutions.

Most Muslim NGOs are directed and managed by Muslims, often but not always for family reasons, but a number of Muslim NGOs in Africa working in education and other development work employ more Christian than Muslim staff and this is not seen as a problem. There are however fewer 'development professionals' working in Muslim NGOs than in secular or Christian ones, partly because the Muslim ones tend to be smaller but also because there is strong reluctance to spend zakat funds on administration.

Like some Christian NGOs, some Muslim NGOs expect their staff to behave in an Islamic manner at all times, to pray during work, not to wear unsuitable clothing, or to drink alcohol, and in general to act as role models at all times within the communities where they work. These rules are of course very similar to those which govern the SKDRDP *sevanirathas*. Other institutions require reasonable behaviour at work, but they consider the lives of staff members their own business after working hours. Most Muslim NGOs do prefer to have a core of Muslim staff, if only because they want to give them the same sorts of opportunities as Christian NGOs offer their co-religionists.

Muslim institutions, and indeed many Muslims themselves, feel somewhat under threat in present conditions. There are many reasons for this, but there are also many very common misconceptions and generalisations about Islam, and Muslim institutions. There are in particular four common views which relate to development work, and which are widely held, but erroneous. The first is that Muslims are exclusively concerned with handout charity for their fellow Muslims, and that assistance which helps people to become independent, particularly non-Muslims, is not provided. The second is that Islam oppresses women, and keeps them out of the mainstream of society. The third is that Muslims tend to solve problems by struggle and violence, rather than by peaceful means. The fourth is that 'modern' financial services, and particularly sustainable credit, are impossible under strict Islamic financial principles. There are many examples of institutions whose work is totally counter to these views, and four particular cases are briefly presented below.

Examples from Bosnia Herzegovina and Hyderabad

Merhamet is a Muslim NGO working in relief and rehabilitation in Bosnia and Herzegovina. It played a particularly valuable role in its area of operation after the war between Serbia and Bosnia Herzegovina, which was a war between mainly Christian and mainly Muslim nations.

Nicholas Burns, under secretary for political affairs in the United States Department of State, at a function on November 2005, said:

'During the darkest days of the war, there were many examples of compassion, of men and women helping friends and neighbours who were in need regardless of their ethnic background. During the siege of Sarajevo, faith-based charities like the Jewish charity La Benevolencija, the Catholic Franciscan charity St. Anthony's Bread, and the Muslim charity Merhamet played a vital role in meeting people's basic needs at a time when no one else could help. Their generosity was available to all, without discrimination. I know that many Sarajevans of all faiths might not be alive today if they had not received help when it mattered most.'

Sevarflije is a small mainly Muslim town in Bosnia. Before the war, it was a prosperous community. Most of its 2,000 people worked in factories in a nearby town, in farming or in local chalk quarries. The people had good relations with neighbouring Serbian Catholic communities. During the war, however, all the houses were destroyed, and the entire infrastructure of the town was ruined.

After the war, while the villagers were still living as internally displaced persons, Merhamet worked with the people of Sevarflije, and many similar places, to restore not only their economic position but also to rebuild the friendship between the two national religious communities. The NGO collaborated with the people of Sevarlije, who had formed a committee to help the inhabitants to return to their pre-war homes. They linked this committee to assistance from the United Nations High Commissioner for Refugees (UNHCR), and the people nearly all returned and rebuilt their homes, often with the assistance of neighbours from their previous enemies, the Serbs.

Nearly all the factories and quarries where the inhabitants used to work were destroyed, and Merhamet assisted the people to go into farming. The available high-quality land had first to be cleared of landmines, but once this was done the people successfully took up farming, and Merhamet assisted them to make market links with nearby food-processing industries. While they were refugees, the people had become accustomed to living on handouts from UNHCR, but Merhamet helped them overcome this demeaning sense of dependency. They have been provided with materials to earn their own livelihoods, and an opportunity to give to others, and have thus recovered their self-respect.

Merhamet provided the returning people with seeds, small tools, machinery, and fruit trees, and helped them to set up a system whereby those who benefit the most, because they are young and can work productively, give food and other assistance to older and less able people in the community. First, they had to grow enough to feed themselves, then they had to keep seeds for the next season, and then they could market their surplus into the growing local and European market and also assist their less fortunate neighbours.

Each family was initially given seed potatoes or other planting material, and they had to return the same amount the following year to enable others to benefit. The community then received a tractor, owned by the community, and this was used both by individual farmers, on rent, and also to increase the general area available for cultivation. The outcome of this and many similar three year rehabilitation projects was that people of all communities benefited. After the three years had elapsed they were able to be totally independent of external assistance and to take care of the needs of the less able members of their own and neighbouring communities.

Merhamet showed that a Muslim NGO could effectively extend its assistance to communities regardless of their religion, and that it could 'put itself out of business' by enabling totally demotivated and destitute people to become independent of further assistance within three years.

The Confederation of Voluntary Associations (COVA), of Hyderabad in India, is a Muslim NGO which believes that the empowerment of women is crucial to building communal harmony. Hyderabad has a large Muslim community, perhaps half the urban population, and is traditionally prone to communal riots. The demolition of the Babri Masjid in Avodhya in northern India in 1992 led to serious riots in the city, and concerned members of the various communities came together to try to establish communal harmony. Their association was later registered as COVA.

Asghar Ali, the secretary of COVA, says:

'There is a powerful connection between communal harmony and empowering women. One is not possible without the other. If a woman is sensitised and empowered, she can be a strong influence on family members who might have got involved in communal conflicts. We believe that empowerment of women is central to the prevention of communal riots. We feel that a woman is empowered if she understands and believes that she has the potential and strength to improve her situation.'
(Kaur, 2007)

COVA does not however require that Muslim women volunteers should give up their veils or all-covering burqas, and most of the Muslim women volunteers of COVA observe purdah in this way.

Noor Jehan, a volunteer coordinator with COVA, says that the veil is not a hurdle to progress. She said:

'My family is known to have extremely stringent norms for its women. But I believe in what I do here and am able to do it. Earlier, my in-laws were dead against my stepping out of the house. But today, they are proud of my achievements. If you really want to do something, you will find a way of doing it. As an organization, we believe that the decision to give up or continue wearing the burqa is a very personal choice. We don't wish to interfere. We seek to instill confidence in women and a yearning to use their lives well.'
(Kaur, 2007)

Manovar Fatima sits on the board of directors of the Mutually Aided Cooperatives Society which was promoted by COVA near Charminar in the old city. This is part of the Mahila Sanatkar wing of COVA, which helps women gain economic independence. The society has its own brand of jute products, artificial flowers, cushion covers, embroidery pieces and handmade paper. She said:

> 'I used to crochet and, after some initial hesitation, I decided to join COVA. The elders at home were unhappy but did not protest too much because my daughter was already going there. Today, not only do I train other girls, I also make new design samples for clothes. COVA has given me the 'himmat' [confidence] that I can do something.'
> (Kaur, 2007)

The interplay between women's empowerment and prevention of communal riots became clear in 2002, when large numbers of COVA volunteers successfully intervened to keep the peace after communal riots in Gujarat. Risking their lives, the women from various communities came together to form a human chain, and prevented riots from starting by simply holding hands. The experience of COVA shows that Muslim institutions can successfully empower and mobilize women not only for economic purposes but in order to deal with sensitive and even dangerous political issues as well.

CAPARV, the Council for Anti Poverty Action and Rural Volunteers, was established in Imphal, in the furthest eastern extremity of India, in 1988. The organization has no official religious or other sectarian links, but all its managing committee and about half its clients are Muslims. CAPARV is involved in a very wide range of economic and social development activities, with a focus on conflict resolution, forest rights and HIV/AIDS. These are particularly important in the remote mountainous area which adjoins Myanmar and is itself seriously affected by separatist insurgents and other similar problems.

CAPARV works mainly with women, and has promoted a number of self-help groups for local women. Many of the more traditional Muslim communities in the area have a strong prejudice against any form of fixed interest charges, and this makes any form of financial intermediation very difficult. CAPARV have therefore designed a simple form of profit and loss sharing lending, based on Islamic *musharaka*. This is basically 'microventure capital', where the lender shares the risk with the borrower, and CAPARV is one of the very few NGOs which has adopted this very equitable and non-exploitative approach to microfinance.

If a Muslim member of a self-help group wants a loan, such as for a small grocery shop, but does not want to take it on a fixed interest basis, she can opt for what is called a 'business share loan'. The CAPARV fieldworker shows her how to keep a simple record of sales and stocks, and the records are checked once a week by the fieldworker. The surplus made on sales of goods which the borrower has bought with her loan are quite easily calculated, and CAPARV is entitled to one-quarter of the total for the period of the loan, usually one year. If the goods do not sell, or have to be sold at a loss, the woman only has to repay the principal, with no extra charges.

Thus far CAPARV has more or less covered its costs on loans of this kind, and the borrowers are also satisfied with the system. There has been no evidence of any falsification of the figures, because CAPARV are widely known and respected in the community, and the women are very aware that these loans have a certain religious significance, because the system has been especially designed to conform to sharia principles.

Akhuwat of Lahore

In early 2001 a group of senior civil servants met at the Gymkhana Club in Lahore to talk informally about the problems of poverty, and the difficulties experienced by both government and non-government organizations which were trying to assist the very large numbers of people in Pakistan who live below the poverty line. Dr Amjad Saqib, one of those present, was managing the Punjab Rural Support Programme, a government institution. He mentioned that one of the many problems he experienced related to the issue of the 20 per cent annual interest which was charged on loans made by his institution. This was a problem for two reasons: first, the cost itself made it more difficult for borrowers to repay, and second, many borrowers were reluctant to pay any interest at all since fixed interest on loans, or on savings, is specifically forbidden in the Qur'an. Some of the staff of the institution, including Dr Saqib himself, agreed on the same religious grounds.

There is endless debate in Muslim circles, as there is indeed elsewhere, about the definition of 'usury', and whether this means excessive interest or any fixed interest at all. We have already referred to the 'liberal' interpretation of the term which is advocated by some Christian authorities, who believe that the sustainability of any financial institution serving the poor is more important than the interest rates it charges. This view is supported by the fact that the returns on investment in petty trading and most other activities in which microfinance borrowers invest their loans are extremely high, averaging around 800 per cent (Harper, 1998) so that the interest paid on microloans is far less important than their accessibility. From a competitive point of view, high interest rates are also not an issue for microfinance institutions, since their only competition is informal moneylenders. In urban Lahore, the area of immediate concern to Dr Saqib and his colleagues, moneylenders typically charge 10 per cent or more per month.

The traditional Islamic view, however, is that it is wrong to charge any fixed interest at all. This is based on the belief that it is unjust for anyone to earn an income purely from money itself, without any labour, and also because a fixed interest rate implies total confidence in the outcome of a business venture, whereas only God can know the future. As a result of this, a alternative system of Islamic financing has been developed, which bases the reward for savings, and the cost of loans, on the cost of the services which have been provided by the lender, and on the actual outcome of the ventures in which the savings or loans have been invested. CAPARV is one of the few institutions which uses this latter method of charging.

There is now a large and rapidly growing Islamic financing sector, in which not only specialized Muslim institutions but also western banks are playing a major part, but Islamic principles have generally not been applied in microfinance (Harper, 1997). The CAPARV experience in Imphal which is described above is a rare exception. There are a number of reasons for this, including the 'western', Christian or secular origins of most microfinance institutions, and the practical difficulties of calculating the profitability of microbusinesses.

One solution to this is not to make any charge to borrowers for loans, or at least only to charge for the operating and transactions costs of the lending operation, and to ignore the 'cost' of the money itself. This is legitimate in Islamic financing, but it requires that the money which is lent out should come free of cost, from a source that demands no return.

Dr Saqib and his colleagues discussed the issue at some length, and they concluded that common charity, ordinary people's desire to give money to help those less fortunate than themselves, could be the answer. One of the people round the table offered Pakistani Rs.10,000 (about $150) there and then, to start a pool of free money for lending to the poor, and Dr Saqib volunteered to manage the process of identifying suitable borrowers, lending the money, and recovering it so that it could be recycled indefinitely.

This first donation was loaned to a woman, on the basis of a guarantee from the other members of a small group which she formed with Dr Saqib's assistance, and the institution took off from that point. Friends of the original founding members contributed a further $1000 within a few weeks, and a few months later a wealthy well-wisher made a donation of $2000, and Dr Saqib, with the help of a few friends, lent this money to the members of five more groups. He followed the same group lending method that was used in the Punjab Rural Support Programme.

At the end of 2001 it was decided to formalize the activity. Dr Saqib and his friends registered it as a society under the 1860 Act, which is fundamentally similar to the Charities Act in the UK or the regulations for foundations in the USA, and they chose the name Akhuwat, which means 'brotherhood', in recognition of the fact that it had been started by a group of friends, and that their intention was to build an institution which would develop a sense of common ownership and community among borrowers, donors and whoever was managing the institution. Akhuwat refers to the period of the Hejira, when financial support was offered to Muslims fleeing to Medina from Makkah by Muslims living in Medina.

Dr Saqib and his friends continued to give their leisure time free of charge to the managing of the new institution, but it soon became clear that it was growing too fast to be managed and run totally on a voluntary basis. They decided that they would charge borrowers a membership fee of 5 per cent of their loans, irrespective of the timing of the repayment, and by the end of 2003 Akhuwat was employing six people, and the pool of funds had increased to approximately $40,000; they had lent out almost $100,000 to a total of 900 men and women in about 40 groups by recycling the funds. There had been no defaults. The 5 per cent administration fee is not levied on loans of less than $60, because such borrowers are felt to be too poor to be able to pay this without hardship.

The group formation and management process was quite time-consuming, for Akhuwat staff and for the members of the groups. Some members, both men and women, complained that the regular group meetings which were part of the system which had been copied from the Punjab Rural Support Programme were taking too much time. Some potential borrowers who were very poor and clearly needed loans to enable them to start or expand their petty trading or other activities found it difficult to form or join a group, and some people, quite often those who were more enterprising than their fellows, did not want to work in groups. They were individualists, and wanted individual loans just like better-off people who did business with banks. Akhuwat's management were also aware that they had competition from other microfinance institutions in Lahore, and that groups were unpopular. Akhuwat might be able to use individual lending as a 'selling point' to attract new clients. It was therefore decided to experiment with individual loans as well as working through groups.

This was an immediate success. The staff had to spend less time on each loan, since they had only to visit the applicant to check on his or her income level and reputation in the community, and on the feasibility of the proposed or existing microbusiness. They had to do that in any case for group members, but they also had to help to form the groups and to attend the weekly meetings.

Around this time there was also some evidence from Bangladesh that lending only to women could cause severe and sometimes tragic social problems. Some Bangladeshi men were very frustrated at what they saw was their loss of prestige, as their wives were able to take over the financial affairs of their households and to marginalize their husbands. There were many cases where men beat up their wives, or even disfigured them by throwing acid on their faces.

Akhuwat's very name implied solidarity and mutual support, rather than conflict, at all levels. In pursuance of this, when they moved from group to individual lending, in order to strengthen family relationships rather than to promote conflict, Akhuwat instituted a policy of lending to households, not to individuals. Wives and husbands were required to sign loan agreements, or mothers and sons, or fathers and daughters, and the loans were known as family loans. Every one in the family knows that the family has taken a loan, and this creates a sense of unity in the household and avoids duplication of loans in the same family. The entire family is liable for the loan, and is also the beneficiary.

Borrowers are also required to bring two guarantors, who are not from the same household, to co-sign their loans, in order to replace the group guarantee. These guarantors do not have to be any wealthier than the people whose loans they are guaranteeing; they have merely to be respectable people in the same communities who know the applicants well and are prepared to stand behind them.

Akhuwat was by this time attracting some attention among practitioners of more conventional microfinance. They had initially been very doubtful whether

Dr Saqib and his friends would be able to attract enough funds to finance any significant expansion, and, if they did, whether borrowers would repay regularly. Akhuwat was not following normal practice in many respects. It relied completely on generous individuals to give funds for onlending rather than raising commercial money, it relied quite significantly on volunteers to give their time, and its five per cent fee, which was the same irrespective of how long the loan was outstanding, seemed to be an invitation to delay repayment. Akhuwat's individual loans, which were rapidly replacing group-based loans, were also made to men as well as to women. This was completely contrary to accepted best practice in microfinance, where the vast majority and often all the borrowers are women.

The many sceptics frequently pointed out these potential difficulties to Dr Saqib and his colleagues. Initially, when Akhuwat only had a handful of clients, they had said that the system would surely break down after it reached a few hundred clients. When Akhuwat achieved 1,000 clients, without major problems, the sceptics said that it could never grow much beyond that number. In 2006 when the figure of 10,000 clients was reached, some sceptics changed their views. Dr Saqib felt that in a modest way Akhuwat was doing for conventional microfinance what Professor Mhd Yunus had done for conventional banking in the late 1970s; it was showing that things could be done differently, and that the 'accepted wisdom' could be challenged.

By 2007 Akhuwat was lending to over 15,000 clients. They still charge a fixed membership fee of 5 per cent of the loan amount, irrespective of the repayment period. Potential borrowers are carefully screened by Akhuwat's field staff, and 90 per cent of them have incomes of below $70 a month, which is close to destitution in the city of Lahore. A small number of better-off borrowers are also accepted, whose incomes may be up to twice this amount, because they wish to start or expand small businesses which can employ others in the same community.

The financial picture of Akhuwat at the end of March 2007 was approximately as follows:

Assets, or uses of finance

Long term loans	$11,000
Loans	$831,000
Cash and bank	$141,000
Total	$ 983,000

Liabilities, or sources of finance

Donations	$983,000
Total	$983,000

Income and expenditure for the year 2005/6

Grants	$8,000
Fees	$57,000
Total	$65,000
Expenses	$75,000
Loss	$10,000

Note: Pakistani Rs. have been approximately converted to US$ at the rate of Rs.60=$1.00.

The operating losses were covered by special grants that were made for the purpose, and it was calculated that the 5 per cent fee would cover the full operating costs by the end of the year as the programme expanded.

All the funds come from individuals. These include large sums from prominent people such as the Pakistani President General Musharraf, the Mayor of Lahore and prominent business leaders, and much smaller donations from ordinary citizens. The Governor of the Punjab has been particularly helpful; he contributed Rs.300,000 ($5,000) from his own pocket and organized three fund-raising dinners at his official residence, as well as introducing Akhuwat to other influential people such as the president. Most of the donors are residents of Lahore, but some are living in the USA and elsewhere, and wish to give something back to the city they have come from.

Not all the donors are wealthy. A local mechanic whose property had been destroyed by a flood had successfully restored his business with the assistance of a loan from Akhuwat, and he then got a job in Dubai. A year later, he donated a substantial sum to Akhuwat from his foreign earnings, in order to enable others to benefit as he had. Many other borrowers have made similar smaller donations when their businesses prospered, because they felt a sense of identification with the institution. In this way the local branches of Akhuwat are slowly becoming self-financing, and local small business people who do not need Akhuwat's loans are also making contributions. Borrowers, donors, volunteers and the paid staff feel that they stand on the same footing. Although the loans are only made possible by the charitable generosity of donors, there is no sense of obligation; all the stakeholders feel that share a common purpose.

Akhuwat deliberately avoids grants from official foreign donors or other similar sources. Dr Saqib and his colleagues feel that these would inevitably come with 'strings attached', and that there are in any case enough generous individuals in Pakistan, and overseas, who sympathize with and understand the basis of Akhuwat's operations. On the same principle, funding has not been requested from the Pakistan Poverty Alleviation Fund, which has been established by the Pakistani Government, with foreign assistance, to finance microfinance institutions. It is unlikely that such funds would be suitable for Akhuwat in any case, since they are generally provided as interest bearing loans. It is possible however that in the future Akhuwat might receive funding from the Pakistani Government's zakat fund, which is financed by contributions from tax payers who prefer to leave the disposition of their zakat donations to the government, rather than identifying suitable recipients themselves.

The average Akhuwat loan is for about $200. This is partly because the institution is growing very fast, and the first loan to any borrower cannot exceed Rs.10,000. Depending on the borrower's need, and repayment performance, larger sums can follow, but the maximum is Rs.25,000 ($420). Akhuwat's lending is restricted by the amount of funds it can raise from donors, and their goal is in any case to relieve poverty and to help people to better themselves, rather than to grow for the sake of growth, or to create permanent dependence.

Borrowers who have reached the maximum loan can borrow again if they wish, but they have to revert to the lowest loan level. They can then climb back up again to the maximum level, but the hope is that this will be less than they need, because their businesses have grown during the three or four years they have been borrowing from Akhuwat, and that they will therefore look to banks or to other lenders for larger sums. Akhuwat has successfully introduced one women borrower to First Women's Bank. The bank was impressed by her record as a good client of Akhuwat, and approved her loan application for $750.

The loan terms are flexible, but the maximum repayment period is 18 months. Most of Akhuwat's loans are repaid in 11 months, and most borrowers repay at the rate of Rs.1,000 (just over $16) a month. If any instalment is overdue more than 30 days it is considered as being in default, and pressure is brought to bear on the borrower, and his or her guarantors, to bring the repayments up-to-date. The most important sanction is the knowledge that those who fail to pay promptly risk losing any chance of receiving loans in future. Up until early 2007, the repayment rate has remained at about 99 per cent.

International experience shows that group loans are more likely to be repaid on time than loans to individuals. Akhuwat's group loans are being phased out in favour of household loans, which are similar to individual loans. The repayment on group loans has been 98.4 per cent on time, and the overall repayment rate for all kinds of loans is 99.7 per cent. This is marginally reduced by the slightly poorer performance of the group loans, and the repayment rate on the individual household borrowers is 99.9 per cent; the difference is very small, but is quite contrary to what might have been expected.

In addition to the 5 per cent fee, borrowers also pay a compulsory 1 per cent insurance charge. In case of death or permanent disability, outstanding loan balances are waived, and needy families receive a $75 cash payment as well as a stipend of $45 a month for three months. This fee has so far been sufficient to cover such problems as may occur, in that by early 2007, after five years of operation, only half the total amount which had been collected as insurance fees had been paid out. The balance of half a per cent is treated as the fee for managing the insurance operation.

Akhuwat 's operating expenses have been maintained at a very low level, in spite of the rapid rate of expansion. From July 2005 to June 2006, around 6,200 loans were disbursed amounting to just under a $1 million. The total of all the costs was about $70,000, including loan loss provision and a substantial donation to the victims of the 2005 earthquake in northern Pakistan. The total income from the 5 per cent membership fees was about $50,000, plus a small amount for the administration of the insurance programme. The cost per rupee lent during the last financial year was thus 7 per cent, and Akhuwat had to provide an operating subsidy of $20,000 to make up the difference. This was drawn from the funds which were donated, both for this purpose and from the general fund.

Management anticipate that as the volume expands costs will eventually fall to 5 per cent, so that the membership fees will cover them and the operating losses will thus be eliminated. This may take some time, however, as Akhuwat is expanding quite rapidly and the costs of hiring and training staff, and purchasing equipment, must be incurred before any revenue is generated.

Akhuwat has eight branch offices in the city of Lahore, and six branches outside the city, with about 60 full-time staff, paid at approximately the same level as they could expect elsewhere. It is Akhuwat's policy, however, to recruit staff from the same communities as their borrowers, and not to hire highly qualified professionals. This reduces costs, and it also ensures that staff turnover is much lower than in other microfinance institutions whose staff are more highly qualified. The operating systems are simple, partly because no interest charges are levied, and success depends mainly on interpersonal relationships rather than professional skills. Akhuwat owns no vehicles; its loan staff can take loans from the organization to buy motorcycles if they wish, and they receive a small allowance to cover the costs of fuel.

Dr Saqib himself is a former civil servant who works on a voluntary basis. He is assisted not only by the full-time staff but also by a large team of volunteers, at all levels. One vendor of perfume and ornaments from a mobile stall at the entrance to a mosque has taken and successfully repaid four loans from Akhuwat, but he also voluntarily helps by visiting other borrowers at their homes to remind them when repayments are due. Several hundred students at a local university have also volunteered to 'adopt' borrower families, to help them with their businesses, to learn from them, and generally to try to bridge the wide gaps between the middle class and the poorer people who borrow from Akhuwat.

Another important way in which costs are reduced and the general spirit of Akhuwat is supported is the use of local mosques as meeting places for loan disbursement. The imam of the Dar-ul-Haq mosque in the township area of Lahore initially offered space in his mosque for this purpose in between the afternoon prayer periods, for Akhuwat staff to discuss any problems and to disburse its loans. This extension of the use of the mosque from purely *ibadat* [worship] to *khidmat-e-khalq* [service to mankind] has become central to the approach of Akhuwat, and it builds and strengthens the links between Akhuwat and the local communities that the mosque serves.

This means that Akhuwat's offices can be very small and inexpensive, since meetings are held in nearby mosques, and it also reinforces the sincerity of borrowers' commitment to repay; nobody likes to break an undertaking he has made in a place of worship. The imams are also pleased that their premises are being more regularly used, and borrowers who come to receive their loans also remain for prayers; this reinforces the position of the mosque in the community. Women do not participate in the prayers if these are taking place before the disbursement, but they sit at the side of the mosque and then move to take their place along with the men to receive and sign for their loans.

Akhuwat has also made use of a local church in the same way to serve its Christian clients; unfortunately the priest who initiated this was transferred to another church outside Akhuwat's area of operations, and his replacement was unwilling to continue the arrangement. The priest is trying to persuade the bishop to encourage priests throughout the diocese to work with Akhuwat in the same way. In the meantime, the Christian borrowers come to their nearest mosque to receive their loans, just like their Muslim fellows, and the few loan officers who are Christians are also welcome in the mosques. Some imams are also reluctant to allow financial transactions to take place in their mosques, but this resistance is being overcome as they see the benefits that it brings to the community.

Akhuwat's expansion depends on continuing donations to finance growth in the loan portfolio, and on the continued willingness of the voluntary staff. There is as yet no evidence that these will stop, and although substantial effort has to be put into fund-raising, and further initiatives will be required in future, there does not seem to be any reason why a programme which depends on brotherhood, generosity and goodwill should be any less 'sustainable' than one which depends on purely financial incentives. In the three years from early 2002 to 2005 Akhuwat raised donations of about $300,000; in the following one year, they raised $500,000.

A number of influential individuals in Rawalpindi and Faisalabad and other cities in the Punjab have observed Akhuwat's success, and have raised local funds to start what are effectively locally managed 'franchisees' of Akhuwat. They and their locally recruited staff and volunteers have spent time in Lahore with Akhuwat's staff, and it is hoped that this will eventually extend the institution's outreach throughout Pakistan, without straining the management or financial resources of Akhuwat in Lahore.

Muslim development NGOs – some tentative conclusions

Islam is in many ways a more prescriptive religion than the Dharmaic religions such as Hinduism, or than Christianity. The Qur'an, together with its various interpretations, lays down quite clear rules of conduct, particularly regarding charity. As in other religions, there are many different divisions and interpretations, and different individuals observe the rules more or less strictly. There are nevertheless certain very detailed rules governing the proportion of one's wealth which should be given to charity, or the ways in which financial services should be provided, which can guide the activities and practices of development NGOs far more definitively than the more general principles of Christianity or the holy books of Hinduism.

Muslims are also under pressure. In recent years the actions of a small number of extremists have put a fierce spotlight on all institutions which are explicitly Muslim, whether they are local *madrasahs* for school children or development NGOs. Their treatment of women, their attitudes to people of other religions and their relationships to governments are all under intense scrutiny.

Islam has also been on the defensive historically. The great European empires were all at least nominally Christian, except that of the Soviet Union, and many colonialists saw the 'conversion of the heathen', including Muslims, as a major justification for their conquests. The more recent cultural, commercial and military world domination of the USA is secular or even irreligious, but the USA is a generally religious and mainly Christian nation, and its leaders frequently invoke a presumably Christian deity in their public announcements.

Within India, home to the world's second largest Muslim population, the Muslim minority are also under pressure. There is debate as to the extent to which Muslims should be included in the quotas of public sector jobs and other benefits which are reserved for historically oppressed minorities such as 'backward castes'. There are many exceptions, but Muslims in India are generally worse off than the majority in terms of all the familiar indicators such as literacy, incomes or longevity. Muslim development NGOs are therefore more likely to focus their work on Muslim beneficiaries than NGOs based on other faiths. Muslims have been oppressed, internationally and within countries, and 'their' NGOs inevitably focus on the redressal of past and present injustices.

The detailed regulations of Islam also tend to confine Muslim NGOs to Muslim beneficiaries. Zakat, the major 'official' source of funding, is believed by some authorities to be intended to benefit only Muslims, and its uses must also conform to more traditional views of charity which are inconsistent with 'sustainability' and profit. This is particularly true in microfinance because many Muslims, particularly in more traditional places, will not accept 'Western' credit systems based on fixed interest rates. The financial products which they offer have to be specifically designed to address this need, and they may be less acceptable, or at least less familiar, to non-Muslims.

Both COVA and Akhuwat have designed their programmes in accordance with sharia principles, and most of their clients are Muslims. Akhuwat in particular demonstrates how 'sustainability' can be viewed in a totally different light from the normal western market-driven sense. Akhuwat is built on generosity, in giving both money and time, and its dramatic success thus far suggests that an institution may be 'sustainable' not just because people are willing to lend it money at market rates of interest or work for it for at market wages. Generosity and voluntarism are perhaps as sustainable a part of society as the market; Akhuwat's future, and its imitators, will show whether this is true.

References

Adamu, F. L. (1999) 'A Double-Edged Sword: Challenging women's oppression within Muslim society in northern Nigeria', *Gender and Development*, Vol. 7.

Gift of the Givers website, http://www.giftofthegivers.co.za/index.php?option=com_content&task=view&id=15&Itemid=34 [accessed 6 April 2007].

Harper, M. (1997) *Partnership Financing for Small Enterprise: Some lessons from Islamic credit systems*, ITDG Publications, London.

Harper, M. (1998) *Profit for the Poor: Case studies in Micro-Finance*, Oxford IBH, New Delhi and Intermediate Technology Publications, London.

Kaur T. (2007) 'Burqa-clad and empowered', India Together, Hyderabad, May.

Langsun Mate, T (2006) 'Microfinance, A Strategy for sustainable development', *The ICFAI Journal of Business Strategy*, ICFAI, Hyderabad.

Nabila Saddiq (2006) *Capacity Building and Islamic FBOs*, INTRAC, Oxford.

CHAPTER 12
Christian development practice and some examples

Abstract

Unlike their Muslim counterparts, some of the larger Christian development NGOs feel it is necessary to downplay or almost to conceal their faith-based origins, in order to avoid being associated with colonialism and conversion. Many others, however, work mainly through local churches and openly associate their religious beliefs with their development work. A German Jesuit priest started 'Catholic Bank', a cooperative savings and loan institution, in Ranchi in northern India in 1909, and it has survived and grown steadily since that time. It works through the local Catholic parish; the priests direct its field operations, and it is chaired by the local bishop. Its field staff and most of its members are men. It operates in a predominantly Catholic area, and membership is restricted to Catholics. In contrast, the Catholic Holy Cross Sisters run a very different institution in a nearby part of the same state. They promote self-help groups and help them to take credit from the local banks, and they also provide other livelihood development services. They have few links with the local churches or other religious institutions, and many of their staff, like most of the group members, are women and Hindus.

'Christian development'

Some faith-based development organizations bear the names of their religions in their titles, and may use their symbols in their logos. Others seem to wish to conceal or even to be ashamed of their religious affiliation, at least in the places where they work, as opposed to their head offices and fund raising. One of the authors had to teach a short course on Christmas Day morning when he was working at a Jesuit institution in India; the aim seemed partly to be to demonstrate that the faith of its founders and senior staff would not be allowed to influence its day-to-day work.

The reasons for this are obvious, particularly for Christian institutions which are the wealthiest and the most visible, and which most often work for people who do not share their faith. Their religion is perceived as 'western', and is inevitably linked with imperialism, whether of the traditional 19th century colonial variety, or the more contemporary hamburger and fried chicken kind.

There is a long history of religious conversions which are actually or allegedly based on immediate incentives such as education, health care or even emergency feeding, and Christian development NGOs continue to be accused of this in India and Nepal. People only decide to join a particular religion in the hope of some benefit. They may anticipate eternal salvation, they may look for enhanced respect by escaping from their traditional caste, or they may want decent primary education for their children. The boundary between 'legitimate' belief-based conversion and 'coercive' conversion are unclear, so the accusations and the resulting sensitivity are inevitable.

There are adherents of every religion who believe that their faith offers the only true path to salvation, and that the over-arching goal should therefore be to bring people into their fold; rural development and microfinance are seen by these people as routes to conversion and strengthened faith, rather than as ends in themselves. These views can be reconciled with 'modern' approaches to sustainable development. Microfinance is an increasingly popular tool for poverty alleviation, but it also poses some quite stark dilemmas for faith-based development institutions. The ways in which these are resolved can reveal a great deal about the relationship between actual practice and religion. Interest charges are perhaps the clearest indicator, since they are direct and quantifiable and cannot easily be 'fudged' with vague statements of good intentions.

Russell Mask (2000) argues that temporary grant-based institutions can harm people, and can also damage the reputation of the church. He suggests that the Old Testament prohibition of usury can be interpreted as being only against excessive interest. However, that may be defined as not against interest in principle. Interest rates must be high in order to cover the high costs of reaching out to remote communities, with very small individual transactions. Repayments must also be kept at a high level, and 'forgiveness', a classic religious virtue, is inconsistent with 'sustainability'.

If interest rates are set at what seems to be very high levels, and prompt repayment is rigorously enforced in order to sustain the institution rather than to make excessive profits for its owners, then that is seen to be acceptable. It is argued that the motivation for the interest rate and recovery methods is what determines whether or not it is exploitative, not the rate or methods themselves.

Mask (2000) quotes World Relief, one of the larger Christian microfinance providers, which uses the notion of the 'triple bottom' line: financial sustainability of the financial system, developmental impact on the client, and spiritual transformation of the client. The word 'transformation' is not defined, but Mask and others argue that there is such a thing as specifically Christian microenterprise development, and Christian microfinance. They do not suggest that other initiatives which are not specifically Christian and do not share this belief in the triple bottom line are bad, but that there is a 'richness' in Christian initiatives which merits the religious label.

Brian Fikkert (2003) goes further, and suggests that all Christian development work, including microfinance, must include a clear presentation of the gospel. Failure to do so denies the poor access to the only real solution to the fundamental causes of poverty, which, he believes, is belief in Christ. Because poverty is about failures of relationships, and people and their relationships are 'sin-marred', credit and financial service alone cannot eliminate it.

This view of the limited potential of microfinance on its own is strikingly similar to the growing trend (see, e.g., Dichter, 2006) to reassess critically microfinance, and to recognize that its potential has been seriously exaggerated. The missing ingredients may be evangelism and discipleship, livelihoods development, training, primary health care or infrastructure and good governance, or perhaps all of them, but microfinance on its own is not enough.

Fikkert's (2003) explanatory footnote on this point is worth quoting in full, since it very effectively articulates a 'fundamentalist' view which is probably similar to that which is held by many faith-based development institutions, including non-Christian ones:

> 'This does not imply that the root cause of all of the dimensions of poverty is the personal sin of the poor. Both the Scriptures and empirical evidence indicate that oppression of the poor is often a factor in their poverty. But oppression is the result of a broken relationship between the oppressor and the victim. It takes the power of Jesus Christ over sin to reconcile this relationship or to remove the oppressor. Without Jesus' death and resurrection, there is no reason to hope that the weak can ever overcome the oppression of the strong. His power is the answer, and the poor need to cling to this hope.'

This view implies not only that development must include a powerful element of evangelism, but also that Christian development work must be closely associated with local churches, for churches are the primary evangelizing authority.

Fikkert accepts that the maintenance of this view is difficult when funds have to be obtained from secular sources, and when development initiatives are under pressure to be 'sustainable', that is, to maintain themselves from their own earnings rather than from donors. It is particularly hard when minimalist microfinance precludes the offering of *any* non-financial services, religious or otherwise.

He concludes that it is impractical even to attempt to build a large microfinance institution and at the same time to maintain the religious mission that is central to his view of the role of Christianity in the development process. It may be possible to achieve some balance by working on a small local scale, by hiring committed Christian staff, by motivating them to provide spiritual as well as financial services, by working with local churches and by using microfinance groups for biblical instruction as well as for financial intermediation. His overall prognosis is somewhat pessimistic, however, and although there are some examples of effective combinations of evangelism with microfinance:

> '...the reality is that increased competition and market forces are likely to make it more and more difficult for the staff of Christian MFIs to engage in such activities in the future.'

Others take a more optimistic view. The Local Enterprise Assistance Programme (LEAP) of the Association of Evangelicals of Liberia found that tithes and offerings to churches which participated in their microfinance programme increased from a low of 30 per cent for a church with only one year of programme participation to over 100 per cent for churches with three or more years of participation (Microenterprise Best Practices, 2001). This demonstrates that development activities which initially involve substantial expenditure on non-religious activities can eventually be 'good business' for the religious institutions which set them up.

Others of the same persuasion suggest more immediate measures to finance evangelical activities. Llanto and Geron even propose that microfinance institutions offering non-financial services, including evangelism and discipleship, might cover the costs of these services by raising their interest rates (Llanto and Geron 2000).

Fikkert and others conclude that the best approach is for faith-based development to be undertaken on a small and local scale, working through local churches and using microfinance groups because of their potential for religious purposes. They suggest that churches and other faith-based institutions should not themselves engage in microfinancial intermediation, since they lack the institutional capacity to operate like banks. They should instead promote and assist local savings and credit groups. These have been shown to be more accessible and useful to very poor people than groups which borrow from a bank or microfinance institution (Allen, 2006), which tend to be used mainly by the not-so-poor, and they have the potential eventually to evolve into credit unions and cooperative banks. Community management and control can be maintained, with the spiritual leadership remaining with the church.

This type of relationship, it is felt, can enhance the local church's ability to embody Jesus Christ by caring for the spiritual and physical needs of its own members and others in its community. The churches do not own the groups, but they remain linked to the church, and can be used for recruitment to church membership and for Bible study. In addition to their purely financial and economic activities, a typical group objective is said to be 'to give glory to God's name through building unity, trust, and relationships in the group and through testifying to God's power in the community'.

Views of this kind are often associated primarily with evangelist Christian groups in the USA, but they are also widely held elsewhere. Ingie Hovland (2005) analyses the tensions between the Norwegian Missionary Society (NMS) and its dependence on secular funding received from NORAD, the Norwegian government's official development assistance agency. NMS apparently recruits only committed Christians, who believe that it is their duty to convert others to what they see as the only true faith. Development, in their view, is a holistic process which includes spiritual as well as material aspects of life, and it is wrong to deprive their clients of this component because this means that their development can never be complete. This has observable outcomes in the field; the Norwegian staff of an NMS health care facility hold religious services on the premises, in working hours, but patients' relatives who sing traditional animist songs in an effort to cure or cheer up their family members are asked to stop.

The debate has apparently received some media exposure in Norway, and one columnist asked, rhetorically, how the Norwegian authorities would respond if a Muslim institution was to engage in welfare work with street children in Oslo, if conversion to Islam was one of its main purposes.

Hovland interviewed a member of NMS' staff, and reported as follows:

> '...Christianity would enable them to access better health care, more education, improved job prospects, and, most importantly, a different mindset – in short, 'development'. In extension of this logic, therefore, he felt that it was in fact directly counterproductive to run development projects without also changing people's religious beliefs – or more precisely, to change people's religious beliefs to Christian beliefs. For him, the Christian God is the God of development, and other gods simply do not measure up.'

Hovland argues that development can never be value-free, and that adherence to a given faith is just one particularly clear expression of values. It is inappropriate, and in any case impractical, she suggests, to try to compel explicitly Christian institutions to separate their religious from their secular work, since the two are inextricably linked and cannot, indeed should not, be separated.

The development activities of the Mennonite Central Committee (MCC) represent a very different and more liberal Christian approach to development assistance. The Mennonites are themselves quite a small denomination, and they are very clear that their intention is not to convert or evangelize. They work closely with local church organizations, and are strongly pacifist in their orientation (Dicklitch and Rice, 2004).

The MCC refuses to take any funding from official US sources, and its only government funding is a relatively small amount of commodity aid from the Canadian Government, amounting to little over 10 per cent of its total budget. Its expenses are kept as low as possible; all its expatriate staff are volunteers, only receiving direct living expenses, and the emphasis of their work is on their core values of accountability and responsibility. They aim to capitalize on and enhance the 'reverence, moral legitimacy and influence' of local faith-based institutions, without supplanting them in any way. As in any institution, actual practices in the field vary according to the individuals who are employed, but all the work of the MCC is certainly informed by these principles.

The Evangelical Social Action Forum (ESAF), of Kerala in southern India, occupies what might be considered a middle point between the extremes as represented by the writings of Fikkert and others, and the programmes of the Mennonites. ESAF was started by a local evangelical group in 1991, as a result of 'a deep conviction that teaching and preaching should go hand in hand with social action' (personal communication with K. Paul Thomas, executive director, ESAF). They have a number of different programmes, focusing mainly on savings and credit groups for income generation. In 2006 ESAF was working with about 44,000 women, and had a microfinance loan portfolio of nearly $4 million.

ESAF believes that 'microenterprise development is empowering the poor in ways that are consistent with fulfilling the purposes of God for their lives and their communities' (ibid).

Most of the ESAF staff are Christian, of various denominations, and they work in collaboration with local churches whenever possible, but their clients include people from all religions in the area. The majority are Hindus, followed by Muslims and then Christians. The client profile more or less follows the profile of the populations of the villages where they work. There is little or no direct evangelical content to their work, apart from the name itself and the organization's clear association with evangelical Christianity. Conversions, if they occur, are presumably incidental to the main vision, which is the promotion of social justice through economic empowerment of the poor.

As might be expected, the nature of Christian development practice varies enormously from one institution to another. Most, if not all, Christian development institutions, however, maintain a strong commitment to their religious origins. We shall now examine an unusually long-established financial service cooperative, which was set up and is still, after 100 years, mainly managed by priests who are self-avowed missionaries. It serves only Christians, indeed only Roman Catholics, but the majority of its 66,000 members are drawn from the very poorest rural communities in one of the poorest states in India, so its policy of admitting only Christians is not 'exclusive' or unjust in any normal sense.

'Catholic Bank', or the Chotanagpur Catholic Co-operative Society

The Chotanagpur Catholic Mission Co-operative Credit and Savings Society, popularly known as the 'Catholic Bank', was founded in 1909 by John Baptist Hoffmann, a German Jesuit who came to India in 1887 and was attached to the Belgian missionaries. Father Hoffmann wanted the society to be the backbone of the overall development of the nascent church, to be a cooperative of the people, for the people and by the people. The early missionaries believed that there should be close relationship between religion and development. They considered that the gospel addressed human beings not as segmented and compartmentalized entities but in their totality - body and soul, material and spiritual, individual and social. Religion for the early missionaries was not only a spiritual message but part of total human development and the fullness of life.

In 1872, well before the establishment of the Catholic Bank, a Lutheran missionary had founded the Chotanagpur Christian Cooperative Bank. This functioned fairly effectively until 1952, when it was voluntarily wound up, but it catered mainly to the better-off Protestant and non-Christian communities in Ranchi and other towns, and did not have any outreach to the poorer rural areas. Although the Catholic Society was and still is generally known as the 'Catholic Bank', it is not a traditional commercial bank, nor a cooperative bank, but is a cooperative society, which is effectively owned and managed by its clients who are also its members.

In 1908 a serious famine struck eastern India. It was not as catastrophic as many famines in the previous century but it led to growing indebtedness among the poor, and one remedy was seen to be improved access to financial services. By the end of 1909 there were already 27 credit cooperative societies in Ranchi town and the neighbouring areas. The rural areas had suffered the most, however, and Fr Hoffmann set up the Catholic Credit Society to serve the rural poor.

The thickly forested hills around Chotanagpur in Jharkhand had for generations mainly been populated by the so-called 'tribals', descendants of the original inhabitants of the Indian sub-continent. There are around 80 million tribals in India, scattered in small groups over many of the more remote and hilly areas in the country from Kerala in the south to the foothills of the Himalayas in the north east, but they are particularly concentrated in the central and eastern states of Madhya Pradesh, Orissa, Chhattisgarh and Jharkhand. The latter two states were separated from Madhya Pradesh and Bihar in 2000, partly in response to demands from tribal people.

When the early missionaries had come to Chotanagpur in the middle of the 19th century they found that the tribal population was suffering from generations of exploitation. Ever since the original Aryan invasions of 2,000–3,000 years before, they had been marginalized. First, they were driven out of the fertile plains into the hills by the Aryans, then the Mughal rulers exacted tribute from them by appointing non-tribal *zamindars* [landowners] to collect taxes, and most recently by the British rulers, who continued the *zamindari* system on a more thorough and organized basis.

The Hindu majority excluded them from their caste hierarchy, ranking them even lower than their own 'untouchables', and the tribals found it impossible to fit into the modern monetized property-owning system. To the tribals, land had always been something which you were entitled to use if you cleared and cultivated it, and the idea of paying somebody else to use their land, or being paid to cultivate their own land, was totally alien. Property was to be enjoyed and shared, and accumulation was an alien concept. They thus easily fell prey to moneylenders, who were also often liquor dealers and traders, and many became bonded labourers on what had been their own land.

The tribals were initially eager to become Christians because this seemed to offer a route to the recognition and self-respect of which they were deprived by the Hindu majority. They responded to the evangelical work of the early Lutheran missionaries, starting in 1845, and then to the Jesuits and other Catholics who arrived some 10 years later and started work in the more remote areas which had not been covered by the Lutherans. The Christians also offered the tribals education, which seemed to be a good route to higher status and might also enable them to understand and fight for the land rights which were being taken away from them, sometimes on fraudulent grounds.

After some time, however, when their new religion seemed to offer no improvement to their economic condition, many tribals left the church to join the *Sardar* movement, which was led by a minority of educated tribal people and was against all oppressors. Its leaders aimed to expel from their own traditional areas all non-tribals, including the Christian churches, the British administrators and the Hindu majority. The missionaries realized that they had to engage in some activities which would be seen as actively pro-tribal and would also address their economic problems. Redeeming tribals from moneylenders was one such activity.

Early in 1909 Fr Hoffmann circulated a booklet among the Catholic missionaries called *Social Works in Chotanagpur* advocating the establishment of a savings and credit society specifically for the rural Catholic tribals which would, he proposed, do the following things:

- Protect the people against exploitation by outsiders, which was reducing them to a state of quasi-slavery.
- Adopt a holistic approach to religion that included spirituality as well as farming and artisan skills.
- Make the tribal churches financially self-sufficient.
- Cover the costs of the missionaries from Germany and Belgium, since financial aid from Europe was likely to dry up in future.
- Show that the missionaries could help the tribals in their overall development as well as in spiritual matters, to discourage them from turning away from the church as they had done earlier under the *Sardar* movement.
- Enable the tribal people to be independent of loans and charity, and to avoid the accusation of converting 'rice Christians' (people who become Christian in order to receive handouts).
- Form a strong economic base for tribals to preserve their identity in the wake of the so-called higher culture and religion, like Hinduism and Islam.
- Attract converts who might otherwise resist Christianity because of its rather strict moral code.
- Facilitate education and employment.
- Use and strengthen the existing parish facilities, which would provide an excellent infrastructure for the handling of credit, with little additional manpower and expense.

The society which was established as a result of Fr Hoffmann's initiative has in part contributed to these objectives, except that it has never been necessary to draw on the society's surplus to support the parishes or the work of the Jesuit missionaries, whether from India or from abroad.

The task of establishing and expanding the Catholic mission in 'Bengal', which consisted at that time of the complete area of the present states of Bengal, Bihar, Jharkhand and Orissa, had been entrusted by the Catholic authorities to the Belgian Jesuits. They identified themselves fully with the customs, language, culture and social struggles of the local people, and they believed that building the dignity and development of the tribal people was an assignment from God. They successfully established a number of institutions, including the society.

Hoffmann and Constant Lievens were the main pioneers in the struggle for changes in the agrarian situation. They started during the last decades of the 19th century by taking up the defence of tribals in the law-courts. Hoffmann in particular was convinced that social justice was an integral part of Christianity, and he was aware that tribals had to be liberated from all forms of oppression – religious, social, economic, and political. He appreciated the important role of the law, and played a vital part in the drafting of the Chotanagpur Tenancy Act 1908, which is still the basis of land tenure for tribal people throughout India. He then launched the Catholic Co-operative Credit Society in 1909.

Hoffmann started to recruit members and build up the working capital of the society in March 1909. He had thought that it would take about two years to collect the necessary capital before loans could be issued, but the first loans were sanctioned in May the same year. One year later, in March 1910, there was a total membership of 2,430 people who had together contributed a share capital of Rs.16,000 ($2,000 at the then exchange rate of Rs.8 = $1). Wage rates at that time were around Rs.1 a day, so this amounted to an average contribution of about one week's wages from each member.

Some members deposited large amounts. Hoffmann relates the case of a Munda tribesman who brought him Rs.600. By March 1913, a total of 3,890 members had borrowed some Rs.60,000 ($7,500 at the current rate of exchange) at an annual interest rate of about 10 per cent. Other banks charged interest at the rate of 18 per cent. Hoffmann calculated that if the members had taken these amounts at the 'ordinary' rate of one anna per rupee per month, or 75 per cent per year, from the village moneylenders, it would have cost them Rs.45,000 rather than the moderate sum of Rs.5,600 they paid to the society.

To build up the initial capital sufficiently quickly Hoffmann had thought it would be necessary to take initial loans from government and from the mission itself. The response of the members was in the event so good that at the end of the first year the members had already contributed Rs.28,000 in entrance fees and shares and had deposited Rs.8,000 of their savings. This made a total of Rs.36,000 ($4,500 at that time), which was an enormous sum relative to the poverty of the area. The first year also brought to the society a donation of Rs.8,000 from Belgium, Rs.3,730 from Bonn in Germany and Rs.3,000 from a Bavarian parish priest. The capital was sufficient to start issuing loans, and the society never had to borrow from the government.

Many cooperative institutions in India have effectively been taken over by government, and have thus been politicized because they have become dependent on government finance. Catholic Bank has never taken loans from government, and its capital has come entirely from members' shares and the deposits of members and non-members who use its facilities. The society has observed the requirements of the Indian Government and the Cooperative Department has not interfered with its activities. As Fr Mvden Bogaert (Van den Bogaert, 1960) puts it, the bank is a 'quiet giant'. It works quietly and reasonably efficiently, just as do the tribals themselves if they are allowed to.

The members of the society were initially the converted tribals, and its present members are their descendants, the Catholics of Chotanagpur. It was founded both to cater to their developmental needs and to deepen their Catholic faith. It aimed at both material and spiritual goals, to rescue the tribal peasantry from the clutches of moneylenders when they needed cash, to teach the Oraon and

Munda tribal people to be thrifty and thus to set up independent cooperative societies in their different villages, to help them to help themselves by managing their own organization, and to benefit from working together even as they built the society.

Hoffmann had originally proposed that the cost of one share should be Rs.10 (just over $1) but this was subsequently reduced to a slightly lower figure. There were some arguments in favour of a higher amount, since the original idea was that the village people would have their own local societies and that these societies, and perhaps some individuals, would then have shares in the apex society. A special class of preference shares was also introduced for outsiders such as the missionaries, which would allow them to have a legal status in the organization and its management.

Tribal life was then and still is community centred, and the *panchayat* or village council played an important role in the formation and management of the society. This close cooperation between the missionary and *panchayat* members was one of the cornerstones on which the society's success was built. Members would bring their savings to the missionary once a month, on a particular day, and the village elders would come with them. The missionary would receive the deposits in an open meeting and enter them in the circle register. If any of the elders could sign their names, they would countersign the missionaries' receipts.

The society helped the tribal people to work together for the own economic benefit and for the strength of their communities. They improved their sense of their own worth through their savings, and as their life-style improved, they were more able to assert their identity as tribal Christians.

The society succeeded, and survived, for many reasons. Some critics had suggested that the tribal people were too 'primitive' for a formal financial institution like the society, but they very quickly realized the benefits and understood that their money was still theirs when it was deposited in the society. The link to their local church and their priest helped them to trust the society, and they differentiated it from the numerous local moneylenders and others who exploited their ignorance of financial matters. They joined in large numbers, and their small individual deposits quickly grew together to capitalize a large and financially strong institution.

The society was and still is closely linked to the church. It works through the local parishes, the priests play an important role, and this gives the society a distinctly religious orientation. The community was directly and heavily involved, as is so unusual in many externally initiated cooperatives, but the members were not themselves in charge. Hoffmann was himself a remarkable man, and he was able to push through a number of highly unorthodox and even technically illegal features through the strength of his personality.

The German *Raiffeisen* system, which was in many ways the basis of the Indian Cooperative Credit Societies Act of 1904, is based on a 'bottom-up' approach whereby local individuals form local societies which then federate into higher level apex societies, and so on upwards, even to the national level.

Control, at least in theory, and in Germany in fact, remains very much with the original village societies.

By starting with the centralized apex society rather than autonomous rural units Hoffmann was acting directly against the 1904 Act, since he was building from the top rather than from the bottom. In doing this he ingeniously exploited the hierarchical structure of the Catholic Church and used the unpaid services of its missionary priests, each of whom became an assistant director in his own circle or parish and supervised the collection of deposits and issuing of loans. The missionary functioned as custodian without being a member of the bank, and could veto the decisions of his *panchayat* if he felt that the members were acting unwisely. Their religious authority enabled them to do this, and at the same time the society worked through the tribals' traditional village councils or *panchayats*; in some sense, this enabled it to have the best of both worlds.

Decision making was genuinely decentralized to the rural unit level, in order to facilitate the anticipated evolution of independent village societies, but the central society maintained a certain degree of control. All decisions of the rural units were subject to the concurrence of the administration at headquarters, but at the same time the headquarters could not issue loans unless they were sanctioned by the rural *panchayats*. The central society headquarters could not admit new members without the sanction of the local *panchayat,* but the *panchayats* in turn could not expel members or punish defaulters without agreement from the society. It was reasonable for the central society headquarters to have the final say on loans, since only they knew the exact state of finances of the bank; the society was in any case the only legally constituted entity and was thus the legal administrator of the whole organization.

The formal structure of the society has changed very little since its establishment in 1909. It is essentially a quasi-democratic three-tier system, combined with the controlling role of the clergy, which is hierarchical. The society comprises three distinct bodies: The Board of Control, the Board of Management, and the rural units, grouped in circles around each Catholic Mission Station. There are in total about 1,000 units, organized into some 50 circles.

The rural units form the basic cells of the bank. They are managed by the managing committee, or *panchayat*, which consists of not less than five members, who are elected annually at the general meeting of the unit. This committee controls the admission of new members, it deals with loan applications and enforces timely repayments, it checks that loans are used according to the purpose for which they were granted, and receives and pays out savings deposits, to members and non-members. The committee also represents the unit at the monthly circle meeting. The decisions of the *panchayat* are made by consensus not by majority voting, which is the traditional tribal approach to decision making.

Around 20 rural units are grouped together in a circle. These are not legal entities, but they form a vital component in the management of the society since they keep the books and carry out the other administrative work of the rural units; effectively, they control the units. The priest of the parish where the circle operates is *ex officio* the manager of the units in his circle, and their success depends on his efficiency and effective cooperation with his circle managing committee.

Each circle has a full-time *munshi* or clerk to look after daily administration, under the supervision of the assistant director. He takes deposits and handles cash, but the actual cash box is kept by the assistant director, the local priest who is the *de facto* treasurer of the circle. The *munshis* are not necessarily members of the circle managing committee but they tend to be elected as circle representatives for the central managing committee and thereby influence the central management body.

The *munshis* are appointed by the director and are employees of the Society. They are paid partly by the society and partly by the assistant director from parish funds, since they also work for the mission station as well as the society. They are responsible to the director through the circle-level assistant director, and can be dismissed even if the circle managing committee disagrees. They are effectively responsible to the priests rather than to the members.

The society also acts as a fertiliser distribution agency and employs some 60 agricultural advisors or *kamdars*, who provide farm advisory services to the society's members. They are employed by the society and are paid from the income received by the circle to which they are attached. The parish priests and their *munshis* assist with the administration of fertiliser distribution, and the society takes a 1 per cent margin on fertiliser sales to cover the out-of-pocket costs which are involved.

A member who applies for a loan is expected to be present at the unit meeting along with the *panches* of his unit, and his guarantors. His past record is examined, and if it is approved and sufficient cash is available at the circle the loan is issued there and then; no funds have to be obtained from head office. All the units' account books are kept at the circle office and are maintained by the *munshi*. This is another case where the central authority overrides the democratic powers of the units.

The supreme authority of the society is nominally vested in the annual general meeting which consists of all the members. Each member has one vote, and the general meeting elects the officers of the society and fixes the rate of interest on loans for the year. It also decides on the distribution of any surplus.

The day-to-day management of the society is under the full-time director. He reports to the general managing committee, which consists of the chairman, secretary and treasurer and one representative from each circle. If the necessary quorum of 10 members is not present the director can take decisions. The director is a priest, like the assistant directors who are the parish priests, and they are necessarily all men. This perpetuates the male domination of the society, which contrasts strongly with 'new paradigm' microfinance which is dominated by women.

A board of directors was set up in 1953 and was originally appointed by the general meeting in order to provide the ordinary members a greater say in the running of the society, but its members are now chosen by the Archbishop of Ranchi, thus strengthening the hierarchical clergy-based aspect of the society's governance. It controls the reserve funds of the society, and provides some counterbalance to the predominance of the *munshis* in the general managing committee. It also decides matters such as the salaries of the *munshis* themselves.

It is clear from the above that the director and his co-executive colleagues play a critical role in the day-to-day management of the society and its component rural units, and also in its overall direction and policy. They are all Catholic priests, and there is no doubt that the clergy are the custodians of the Society. Fr Hoffmann secured the government's approval for this when the society was first established, and it is included in the official bylaws. In rural areas people still have faith in the clergy, and local people say, 'Take away this role of the clergy, tomorrow the people will withdraw their money and in no time the society will collapse.'

The director and the vice-director are both priests, and are nominated by the Catholic Bishop of Ranchi, who is *ex officio* the president of the society. The priests in charge of the parishes where the circles are based are *ex officio* the assistant directors, and are also nominated by the Bishop of Ranchi. The director has wide powers. He can veto proposals for non-member deposits, and he can also veto any local unit decisions to expel members, for whatever reason.

The assistant director at the circle level, who is also the parish priest, organizes the members in his area into units, and has to agree and sign off on all loans after they have been sanctioned by the circle managing committee. He is also the effective treasurer of his circle. He keeps the cash box in his custody and is helped by the *munshi* who brings the cash book up-to-date, tallies it with cash-in-hand, and entrusts it to the assistant director, who locks it in the safe of the mission bungalow. The assistant director has a very powerful role, since he controls the cash and must examine, sanction or veto every loan.

There are 17 staff at the head office, as well as a *munshi* at each circle. They wield enormous *de facto* power because of their knowledge of the working of the society, and because they are the main channel of communication between the members and the priests. The staff are not highly qualified, and many of the *munshis* have not gone beyond primary school, but they attend a training course every year. The farm extension staff also receive regular training.

The staff are paid quite low wages, in line with their modest qualifications, and the priests at the circles and in head office work on an honorary basis. The assistant directors are entitled to an expense allowance according to the volume of business in their circles, and the director and his colleague have a small travelling allowance. This means that the running costs of the society are very low, in relation to the amount of business transacted. The society is also subsidized quite heavily, through the unpaid assistance in kind it receives from the Catholic Church such as management, premises and transport.

The head office and housing for staff are provided rent-free by the Arch-diocese of Ranchi, and the stipends of the priests who manage the society are also paid for by the diocese. The society has only to pay their routine expenses and the cost of basic facilities, such as water, electricity and maintenance. At the circle level, the *munshis* are paid by the society, but their facilities, as well as the cost of the local priest, are paid for from parish funds.

The society does rent temporary seasonal storage space for its stocks of fertilizers, but these costs are quite modest, and very little capital is sunk in buildings and their upkeep.

From an organizational point of view, the society has changed very little since it was established. A few minor changes were made in the earlier years, and in 1943 the society adopted a formal set of objectives as follows:

• To unite the Catholic aborigines of Chotanagpur in one cooperative society with a view to provide them with financial assistance for their material uplift.

• To encourage thrift among the Catholic aborigines by placing within their easy reach a bank wherein to deposit their savings.

• To impart to them moral and economic training enabling them to manage their own financial business.

Since 1943 no further changes have been officially registered with the government registrar of cooperative societies. This was because the system had stood the test of time and operated reasonably well, and also because management knew that if further important changes were introduced it would draw attention to the society and might lead the government to demand changes which the members might not like, such as the division of the society into smaller units or opening the membership to non-Catholics.

One other change has been the acceptance of a permanent managerial role for the church. It was originally stated that the clergy would assist for the first 15 years, and that the society would then be broken into smaller self-managed local institutions, but this deadline was dropped and it was accepted that the interests of the society, and perhaps also of the Catholic Church, would be best served if the relationship was permanent.

The members, most of whom are men, nevertheless feel themselves to be the real owners of the society. The clergy only help them with management, and the director and his assistants at the circles are not allowed to be members themselves. The members are very much aware that they are the owners of the society. In some of the more active parishes it is very clear from the way it functions that it is owned by the members and not by the clergy. They accept and indeed welcome the clergy's management role, and in spite of the rather tight control exercised by the Church, the people right from the beginning called the society *hamlogon ka bank* [our Bank], rather than 'the Fathers' bank'. All the money deposited remains in the ultimate control of the members, and not the moneylenders, and they can also borrow money when they need it at much lower rates than from moneylenders.

During the 97 years from 1909 to 2006 Catholic Bank grew fairly steadily in financial terms, and by 2006 there were some 66,000 members, with a total savings balances of Rs 445 million ($10 million). The share capital and accumulated profits of the institution amounted to a further Rs.112 million, so that the total funds of the society amounted to $12 million. The following very simplified figures show the approximate financial position in 2006, and the earnings and expenses for a full year.

Approximate rounded accounts for Catholic Bank (CCCS), Ranchi:

Balance Sheet as at 31.03.2006

Assets

Cash	Rs.10.4 million
Fixed deposits	Rs.499 million
Savings account	Rs.18.9 million
Fixed assets	Rs.30,000
Loans outstanding	Rs.28.4 million
Total	**Rs.557 million**

Liabilities

Members' savings	Rs.444.6 million
Share capital + surplus *	Rs.112.4 million
Total	**Rs.557 million**

Income and expenditure for the year ending 31.03.2006

Income

Interest on loans to members	Rs.1.2 million
Interest on savings and deposit accounts	Rs.28.1 million
Total income	Rs.29.3 million

Financial expenditure

Interest on members' shares	Rs.30,000
Interest on members' savings	Rs.24.2 million
Total	**Rs.24.23 million**
Gross 'spread'	Rs.5.07 million

Operating expenses

Director's honorarium	Rs.50,000
Parish level clerks' salaries	Rs.4.3 million
Transport and stationery	Rs.30,000
Administrative wages and salaries	Rs.20,000
Total	**Rs.4.85 million**
Net surplus	Rs.22,000

* = balancing figure

Note: the figures are given in rupees. This converts to US$ at the rate of Rs.1 million=$16,600.

These figures show one remarkable change that has occurred during the life of the institution, in addition, to its growth. Initially the main purpose was to provide loans, and the first members' savings were quite quickly lent out as loans. Now, the total of the outstanding loans is only about $500,000, whereas the total of members' savings is about 20 times this amount. The society has to deposit these unused funds with other banks, and very little of the members' money is being invested in the local economy.

There are a number of reasons for this. The economic condition of the tribal people is still not good, but it has greatly improved since the time the society was set up, and most families have at least one member who is employed in Ranchi or elsewhere. The tribal people are generally risk averse, and they prefer to be employed, even at very low wages, rather than to be self-employed. They are reluctant to become indebted, and even if one man does want to borrow he also finds it difficult to persuade three others to be his guarantors, as the society's rules require.

The procedure for taking a loan is also quite slow and complex. Prospective borrowers have to submit their loan applications to their units. If they are approved they are then passed to the circle for further scrutiny, and then to the head office. The application is then checked to ensure that the applicant is up-to-date with his compulsory monthly savings of Rs.10, and that the guarantors are similarly members in good standing. If these conditions are satisfied, the loan is automatically approved, unless it is for over Rs.10,000 ($200) in which case the director must sanction it.

The society has also generally succeeded in maintaining a high recovery rate, partly by restricting the availability of loans. If a unit fails to hold regular monthly meetings, no loans can be authorized to its members and some whole circles are debarred from taking loans because one member of one unit is in default on a loan of Rs.500 ($10). All the units under the parish of Noadih, for

---

Box 12.1 Raphael Kullu, a typical member

Raphael Kullu is typical of the members who do not want to take loans. He joined the society in 1980 and has been saving regularly since that time. His father Paulus Kullu was a member before him. In May 2007 Raphael had a balance of just over Rs.1,000 ($20) in his account, and he withdraws money as and when he needs it. His son has a government job in the city and sends money regularly to his parents, and Raphael lives quite comfortably from this and the crops he grows on his small plot of land.

He likes doing business with the society, which he calls the 'Catholic Bank'. It is easy to deposit and withdraw money, he trusts the society's staff and management because they are his own people, and he feels his money is safe because the church stands behind it. Every member can vote on decisions such as admitting new members, and sanctioning or recovering loans, and the society helps to maintain the unity and cooperation of the community as a whole.

Raphael would be happy if the society could help to find new ways for the community to grow, economically, culturally and educationally, but he is not sure how this could be done and is generally very satisfied with the service he receives.

Box 12.2 Thomas Beck, a regular borrower

Thomas Beck has been a member of the society since 1970, and has taken four loans during that time. One was to pay for improving and fertilizing his land, one to buy a pair of bullocks, one to help with the cost of his brother's marriage and one for an irrigation pump. In May 2007 he had a balance of Rs.1800 ($36) in his savings account, and still owed Rs.4,000 on his most recent loan. Thomas also buys fertilizer from the society; he finds it cheaper and more convenient to buy it there than from any other source, and he can also buy it on credit if he needs to.

In general, Thomas is very pleased with the service he receives. He can get loans quite quickly if he needs them, and the 5% interest charge is much lower than is available elsewhere. He also receives 4% interest on his savings, which is as good as he could get from a bank; it is much easier to make deposits and withdrawals, and it would be very difficult to get a loan from a bank. The terms are also very reasonable. Loans of $10,000 or more can be repaid over a period of up to five years; smaller loans have to be repaid within a year.

Thomas has also found that members of the society cooperate with one another in times of difficulty, for their own good and also for the good of society as a whole, and he is grateful for the help that the society gives to help pay the salaries for private school teachers in the poorer villages which do not have good government schools.

He would like the society to offer training to its members in topics such as better farming, health and sanitation, and he wishes that it would also be able to do something about the low prices which the members get for their crops. Otherwise, he is generally content.

---

instance, were debarred from loans for 15 years, but these defaults have recently been cleared, and the members are saving and borrowing once more.

Loan recoveries are generally left to the units and their members, and they generally take this seriously since badly performing units are debarred from further borrowing until any arrears are cleared. The society does not as a matter of policy take defaulters to court, since this involves confiscation of people's houses and their arrest. The members usually use 'camping' as a last resort, which generally succeeds except when the defaulter is a powerful local figure and can resist it. Twenty or so members of the central committee go to the house of the defaulter as 'guests' and demand food and drink. They eat and drink their fill and tell the defaulter that if he fails to return the loan they will come back again. They continue this process until the defaults are paid up.

There have been relatively few problems with defaults. At the end of 2006, only Rs.800,000 worth of instalments were overdue out of a total of Rs.28 million outstanding. This figure of under 3 per cent defaults is immeasurably better than the experience of the banks in the area, and is similar to the achievement of the more 'modern' microfinance institutions which have been started elsewhere, such as SKDRDP. Most members use the society as a savings bank, a safe, convenient and modestly remunerative place to keep and when necessary withdraw their own money.

The society did run into some difficulties during the 1950s. Large numbers of members were at that time migrating to Ranchi town for work, and the society gave them loans against the security of their family land, which could actually not be sold. The society suffered a liquidity crisis, and this was burned into its institutional memory so that loans are still only granted with some reluctance.

A significant proportion of the 66,000 members' accounts are 'dormant', because the member has failed for five years to make his monthly Rs.10 savings contribution. Such members can be reinstated if they show their passbook and make a single Rs.120 ($2.40) deposit. Some of the dormant account holders are content to leave their savings balances untouched for years at a stretch, confident that they can if they wish withdraw their money at a moment's notice, and others have moved away or died, leaving their shares and possibly some savings unclaimed. The dormant membership further limits the number of borrowers.

Given the large number of quite widely scattered rural units and circles, it is not surprising that their performance is mixed. A small number may be more or less closed down because of poor repayments, but larger numbers are relatively inactive.

Social and economic inequity has led to problems in some circles since the more affluent members have defaulted and the poorer members, along with the *munshis* who are also poor, are unable to influence their behaviour. The Noadih and Patrachauli circles were closed for many years, and in Patrachauli three-quarters of the loan balances had eventually to be written off in order to allow the society's operations to restart there. Two members there had taken large loans and they refused to repay; they had become fairly well-off, partly with the help of their loans, and although they could easily have repaid they refused, being confident that their relative wealth and status would protect them from their poorer fellow-members.

There have also been a few cases of theft by dishonest *munshis*, since many parish priests lack the skills needed to supervise them, and the society's control systems rely on manual methods with no computers or modern accounting methods. The most important determinant factor, however, is the enthusiasm and interest of the priest who is in change of each circle. Traditionally, as in the church itself, the priest has been responsible for all the religious and the socio-economic development work in his parish. If he was interested and innovative, progress was possible.

Attempts have therefore been made to help the parish priests take a holistic pastoral approach, which involves the spiritual care of the parishioners and their overall socio-economic development and empowerment. It is made clear both to the priests and to their parishioners that both must play a role in the functioning of the society in the parish. The parish priest is its coordinator, and the parishioners are its members and implementing partners. In circles where this has been successful, the members have begun to follow the rules when they save and borrow, the money generated through savings is invested in improved farming and other social needs, and the circle grows accordingly. The success or failure of the society depends on whether the parish priest plays his role as its coordinator at the parish level.

There are other problems. Only Catholics are allowed to be members. This has reinforced the unity and strength of the society, but it discriminates against other churches and non-Christian tribals. It also limits the numbers of potential members, particularly in parishes where there are few Catholics. The rule is however regarded by the leadership as being both strategic and practical. The society's structure is closely linked to that of the Catholic Church in the area, from the level of the bishop down to each priest and village, and the membership rule did not imply that the early missionaries, particularly Hoffmann, were unconcerned about the non-Christian tribals. His main concern was for the Chotanagpur tribals, over 95 per cent of whom are Catholics. In a few urban circles such as Doranda some non-tribal Catholics are members, but they are very few in number and play no part in the governance of the society.

The society has given the tribal Catholics a sense of pride, unity, achievement and belonging. In many rural areas large numbers of people come to mass in order to attend the monthly meeting of the society. Both their spiritual and their material needs are satisfied together. In 21st century India the tribals are still marginalized, and government attempts to remedy this by reserving certain proportions of jobs and place in educational institutions for tribals, along with a whole range of other concessions. The oppression of 3,000 years cannot be corrected overnight. The society's working methods, particularly at the unit level, are also designed to fit traditional tribal customs such as avoiding confrontation and working for consensus.

One of the strengths of the society is that its members are a fairly homogeneous group of people, bound together by a common culture, which is reinforced by the fact that they are all Roman Catholics. The restricted membership may seem discriminatory, but the security which the members contribute, and the force that ties the members together, is not money but the unity of the members in a group.

The membership restriction was discussed several times during the first 30 years of the society's existence, but every time a proposal for change was put to the vote it was turned down almost unanimously. The priests were not against the idea, and several were in favour of change, but the ordinary members would not hear of it. One reason for the society's survival has undoubtedly been the strong bond of a common religion, and role and authority of the clergy who are managers and also spiritual leaders. Had the priests been withdrawn, as would have been necessary if the society had broken its links with the church, the society would probably have collapsed long since, as have the societies which were opened by two other Christian churches in Ranchi, which were open to all. The Catholic tribals would have found it difficult or impossible to manage the bank on their own in 1909, and it would today be very difficult to change. The restricted membership and the contribution of the priests go hand-in-hand. The society has failed in parishes where community life has been weak, and where individualism and lack of transparency have taken over from openness and unity. Where the church is vibrant and works well, so too does the society.

In the context of tribal culture, it is only the moral pressure of the local elders, or *jor-julum* as the members call it, backed by the authority of the local priest, which compels the members to pay back their loans. This *jor-julum* would not have a hold on non-converted tribals or on Christian tribals belonging to other Churches, let alone the non-tribals.

The society brought with it a sense of belonging to the larger unit of the Catholic Church. To the often deeply religious tribals, the society was an establishment of the kingdom of God. It demonstrated the further possibilities of spreading the kingdom through overall development rather than conversion.

When Fr Hoffmann attended a conference on cooperatives at Calcutta in 1911, other participants asked how he had managed to avoid taking money from government and to raise the necessary share capital and savings from the Chotanagpur tribals when so many other cooperatives had failed even with much better-off and more developed communities. A Bengali lawyer is said to have remarked, 'We will never get such results, this requires an organization as only the Jesuits have'. Hoffmann's plan effectively integrated the tribal people's traditions with their Catholic faith and the society has survived for 100 years as a result.

The Holy Cross Social Service Centre, Hazaribag

'The need of the time is the will of God' is the motto of the Sisters of Mercy of the Holy Cross, which was founded in Switzerland in 1856 by Fr Theodosius Florentini, a Capuchin priest, along with Mother Theresa Scherer. The founders recognized the will of God in the needs of the people. With a clear vision to fulfil the will of God, they started the congregation of Holy Cross Sisters to respond to the needs of the poor and the neglected. Education and health care were the most pressing needs at that time, and the Sisters started work in these two fields.

Even from its earliest days, they tried to alleviate poverty through the involvement of the sisters not only in and around Europe, but in other continents as well. As Fr. Theodosius said, 'I wanted to organize this congregation in such a way that it fits in everywhere, finds acceptance everywhere and is able to integrate itself into any condition and situation' (www.holycrosssisters.org).

Cheerful willingness to put up with all types of difficulty has been a hallmark of the Holy Cross Sisters from the very beginning. Mother Theresa Scherer was never afraid to take risks if the need arose, and she guided the congregation for 31 years as its mother general and co-founder. Her main concern throughout was to build up groups of Sisters so that they could reach out to people in need, wherever they were. She said, 'We hurry to wherever human need calls us to be' (Dom Antoine Marie, 2005).

In the 150 years since its establishment, the Congregation of Sisters of Mercy of the Holy Cross has spread its work into 15 countries. In 2006 there are over 4,000 Sisters, living in 450 convents across the world.

Four Holy Cross Sisters arrived in India in 1894 as missionaries. They started work in north Bihar, then, as it still is, one of the poorest regions of the country. Three of the four Sisters died in a cholera epidemic while they were nursing the poor and taking care of children who had been orphaned by the epidemic. Two years later five more Sisters joined the survivor, and they established Holy Cross outposts not only in Bihar but also in Jharkhand, west Bengal, Madhya Pradesh, Chhattisgarh and several states in southern India.

The Sisters started their work in India in government hospitals in Bihar and Jharkhand, even as they do today. They also established girls' schools. As the years went by and it became clear that there was a continuing demand for committed development workers in India, they decided in 1952 to admit Indian girls to the congregation. By 1955 the first seven candidates from India had been trained and had taken their first vows as Holy Cross Sisters. By 2006 there are nearly 1,000 Indian Sisters, working in 17 different states, with their regional headquarters in Bangalore in the south and in Patna and Hazaribag in the north. The latter are located in two of the poorest states in India, where many NGOs, microfinance institutions and other development agencies have no presence. Only seven foreign Sisters remain in 2007, all of whom are in their seventies.

The Holy Cross Institute of Hazaribag was set up as a religious society and voluntary organization, to work in education, health and social work. The activities of the Sisters include nursing schools and colleges, hospitals, dispensaries, mobile health projects and health awareness programmes. They also run old age homes, orphanages and asylums for destitute women and for HIV/AIDS patients.

A governing body, which includes nine Sisters, administers the institute and its work is divided into 15 functional units. The Holy Cross Social Service Centre (HCSSC) is one of these units, and was established by Sister Rosily in 1982 to work in some of the most remote and indeed dangerous parts of what used to be Bihar including Hazaribag, Ranchi, Chatra and Giridih districts. Since that time its activities have also been extended to the states of Madhya Pradesh, Orissa and Chhattisgarh. HCSCC is administered by a managing committee of seven members, which includes two members of its staff and Sister Rosily, the executive director.

The vision of HCSSC is to work towards an equitable, peaceful, just and value-based society, free from any discrimination based on economic status, gender, caste or religion. The institution has always worked for the development of poor and marginalized people, irrespective of their caste and religion, and with special emphasis on women. Its mission is to organize and empower marginalized people, through initiatives which enable them to manage their own economic, social, educational and political affairs in an ethical and sustainable manner.

Sister Rosily came to Hazaribag from the state of Kerala in southern India in 1971 and joined as a candidate at Holy Cross Institute. After seven years of intensive training, she took her first vows as a Holy Cross Sister in 1978. She worked as a science teacher for two years, before joining the Xavier Institute of Social Service at Ranchi, where she studied for a postgraduate diploma in management. After her management studies she was appointed as course director of the rural development department of Holy Cross Vocational Training Institute in Hazaribag. She set up HCSSC in 1982, and has been managing both for 25 years.

Sister Rosily set up the Social Service Centre in order to reach out to the poorest villages in the region, following the precepts of the congregation to go to wherever there was a need. The religion of the people played no part in the choice of villages to work in. What mattered was their need for development, irrespective of their religious faith.

In the initial years, HCSSC worked in just nine villages in Hazaribag district. They focused on the problems of the lower caste *Harijans*, such as untouchability, illiteracy, and ill health. The *Harijans* were also oppressed by the landowners and moneylenders, who kept them in bondage for many years, or even over generations, when they failed to repay even quite small loans which they had taken for emergencies. The HCSSC team worked with the *Harijans* on primary education, health, farm development and income generation.

Sister Rosily recalls that when they started work in 1982 many of the men and the women were drunk, even during the day. They had innumerable meetings, and campaigned against the preparation, sale and drinking of alcohol. After two or three years of constant effort all the women stopped drinking altogether, and only a very small number of men still drink during the day, apart from occasional feasts.

In the early days 28 bonded labourers were released from the first two villages where HCSSC started working by paying off their debts, and they helped them to rebuild their livelihoods by levelling and irrigating the sloping and barren government land they had been given. The HCSSC team provided improved health and sanitation services, and they started a nursery school and a primary school. In addition to drunkenness and bondage, they had to struggle against illiteracy and threats from the landlords who were losing their free labour, their market for alcohol and their general influence, and there were also many legal challenges to the people's land ownership.

The situation in the villages where HCSSC started work in 1982 is now completely transformed. The economic situation has improved, the houses and the peoples' lifestyles have changed, the children are going to school, the villagers have become conscious of their rights and their duties, and the women have been empowered. Untouchability has more or less disappeared, along with the general sense of powerlessness and helplessness, and these villages have become a model for the other communities where the organization is working.

HCSSC focused during its first three years mainly on free welfare services, but Sister Rosily and her team soon came to see that this was a mistake since the people became dependent on them for all their needs. They changed their policy and decided to work with, rather than for, the people, and to treat them as partners in development rather than as beneficiaries.

Between 1985 and 1989 Holy Cross expanded its work to 50 villages which were mainly inhabited by the *Santhals*, a severely marginalized tribal community. They 'adopted' the tribal villages and worked with the people in health, education, irrigation management, agriculture and income generation.

HCSSC also linked a few villagers to the Development of Women and Children in Rural Areas (DWCRA) programme, a government-sponsored initiative which encourages group economic activities for poor women. The tribal women were trained in various income-generation activities such as jute handicrafts, soap making, weaving, leaf plate making, mulberry cultivation, silk rearing and reeling, bamboo products and block printing. They were generally unsuccessful because of the difficulties in buying raw materials and marketing the products, and because of the interpersonal problems which arise in most group businesses.

Their work with small farmers was more successful. They worked in irrigation, input supply and improved farming practices, and many marginal farmers significantly improved the productivity of their land. The benefits of this did not reach the poor, however, since they owned no land and worked only as sharecroppers and bonded labourers. The landowners and moneylenders captured all the benefits.

Sister Rosily and her team felt that the best way to address these deep-rooted problems was through the women, by organizing them into self-help groups for saving, credit and social empowerment. The women's husbands strongly resisted this at first, but the fieldworkers persisted. Eventually the women mustered the support and cooperation of their husbands and other household members and started to set up effective self-help groups. During this period, the HCSSC team shifted from welfare to self help, and from a family-centred to a group-centred approach. They also realized the vital importance of working with women.

When it became clear how the self-help groups could both empower their members and help them financially, the team started to form groups more rapidly. They started in 1993 with 47 groups in about the same number of villages, and by the end of 2006 there were over 2,000 groups, in some 550 villages, with 34,000 members. The members of the original groups became the leaders of the movement, and they worked with Holy Cross to motivate their neighbours to form groups of their own.

By 1995 some of the members of the groups wanted to take larger loans than the groups' own savings would allow, and the HCSSC team started actively to assist them to get bank loans. This enabled the members to get bigger loans from their groups and to redeem the land they had pledged to the moneylenders. They both regained their land and stopped having to pay interest charges of as much as 10 per cent a month. By the end of December 2006, 1,500 groups had borrowed a cumulative total of Rs.55 million from banks (rather more than $1 million).

Box 12.3 Sobhani Devi and her handful of rice

Sobhani Devi lived in Danto Khurd village in Hazaribag. Her family owned a small hut on one-tenth of an acre of unirrigated land. Her husband was an alcoholic and could not work. Their six sons had never been to school, and the family survived from their earnings as casual labourers, when they found work. They also made a little extra money by collecting and selling firewood from the nearby forest. The family had no other income.

Fifteen of Sobhani's neighbours had come together and formed a self-help group with assistance from the Holy Cross Sisters. There were 10 Catholics, two Muslims, two harijan untouchables and one upper caste women in the group, but they were all poor. They held their meetings every Sunday and saved Rs.5 ($0.10) a week each.

Sobhani was keen to join the group. She wanted to learn to save every week so that her family would have some money in case of an emergency. But she did not dare to ask the group members if she could join, because she was afraid that she might not be able to save even Rs.5 every month.

She was desperate to join the group, however, and she discussed her problem with the parish priest. He advised her to start by saving just a small handful of rice whenever she was cooking food for her family. She could sell the accumulated rice for Rs.5 every week, and have enough money for her contribution to the group. She started at once, and soon asked the group to accept her as a member. They were impressed by her willingness to save in this way, and they accepted her as the 16th member of their group. She has been able to save regularly ever since, and she has taken a number of small loans which have helped her family to improve their condition and to start small income-generating activities.

As a result of their success with women's self-help groups, HCSSC ensured that women's groups participated fully in all their development initiatives. They then moved on to federations. These groups of groups were able to address broader issues, such as struggling for their rights under government programmes, of which they were so often deprived. The Sisters became fully convinced that the self-help group is the best platform on which to base development work for the poor in rural areas. They found that very poor and illiterate women from very backward regions are able with some guidance to manage their finances very successfully.

Self-help group promotion is the flagship of HCSSC, and occupies about half of the institution's staff time. The rest of their time is devoted to assistance for farming, for watershed development, for education and health, and for non-farm income generation activities. The general public and the government have come to perceive Holy Cross as a competent development organization. They are of course fully aware of its religious background, from its name, and indeed even from the very distinctive nuns habits. But its work is wholly secular, it has no official association with local churches, and the people for whom it works come from all religious backgrounds.

The state officials and political parties in Bihar have always been very sensitive to any suggestion that Christian institutions are involved on conversions, or to any implication that poor people are attracted to a particular religion because

---

Box 12.4 Parvati and her mortgaged land

Laskari is a tribal hamlet in Hazaribag district, 70 km from the nearest town. Over the years, many local tribal families took loans from moneylenders, and failed to repay. They had mortgaged their land as security, so the landowners took possession and employed the previous owners as labourers to work on what used to be their own land.

Parvati Hansda was a typical case. She borrowed Rs.1,200 ($24) in 1985 from a moneylender, at 10% interest a month. She was quite unable to repay, since the interest alone amounted to Rs.1440 a year, so she mortgaged her family's three acre plot to the moneylender. She and her family then had to work in what had been their own field as sharecroppers; the moneylender took half the crops in lieu of interest, and this went on for 10 years.

In 1992 the HCSSC helped Parvati and six other women to start a self-help group. Soon seven more women joined them. In 1994 the group borrowed Rs.10,000 from the local branch of Bank of India. They used most of the money to clear loans they had taken from moneylenders. Parvati borrowed Rs.1,800; she paid off the principle of her loan with Rs.1,200, and had to pay another Rs.600 as a fee to release her land.

After recovering the land, the family was much better off. They dug a well and installed an irrigation pump so that they could grow paddy, wheat and vegetables. They bought two bullocks, five goats and a few hens. Her son was able to stay in school up to intermediate level, and he got a job as a teacher in the village. His wife works as an assistant to the government village level worker. Her granddaughter is in the sixth year of primary school.

Parvati has dreams for the future. She wants her daughter-in-law to study further and to become a teacher like her son. She wants her grandchildren to go to good schools. She wants to marry her three daughters into good families. She wants to buy two more acres of land to grow vegetables for sale. And she wants to build a better house.

Eight other women from Parvati's group have done as she has, and the whole group are transformed. They are confident for themselves and for their children, and they want to educate their children, so that they do not fall prey to the moneylenders as their parents did.

---

they have the impression that they will receive favourable treatment if they are of the same religion. Some Christian missionaries, and development workers also, have been expelled from Bihar because of such allegations, but HCSSC has never faced criticism of this kind.

Bihar, and the recently created state of Jharkhand, are two of the poorest states of India. In spite of their great mineral wealth and their fertile land, the area has for many years been known for its corrupt politicians and general lawlessness. The large population of tribal people is particularly affected by this. State government agencies find it very difficult to implement the many very generous programmes which are available from the central government, because much of the money 'leaks'. There are many such programmes which are designed specifically for the tribal people since there is a major national commitment to improve their position, along with that 'scheduled castes' or 'untouchables'.

Self-help groups have been identified throughout India as effective channels for delivering development assistance. Although the people of Bihar and

Jharkhand need such groups and the assistance they can bring, the two states have lagged behind other parts of India in the numbers of groups formed or linked to banks. Holy Cross has become well-known as an effective promoter of such groups, and many state government departments have requested them to implement various projects. Offers of this kind have poured in from government departments from almost all the districts of Bihar and Jharkhand, but the HCSSC team refused to move beyond Hazaribag and Ranchi districts because there was so much to be done near to home.

Similarly, many international funding agencies have approached Holy Cross with offers of funding. These too have been declined, apart from the ongoing support for establishment costs from the Swiss Development Co-operation, which was provided for 12 years from 1982 to 1994, and later from Cordaid, the Netherlands-based Catholic voluntary agency. In 2006, 87 per cent of the institution's total funding of about $160,000 came from Cordaid. The balance was from Indian government programmes such as support from the National Bank for Agriculture and Rural Development (NABARD), the initiator and promoter of the self-help group bank linkage movement, which paid for SKDRDP's training programmes for leaders of SHGs. This support is offered on a standard basis to any group promotion agencies. Holy Cross works in partnership with 16 small local NGOs, of which four are Christian and the rest are secular.

HCSSC has never considered development work as charity. Since its inception, the team have involved the people in the planning and execution of projects. They are deeply concerned about the sustainability of the projects which they have implemented, since so many similar activities fail to survive once the promotion agency has left the scene. In all their farm development projects, the HCSSC team insist that the farmers contribute their labour and thus cover at least a fifth of the cost. Even when the state government provides all the money required, HCSSC insists that the farmers should contribute at least 10 per cent of the cost, and this is kept to cover future maintenance costs.

The members of the self-help groups which Holy Cross promotes have to pay Rs.2-4 ($0.05) a month each into their group fund, in addition to whatever weekly savings they make, in order to meet the administrative cost of the group. This is very unusual in India, but the Holy Cross Sisters believe very strongly that people should take responsibility for their own future. The Sisters are not concerned in the same way about the future of their own institution, since they believe that God will provide for them and in any case they hope that their own work will not be permanently needed in any given location. Holy Cross does not collect any fees from the group members to cover its own costs.

The Sisters believe in handing over projects to communities as soon as possible. All the farmers who benefit from their water management and watershed development projects are organized into user groups. The self-help groups are federated into clusters and federations for the same purpose, and all the groups which have been in existence for more than six or seven years are managed by the members themselves, with occasional advice and monitoring by Holy Cross.

Box 12.5 Learning from bitter experience

Some self-help groups employ literate local youths to maintain the records of their meetings and the books of accounts. They usually pay them Rs.20-30 a month for this, out of the small contributions which Holy Cross advises them to make in addition to the regular savings. In most cases this works very well.

On some occasions it does not. Holy Cross audits its groups' accounts from time to time, and they discovered some cases where the groups' records did not tally with those of the bank where they had their account. One group in Ragania hamlet had appointed a young man who was the son of one of their members to keep their books for them. The group met every month, and he was paid Rs.30 ($0.60) per meeting for the work.

The group leaders were meant to take turns to carry each month's savings and loan repayments to the local bank branch 5 km away from their village, but they used to ask the boy to take it for them instead. Once in 2003 they collected Rs.30,000; they gave the cash to the boy to take to the bank as usual, but he disappeared with the money and never returned. The group members tried to get back the money through his mother, who was also a member, and it took her almost two years to pay it back.

All the groups were told about this incident, and they realized that they had to take responsibility for their own money and that it was wrong to put temptation in anybody's way. The Ragania group blamed themselves, not the young man or his mother.

HCSSC pioneered the formation of self-help groups in Bihar and Jharkhand. The Sisters believe that these groups are the most effective way to empower women, and that clusters and federations of the groups can be an extremely powerful platform for the execution of any development activity, even one which does not traditionally involve women. If women are involved in any project of any kind, such as watershed development or horticulture, the work can be completed more smoothly and sustainably.

There have been some failures. Between 1988 and 1994 HCSSC was involved in a state government-sponsored project to cultivate mulberry trees for feeding silk worms, with a group of very poor lower caste and tribal people, who between them owned about 15 acres of land. It was very difficult to persuade the farmers to grow mulberry since they knew nothing of it, the land was of poor quality, and there was no water for irrigation. The Holy Cross staff and the farmers worked together to build ponds and wells, and they fenced the fields and planted the mulberry seedlings. They were also able to breed silk worms and for two years they produced a small amount of silk cocoons. It then proved impossible to find a good market for the cocoons, and the project was ultimately abandoned.

Holy Cross's work has also involved struggles for women's legal and personal rights, as well as for their economic improvement. Sister Rosily recalls an incident in Barkatha village in 2002 when a low caste woman was raped, and her mother and father-in-law were severely beaten up. The other people of the same caste complained and tried to bring the culprits to justice, but the landlord's friends tied up the two women along with their 4 year old child, and forced them to walk up and down the village street for two or three hours as a punishment for daring to protest.

The victims were not members of a self-help group, but the Sisters called together the nearby women's group federation to discuss what could be done. They decided to condemn the incident, to fight for their rights, and to arrest the culprits. They took the women and some press reporters to the victim's village, and gathered some information about the incident. They then met the victims, who had fled to another village to take refuge with their relatives.

All the federation's group members informed their colleagues, and four days later 5,000–6,000 group members and others marched down the main road of the local administrative headquarters town with black ribbons pinned on their shoulders. The whole crowd ended up in the government office compound, and they stood in dead silence with tears running down their cheeks as the victims spoke about what had happened. The federation leaders said that they and the other women would not tolerate any such incidents in their areas, and they submitted a memorandum of complaint to the chief minister of the state and to the Human Rights Commission.

The Human Rights Commission and the police department took action. The culprits were arrested and the victim's family was given some compensation. This incident was widely publicized and made everyone realize how strong the women could be if they took up a cause together. Since that time, there have been no further incidents of this kind.

There are 70 people working for the Holy Cross Social Service Centre in total, including 12 volunteers. Of these 23 are women, including many of the fieldworkers. This is very unusual in Indian NGOs, even for those working mainly with women's groups. The fieldworkers are nearly all tribal or lower caste people, and the middle-level and senior staff are a mix of Hindus and Christians. There are 34 Christians altogether, of whom two are Protestants and the rest are Roman Catholics. There are 31 Hindus and five Sarna staff (see below). They are all Indian, and no foreigners are employed, even as volunteers. Sister Rosily is the only nun; all the other staff are lay people. Trainee nuns sometimes work with HCSSC for short periods as part of their training.

Holy Cross does not have any preference for its staff to be members of a particular religion, but they are all religious people, and believe in the divine purpose of God in some way. They have to be deeply committed to serve the poor, and the nature of the work is such that those who do not share the same level of commitment are unlikely to apply, or to join. The organization is very informal. The staff are paid higher salaries than they might expect with other NGOs doing similar work, and they have many opportunities for training, and to learn on the job. As a result of all this, the rate of staff turnover is very low.

About 50 per cent of the people who live in the areas served by Holy Cross are Hindus. Another 30 per cent are Sarnas. This is a traditional monotheistic faith, closely linked to the tribe and its area, with a benevolent God, sometimes called Singbonga. One major emphasis of the Sarna faith is the preservation of tribal identity by the prevention of marriage with outsiders. There are some similarities between Christianity and the Sarna faith, which have been used by missionaries in the past as a basis for conversion, and are thus strongly resisted by Hindu fundamentalists. In February 2007 this culminated in a demonstration in which effigies of the Archbishop of Ranchi Cardinal Toppo, the first tribal cardinal and one of only five Indian cardinals, were burned because, it was claimed, he had attempted to prevent tribal people from stating their religion on the certificate of their tribal identify, which entitles them to various benefits. The majority of the rest of the people are Muslims, and only about 3 per cent are Christian.

The Sisters make no attempt to influence the religious beliefs of their clients. They choose remote poor areas for their work, irrespective of the religious faith of the inhabitants. Their clients are all poor families, who are generally farm labourers or marginal farmers. The only bias of Holy Cross is towards the untouchables and tribals.

In the early 1980s, when the Sisters started working with the rural people of Hazaribag district, there was some apprehension that the institution might be planning secretly to convert them to Christianity. It soon became clear, however, that the Sisters were only interested in development and in encouraging the people to participate and cooperate with one another. They obviously had no interest in changing their religious faith. Since 1982, there has not been a single case of change of religious faith among any of the people they work with. The people have perhaps strengthened their faith in whatever religion they belong to, and have become more religious in general, because of their association with Holy Cross, but they have not become Christians.

Catholic Bank and Holy Cross – some comparisons

These two institutions have many common features. Both are Roman Catholic, both operate in the same part of India, with marginalized tribal people, and both groups of missionaries came to Bihar at about the same time. The Jesuit priests who now manage Catholic Bank are at pains to point out that it is not a 'development project' in the modern sense, but it was started by foreigners, not for their profit but in order to improve the economic position of the tribals and it is still indirectly subsidized by the church. It is unlikely that many of the not dissimilar institutions that are being established nowadays by government, or by faith-based or secular NGOs, will survive as long, whether subsidized or not.

There are, however, many important differences, which may explain the very different ways in which the two institutions have evolved and are now operating. First, and most obviously, Catholic Bank is heavily male-dominated; it was started by a remarkable visionary man, for tribal men, and most of its members and all its staff, whether they are priests or lay employees, are still men. Holy Cross is a female order and its 'social entrepreneur' Sister Rosily is a woman, like most of its staff. Nearly all of its self-help group members are women.

Catholic Bank is probably the only faith-based institution which we have examined whose members must be adherents of the same faith. The people who are served by some others, such as the SKDRDP itself, are mainly of the same religion because most of the population of the area covered by the institution are of that faith, but the management and staff of the institutions are very anxious to serve people of other faiths. Holy Cross serves mainly non-Catholics because they are the people who need its services, and its staff are more or less 'faith-blind'; they often do not even know the religion of the people whom they are serving.

Catholic Bank works through and is very dependent on the village priests and the parish system, and its head office is staffed by and located within the 'apex' of the diocesan structure. It is almost a part of the church itself. Holy Cross, on the other hand, has no direct links to the local parishes or their priests; the sisters work directly with the people. They also support and work with government programmes, such as the self-help group linkage movement. Catholic Bank remains strictly separate, in its staffing, its operations and its membership.

Catholic Bank appears to be male-dominated, narrow, closed, hierarchical, self-protective and old-fashioned, like some of the more traditional aspects of the Roman Catholic faith itself, but, like Catholicism, it is also durable and reliable. The Holy Cross Sisters work flexibly with the mainstream of society, and they attempt to address all the problems which afflict their clients. They are not concerned with the survival of their institution itself, as something separate from the well-being of their clients. The Sisters hope that the self-help groups which they have promoted will be genuinely sustainable without continuing assistance, and that their members will become independent of Holy Cross and will themselves maintain and enhance their social and economic progress. Only time will tell whether these achievements will survive as long as Catholic Bank.

References

Allen, H. (2006) 'Village Savings and Loans Associations – sustainable and cost-effective rural finance', *Small Enterprise Development*, volume 17.

Dichter, T. (2006) *Hype and Hope, the worrisome state of the microcredit movement*, South African Institute of Economic Affairs, Cape Town.

Dicklitch, S. and Rice, H. (2004) 'The Mennonite Central Committee and faith-based NGO aid to Africa', *Development in Practice*, volume 14.

Fikkert, B. (2003) 'Christian Microfinance: Which way now ?', Working Paper 25, presented at the 20th anniversary conference of the Association of Christian Economists, Washington.

Hovland, I. (2005) *Who's afraid of religion?*, Proceedings of the Development Studies Association Conference, Development Studies Association, Milton Keynes.

Llanto, G. and Geron, M. P. (2000) *Can Christian Microfinance Institutions Pursue Kingdom Building Activities and Remain Viable?*, Centre for Community Transformation, Manila.

Mask, R. P. (2000) Christian Microenterprise development: Counting the cost and building the kingdom, Covenant College, Lookout Mountain, GA.

Microenterprise Best Practices (2001) *Finance following conflict*, brief number 3, MBP, Washington, DC.

Van den Bogaert M, (1960) *To Stand Together and to Sit Together: A case study of the Chotanagpur Catholic Cooperative Credit Society as a peasant organization for tribal farmers*, University of Ranchi, India.

CHAPTER 13
Conclusions

Abstract

Faith-based development institutions benefit from the continuity and tradition of the faiths to which they subscribe, even when few of their staff and perhaps none of the people whom they try to assist are of the same faith. Their network of co-religionists provides a network of solidarity which can be used for fund-raising and staff recruitment, as well as providing existing physical facilities in the field. This continuity in some sense replaces the charismatic leader who usually establishes NGOs, and whose succession is often a major problem. Hence, faith-based NGOs are not 'projects', they are permanent institutions, and are able to succeed even if they break many of the rules of best practice to which secular institutions adhere. Their staff are generally willing to work for lower salaries or even for nothing, and to commit themselves in a way that is very unusual in secular institutions. Faith-based institutions can use and build spiritual capital in addition to the more familiar forms of capital, and can thus achieve success in circumstances where other institutions might fail.

Some common features

We have examined a number of faith-based development institutions, in more or less detail. Our sample is small and in no way representative, but are there any common features which distinguish them from other secular development initiatives? What can similar agencies, faith-based or otherwise, learn from them?

First, and perhaps most important, none of the institutions are development 'projects'. They may carry out many of the same functions as such projects, and they are often funded by local or foreign development aid, but they have a continuity which goes beyond their immediate 'aims and objectives'. Their existence is based on more than a 'log frame' or a five-year plan. This has important affects on the vision and the day-to-day work of locally funded faith-based institutions as well as those which are partners of more recently arrived foreign institutions which share the same faith.

The churches, mosques, temples and the religions they represent have been familiar parts of every community for generations, and interventions which come through these local entities, or which are linked to them, can be accepted by the community more quickly and more easily than purely external initiatives. Even when the majority of the clients are of a different faith from that of the development institution, the religious basis of their work offers some element of permanence which goes beyond the transitory life of a project, which is defined by having 'a beginning, a middle and an end'. Institutions are designed to last, like religions themselves and as Catholic Bank and SKDRDP have lasted. Faith-based institutions can aspire to something more durable than 'sustainability', or perhaps a rather different form of it, and can share the permanence of the faiths which underpin them.

Most NGOs are established and managed by so-called 'charismatic leaders'. These are social entrepreneurs, people who have the vision and ability to set up new institutions, who are driven not by the desire to get rich but to 'do good', to achieve social goals in which their leaders passionately believe. These goals may be unpopular or unfamiliar, and the tasks involved in achieving them can be unpleasant and even dangerous. The problems of raising money, recruiting staff and managing operations are similar to those involved in building a commercial business, and there is a limited supply of people with the necessary skills and motivation.

These people can also be a liability. Like many business entrepreneurs, they are not always able to manage the institutions they have established once they grow beyond a certain size, and even if they are competent manager as well as initiators, it is difficult to find people to share the founders' vision and motivation and can take over when they leave.

This is less of a problem for faith-based institutions, even if it cannot wholly be avoided. They can share the permanence of their religion, and of its institutions. SKDRDP owes its origins to a 600-year-old temple, and even if Veerendra Heggade's successors do not share his talent or his enthusiasm for development the development arm of Dharmasthala is likely to maintain its work because of the continuity of the dynasty and its religious base. Father Hoffman's Catholic Bank has survived for almost 100 years, and it is remembered not by his name but by the name of the faith which inspired him and the church to which it effectively belongs. Sister Rosily is a classic social entrepreneur, but the institution she has built is not a memorial to her or to some general principles, but to the Holy Cross order and her faith.

Faith-based institutions can be deeply rooted in local communities, but none of the institutions which we have examined can genuinely be called 'community based' or 'people's institutions'. They were started by outsiders, or sometimes by a member of the local elite, not by 'the people', and certainly not by the same groups of people who benefit from their activities. There may be cases of faith-based cooperatives or other associations which have initiated development activities, but this appears to be an uncommon occurrence. Religions and their institutions are hierarchical by nature. Local churches, mosques and temples are led by pastors, imams or priests, who are themselves at the bottom of a complex hierarchy which is headed by senior members at a national or super-national level. There may be very clear direct lines of authority, as in the Roman Catholic Church, or the authority may be doctrinal rather than administrative, but local religious institutions are not community-based in the sense of local cooperatives. They are also a great deal longer-lasting.

This can be a weakness as well as a strength. The hierarchy can and often does maintain the position of a local priest or development worker even if he is quite out of sympathy with the local community, and development activities may be frustrated through lack of interest or distorted for religious reasons which have little to do with community realities. The initiators and leaders of the institutions we have examined have little or no personal experience of the poverty or other deprivation which they want to alleviate, and they can also be authoritarian or patronizing towards the poor. Effective secular development institutions usually aim to 'put themselves out of business' by empowering the people with whom they work so that they can take over the development activities themselves or will no longer have any need for them. The Holy Cross Sisters are the only example described in this book of a group which works towards this end.

Strengths and weaknesses

One of the main strengths of faith-based institutions is that they automatically belong to strong networks which transcend social and gender boundaries, and include their donors, their employees and their clients. A wealthy donor to World Vision, Catholic Relief Services or Islamic Relief in Europe or the USA, a local employee of a faith-based development agency in Asia or Africa, and the poverty-stricken clients of the agency, have little or nothing in common. If they are all members of the same religion, however, they can all say 'we are Christians' or 'we are Muslims'. This provides a common 'vertical' identity, even if it is not necessarily as strong as the 'horizontal' ties of community or family, and it can be a basis on which mutual trust and working relationships can be built. The staff of secular agencies can of course also build such relation-ships, but their counterparts in faith-based institutions have a 'flying start'.

We saw that the staff and chief executives of faith-based multinational 'BINGOs' are willing to work for rather lower salaries that those who work for secular institutions, but the spirit of voluntarism stretches much further. Akhuwat in Lahore is perhaps the best example of this, in that its funding is totally voluntary, its chief executive receives no financial remuneration, and many of its staff, particularly at the senior level, are also volunteers. Some of its clients have also become voluntary donors, thus completing the cycle of voluntarism.

The SKRD *sevanirathas* are well paid, but they are expected to devote themselves to their jobs so completely that their actual pay per working hour must be well below that of most of their contemporaries. Nuns and priests, such as the Holy Cross Sisters or the parish priests who manage the 'circles' of Catholic Bank, are supported by their churches or their religious orders, but they receive no salaries in the normal sense, and they in any case are bound by a vow of poverty that prevents them from accumulating any property of their own.

Volunteers are in many ways more difficult to manage than paid employees because their manager lacks the final sanction of dismissal which underlies all paid staff relationships even if it is rarely mentioned and even more rarely used.

They do nevertheless reduce costs, and if they are driven by religious conviction they may work even harder and for longer hours than those who are paid. The 'charity shop' fund-raising model that is used by so many faith-based development institutions, as well as secular ones, is fundamentally dependent on volunteer workers, and local faith-based institutions are able to extend their use of volunteers into their field operations.

The Akhuwat case again provides a good example of this, where some of the clients of the institution have also become its volunteers. They assist with debt collection to help the institution, not because they are guarantors of other group members' loans, since Akhuwat does not work through groups. And there are even cases where a successful client has himself become a donor of funds to the common pool. This is a 'double bottom line' at a personal level, and the shared faith makes it even more powerful.

All these features make it possible for faith-based development institutions to 'break the rules', to do things that others cannot do, and also to go where others are generally unwilling to go. Both Catholic Bank and the Holy Cross Sisters work in the tribal areas of what used to be Bihar. The new state of Jharkand has only recently been split off from it. This is by some measures India's poorest state, in spite of its mineral wealth. The area has a long tradition of violence and inter-caste conflict, and in spite of its poverty and obvious needs it has received less attention from development agencies than the more prosperous and less dangerous south and west of the country.

The self-help group microfinance programme, which plays a very important part in both SKDRDP's and the Holy Cross Sister's work, is an India-wide initiative but its outreach has been very limited in Bihar. A typical self-help group has between 10 and 20 members, but there were in 2004 over 2,500 officially poor people for every self-help group in Bihar, as opposed to the all-India average of 363 people, and 168 people in Karnataka where SKDRDP's work is concentrated (Harper and Nath, 2004). The Catholic Church has been working in Bihar for over 100 years, and this in itself breaks what is almost a rule for development institutions from overseas – to work mainly in the south of India.

'Sustainability', of a different kind

Akhuwat also breaks most of the rules of microfinance. It does not work through groups, it works with men as well as women, its interest rates are below local 'market' rates (even though loans at these rates are not generally available to people such as Akhuwat's clients), it charges even lower rates for the smallest loans and its basic philosophy is quite contrary to the goal of 'sustainability' towards which microfinance institutions are supposed to strive. Both its finance and its staffing are heavily dependent on charity, voluntarism or personal 'subsidy'. The well-known 'subsidy-dependence index' quantifies the extent to which institutions are dependent on non-market-based resources, and it is implied that large scale impact and long-term survival can only be achieved by eliminating such dependence.

When Akhuwat started, many people suggested that it would not last very long or reach large numbers unless it adopted more traditional commercial principles, like other microfinance institutions in Pakistan. It now reaches almost 20,000 people, with a $1 million portfolio, and its growth rate is similar to that of other more conventional development institutions. 'Sustainability' may have broader dimensions than the purely financial.

Not one of the faith-based institutions we have examined is in fact fully sustainable is a financial sense. It is planned that SKDRDP should cover its direct costs within a few years, but it is clearly planned that it should remain part of the family of institutions linked to Dharmasthala. Some aspects of its work such as the stipends to destitute families will continue to depend on the Dharmasthala Temple Trust and the Heggade dynasty, not only spiritually but also financially. The Holy Cross Sisters aim eventually to make themselves redundant with their present clients and to transfer their efforts to more needy people, but there is no intention that their social service organization should ever cover its costs from client fees.

This lack of sustainability, or of plans to achieve it, is perhaps the most remarkable common feature of all of these institutions, and others like them. If sustainability means survival, growth and continued productive work, then they have all reached it to a substantial degree. But if it means covering their costs from user or client fees, none of them have done so, or intend to.

This does not of course mean that their clients do not achieve sustainable livelihoods. Unlike many secular institutions which aim to retain their more successful clients and thus to earn profits from continuing to serve them, institutions such as Akhuwat and the Holy Cross wish genuinely to 'empower' their clients, to help them to 'graduate' and to be independent of charity, or even, as in the case of Akhuwat, to volunteer their money and time to help others in turn. The traditional and unfashionable notion of charity, or perhaps generosity, and dependence on goodwill rather than the market, seems to be an essential part of the way these institutions operate. They transcend the market and draw their sustainability from quite different motives, which may in the long term be far more 'sustainable' than earnings.

The lessons of experience

There are many lessons to be drawn from the material in this book, by managers and staff, and supporters and critics, of both faith-based and secular development institutions. The stories are diverse, and every reader will be able to find some support for whatever view or prejudice he or she holds. The examples have been chosen because they are generally successful. This does not mean that institutions with a religious foundation always succeed, and there are probably as many faith-based failures as there are successes.

There are many places of pilgrimage in India which are similar to Dharmasthala, and many of them have also accumulated large sums of money from pilgrims' donations. Some of these are of recent origin such as Sai Baba's

Puttaparthi, and others are as old or older than Dharmasthala, such as Tirupatti in Andhra Pradesh or Puri in Orissa. The administration of many of the wealthiest temples has effectively been taken over by government, as was threatened at one time for Dharmasthala, and this probably prevents them from engaging in anything other than traditional charitable activities, such as running hospitals and colleges.

There are also, however, large numbers of smaller but still wealthy institutions with large and increasing endowments, and strong local community links. It should be possible for some of these to learn from the experience of Dharmasthala, and to offer similar professionally-managed development programmes in their neighbourhoods. This could benefit the local community and reduce the all-too-familiar groups of beggars who congregate around the entrances to such places, but notably not at Dharmsthala. It could also enhance the reputation of the religious institution. As society becomes more secular the traditional Indian temple pilgrimage may become less popular, and the institutions may also lose the loyalty of the local people who live around them. Dharmasthala has pre-empted this problem through the work of SKDRDP.

In a broader context, however, faith-based institutions appear able to 'break the rules' and to serve a variety of clients with a range of different services in a way that is their secular counterparts find very difficult. The same SKDRP *sevaniratha* who disburses and recovers market-priced loans from some clients also provides outright charity for destitute people, without compromising his or her ability to serve those who can afford to pay in a business-like way. Catholic Bank lends at very low rates of interest, and provides farm supplies as well as financial services, which most contemporary secular microfinance institutions, and even farmers' cooperatives, fail to do successfully, and Akhuwat also provides loans to poor people at a cost which is far below what better-off people pay. The accepted wisdom is that such loans will inevitably be 'hijacked' by better-off people, and this has indeed been the general experience with subsidized credit. Akhuwat and 'Catholic Bank' are in some way able to do what seems intuitively to be right but is sadly very unusual – to provide low-cost financial services to poor people.

Donors and governments should take note of the peculiar strengths of faith-based development institutions, and should try to work with them to reach the unreached and to deal with the hard core poor in the most deprived areas, who have thus far benefited little from development programmes. Our examples have shown that institutions which are firmly and explicitly based on a religious faith can access funds and staff, and establish relationships with their clients in ways which are not possible for their secular counterparts. The identity of the faith is immaterial; the extra dimension of a shared belief in the value of charity transcends the relatively minor differences between one religion and another.

References

Harper, M. and Nath, M. (2004) *Inequity in the self-help group movement – a view from India's centre,* Shelter, January.